Weary Throats and New Songs

Black Women Proclaiming God's Word

Teresa L. Fry Brown

Abingdon Press
Nashville

WEARY THROATS AND NEW SONGS
BLACK WOMEN PROCLAIMING GOD'S WORD

Library of Congress Cataloging-in-Publication Data

Brown, Teresa L. Fry, 1951–
  Weary throats and new songs: Black women proclaiming God's Word / Teresa L. Fry Brown.
    p. cm.
Includes bibliographical references.
  ISBN 0-687-03013-7 (alk. paper)
    1. African American women—Religious life. 2. Singing—Religious aspects—Christianity.
3. Evangelistic work. I. Title.

BR563.N4B765 2003
277.3'08'082—dc21

                                                                            2003007073

Scripture quotations, unless otherwise indicated, are from the *New Revised Standard Version of the
Bible*, copyright © 1989, by the Division of Christian Education of the National Council of the
Churches of Christ in the United States of America. Used by permission. All rights reserved.

Scripture quotations noted The Message are from *THE MESSAGE*. Copyright © Eugene H.
Peterson, 1993, 1994, 1995. Used by permission of NavPress Publishing Group.

03 04 05 06 07 08 09 10 11 12—10 9 8 7 6 5 4 3 2 1
MANUFACTURED IN THE UNITED STATES OF AMERICA

To God for the call, authority, vision,
and ministry

Pastor Thelma Ray Shockley—grandaunt and
spiritual foremother

Dr. Carrie Lee Dunson—a sistah who believed
in me from the beginning

Sis. Veronica Tinsley, my daughter, and
Sis. Rikesha Fry, my niece—
the next generation of sistah proclaimers

Sistah proclaimers named and unnamed
yesterday, today, and tomorrow

CONTENTS

Acknowledgments

Black preaching is a dialogical process. The call of God through the preacher to the people of faith and the response channeled back to God through the preacher is the essence of the preaching moment. In this moment, acknowledge the cloud of witnesses who have made this proclamation a reality. This book is written for all my sistah proclaimers and preachers across the ages whose call was stillborn. It is for all the contemporary women of faith who are still trying to find their voices and a place to sing their songs. It is written for women everywhere who know who they are and what they have to do to make their ministry a reality.

Thank you to the late Reverend Dr. Prathia Hall, my first female mentor and role model, who showed me I could be a woman, a mother, and a preacher. Thank you to the Reverend Dr. Jacquelyne Grant, who taught me how to navigate the ecclesial waters and stay afloat. This book recognizes all the men, the brothers, who have affirmed women's call to preach at a cost to themselves but with a burning desire to do justice, love mercy, and walk humbly with God. I want especially to thank each sistah who trusted me enough to contribute to this project. Keep on singing.

This project began over twenty years ago when I answered my call to preach. Specifically it has gelled since November 2000 at the American Academy of Religion meeting in Nashville. I had an idea for a book, spoke with a couple of editors, went back to my room, prayed, and outlined a proposal. I wish to thank my colleagues Gail O'Day, Alton Pollard, Luther Smith, Charlotte McDaniel, and Barbara Day Miller for challenging me to do this project even when my plate seemed more than full. I am grateful to the administration, faculty, students, and support staff at the Candler School of Theology at Emory University for spoken and unspoken support and critique of my work. I am appreciative of Thomas Troeger who encouraged me in 1995 to begin this special work. I give honor to Ella Mitchell, whose editing resulted in my first professional published work. Jana Childers and Christine Smith continue to amaze me and provide opportunities for me to be heard.

I am thankful for research assistants over the years who spent long hours in research centers, are excellent proofreaders, and love me enough to tell me the truth. Thank you Kimberley Detherage, Lela LeFlore, Patrick Clayborn, and Sheri Smith Clayborn. I am captivated by words but a little weak on technology. Thank you to Richelle Fry Skinner for taking those long distance calls for technical advice. Love you, Sis. Thank you to Veronica Tinsley for stopping your homework to help me figure out which button to push. Love you, Baby Girl.

I have a wonderful church family. I want to acknowledge the love, prayers, and support that the Reverend Mark Thompson, Sister Stephanie Thompson, the Reverend Zelia Brown-Harvey, NBC Bible Institute, and the entire New Bethel AME Church membership have given me on this project. God is able.

I am eternally grateful to my husband, Frank David Brown. It takes a strong brother to walk with a sistah like me. I know that my teaching, preaching, and writing mean great sacrifice for you. Thank you for being the man God knew I needed. Love you.

INTRODUCTION

"You need to do more."

"What do you mean?"

"You need to do more."

"But I already teach Bible study, supervise the Sunday school, sing in the choir, visit the sick, pitch in whenever possible for church dinners, work whenever the pastor asks and Veronica is only two weeks old."

"You have more to do."

"What more can I do? I am thirty-one years old. I barely have enough energy for life now."

"I want you to teach, preach, and write."

"You want me to do what?"

"Teach, preach, and write."

The conversation started as a nagging whisper as the plane cruised to 25,000 feet on the way to Kansas City, Missouri. The intensity of the conversation grew with every exchange and left me bewildered. It was not a deep, baritone voice, stereotypic of what God should sound like. As a speech pathologist, I could usually detect a dialect after the first six words or so. I had worked with persons with a variety of mental health issues and began to think that I was in the grips of postpartum depression. After all, my daughter was there cooing in my arms as I traveled to meet with my family regarding my mother's deteriorating health. Surely I was just fatigued or stressed beyond my usual "I can handle anything" status. But this conversation would not leave me. "Either I'm crazy, or God is having fun." I was told by an androgynous voice that I was to teach, preach, and write. Nothing about why. Nothing about where. Nothing about how. Just a simple parental "Because I said so." Just a short flight from Denver, but my life changed in more ways than I could ever have imagined. I could not shake the command to change my life, to truly step beyond everything I had ever been taught as a good Baptist or experienced in church to become a woman preacher.

I had heard about those "uppity" women who "looked and sounded like men" and were said to try to take over pulpits. They surely were not really women. I knew that my Aunt Thelma was a preacher. She was just a regular woman, a mother, a grandmother with a special job. She was my grandmother's sister, and I knew that she was the exception to the rule, that a woman's place was in the home, classroom, or kitchen. I had watched as she entered churches in Missouri and was relegated to the front row but never was invited to the pulpit with the great men of the church. She just kept on doing her work, preaching in her own church and ministering in her community.

I went back to Denver a week later to meet with my pastor. When I told him that God had told me that I was to teach, preach, and write, he said, "Are you sure?" and "Let us pray." He instructed me to go back home and think about it. He had not experienced a woman talking about being a preacher and had to think about the consequences. I left, went home, and called my grandparents. I did not even discuss it with my husband until I consulted my wise counselors. I was afraid, nervous, and mostly confused. After all, I was a speech pathologist, a new mother, a law school student, and a good Christian, and I had a comfortable life planned. I spoke with my grandmother first. She said that I had a great aunt, as well as her sister, who was a lady preacher. She said that people talked about them, but she believed that God knows whom God wants to do the work. She said that there were men who did not make good preachers. God calls people who God knows will do the work. I then reluctantly talked with my grandfather, the president of the Missouri Baptist Laymen Association. I thought, "He'll never go for this." He took the phone and said, "You are not the first one." He then began to tell me about all the women in the family and those he had known over the years who were evangelists and speakers. Daddy Lyman said that they did not pastor big churches—usually storefronts or in their homes—because church law said they could not lead or teach the men. He said he believed that God calls whomever God wants. He said that if I was sure God said I was to enter ministry, I should tell them all that was what I would do, no matter what. Relieved, I told my husband who was minimally surprised but not happy for me. He had been in ministry for two years and began to think about what people would say about him. That was a foreboding that I should have paid attention to but chose to ignore at the time.

I went back to my pastor, who immediately asked me what my husband thought. Here I was trying to live into what God was telling me to do, and the person I supposedly should have consulted was discouraging me. I had always been a bit of a rebel, so I said that I saw no reason not to enter ministry and other people's opinion of me was irrelevant. I had to do what God said, regardless of the consequences. We had prayer again, and he began to explain how hard it would be for a woman, especially with a newborn, to enter ministry and be successful. There were dramatic failure examples. I was undaunted. After a period of time, he began publicly to support my decision. He then scheduled my trial, or initial public sermon, *Conjunctivitis: Too Many Ifs, Ands, and Buts*, based on Judges 7:1-7 regarding the excuses given for denial or avoidance of God's call on one's life.

In the congregation, the perception, by most, was that I was either frustrated with my family life, I did not have anything else to do, or I was really answering my husband's call. Nevertheless, I began the process with trepidation and prayer. At first, several people who I thought were my friends stopped talking to me. Older women at the church would literally turn their chairs around or walk out when I prayed or read Scripture. Some were curious and others just looked at me like I was crazy. What business did I have in ministry? Charges that my child would become dysfunctional, my marriage would collapse (a true prediction), men would think I was a groupie or whore, and my sexuality had changed, abounded. I was told that although I already had a master's degree in speech pathology and audiology, I had to begin seminary immediately if I wanted to go through ordination. It did not seem to matter that the men in my class of ministry did not have the same level of education, but since they had families they were exempt from further study. It seemed as if the more I tried, the more barriers were erected. The road was lonely, but God kept on pushing me.

Even my attire—too much or too little makeup, too long or too short hair, too colorful or too dull dress, too low or too high shoes, too long or too shiny earrings, or too long or too red fingernails—was the source of criticism. My mannerisms were also evaluated—smiling too much, crying too much, speaking too loudly or too softly, being too happy or too sad, reading too properly or with too familiar language. There was a flood of criticism and a drought of affirmation. I knew that the price of being the first and only was high, but this was the church! I was too naive for words when it came to Christian acceptance of God's call in unexpected places and in the lives of unconventional people. I became tired, angry, confused, and yet more determined. My grandmother, Mama Tessie, once again provided balance. There was a woman at my paternal grandfather's funeral dressed in a collar and severe black suit, hair pulled tightly into a chignon, low-heeled, clunky shoes, scowling face, and whose "manly" sounding raspy baritone voice intoned the prayer at my grandfather's funeral. She was sitting in the pulpit of Quinn Chapel African Methodist Episcopal Church although I was told she was a Holiness preacher. I remember Mama Tessie saying, "Don't you ever look like that. You are a woman. Don't ever act, sound, walk, stand, or dress like a man. You can be a woman and be a preacher."

The seminary experience was a blessing in disguise. I met women there who were also seemingly "thrown into this ministry thing" without warning. They were seeking ways to stabilize lives that were in a vortex of "whys," "why nots," and "what ifs." It was in seminary that I began to research the lives of women in history and ministry. I had practiced as a speech pathologist for seventeen years and began to teach classes on voice and diction and preaching as a student at the Iliff School of Theology in Denver, Colorado, in 1986. I had access to the lives of preachers in the church, seminary, and academic conferences. I was able to listen to the stories of women who were not the first and not the last to walk over glass on the way to actualization of God's call.

As a child of the black church, I had listened to black preachers boldly denounce the horrors of discrimination and oppression and pronounce the biblical mandate for equality before God. My experience, however, led me to listen beyond the words and see the reality of praxis. I began to question the chasm between words and deeds in roles of women in the church. The role of women seemed to be chief cook and bottle washer, child care specialist, financier, teacher, musician, and caregiver for the pastor. I began to wonder why women who talked of the grace of God, memorized the Bible, led so many to community activism, ensured that not only their children but also their husbands were saved, could not enter the pulpit. They seemed to be functioning in a specialized category of saints who ended at the bottom step of the pulpit.

I needed answers to the cognitive dissonance of freedom talk and freedom walk. I was thirsty to know about black women's religious lives in general and black women in ministry in particular. The more I worked in the church, black or white, the more I felt as if I was in the desert with no oasis in sight. Restrictive signs of "Men Only" reminded me of the segregationist signs of my youth. Charges of my inability to sit in certain places or to be who I was reminded me of the necessity for lunch counter sit-ins and department store boycotts. Surely I was not the only one experiencing discrimination, oppression, and deference in the cradle of liberation, in the land of the free and the home of the brave. Certainly there were other voices I needed to hear, not just for the sake of a pity party, but to help me understand the "whys" and "wherefores" of the experience of being a black woman who happened to be called to ministry. I began to read everything I could about the history of black women: those women who worked for women's suffrage but were denied the right to vote; the behind-the-scenes heroes of the Civil Rights Movement, who, for the sake of the race, had to pretend they required less freedom than the male martyrs; the mothers of the faith who kept churches open with chicken dinners and choir fund-raisers and pastor's aid societies; or those sisters who had to preach in storefronts and founding churches, only to see those churches given over to men when the congregation grew. The initial research began to yield a sense of empowerment in my life as a person in ministry. Many had walked the path before me. My proclaiming foremothers endured beatings, physical removal from churches, verbal castigation for "trying to be a man," their families decimated when husbands or in-laws did not understand their call, critiques of their sexuality, and even death for the cause of Christ. Comparatively, my proclaiming life was easy because of their sacrifices. Many had broken the path for me. I had an obligation to ensure that many would follow.

As a sense of empowerment began to grow, I began to appreciate the challenge of preparing and delivering liberating messages. I affirm the message of liberation in the black church. My preaching passion is liberation for all of God's people. Social and individual transformation permeates every sermon I have preached in the past twenty years. As I began to preach more and more, I understood the intense vulnerability of the preaching moment. I became aware of the transparent nature of preaching as one displayed her or his beliefs, preparation, and personality before a listening congregation of believers and unbelievers. One may be weary because of resistance to her or his call but has to be able to sing a song of

God's justice, mercy, love, and grace in that mysterious meeting of dust and divinity called preaching. People's lives depended on preaching a living word. I came to know that all the fatigue in the process, all the name-calling, long hours, research, tears, fears, loneliness, debt, lost sleep, alienation, and denials of personhood were like suspended animation as I stood to "say a word" for the Lord. My throat was sometimes parched due to human machinations, but I was able to sing a new song when God's word coursed through my marrow. There was life on the other side of the church restrictions. There was a light in the tunnel of discrimination. There was energy in the midst of fatigue. There was an "anyhow" in the gift of preaching. There was a dialectic balancing of the weary throat and the new song. Preaching, teaching, and writing God's word made the journey worth the struggle.

The Psalmist writes, "Oh, how could we ever sing God's song in this wasteland?" (Psalm 137:4 The Message). This is a question asked and answered by countless African American women for centuries. Beaten, ostracized, ridiculed, and dismissed, black women have sung passionate, joyous praises about the goodness of God. They have melodically lifted up the name of Jesus in spite of barriers such as race, class, denomination, education, and gender. Responding to a sense of deliverance from evil and to answered prayers, they have related their faith and trust in God in sacred places such as ships, fields, homes, barns, factories, hospitals, stores, schools, pulpits, churchyards, missionary societies, choir stands, and over kitchen sinks. From the spiritual narratives of Elizabeth in 1808 to twenty-first-century ordained and nonordained speakers and preachers, African American women continue to "Say a Word" about God even when they are disenfranchised in the religious communities they helped create.

There are several books about the history of women preachers, such as *This Far by Faith: Readings in African American Women's Biography*.[1] *Preacher Woman Sings the Blues* provides nineteen autobiographies of black women evangelists and the effect of race and gender on their lives.[2] *Religious Institutions and Women's Leadership, Black Women in Nineteenth Century American Life*, and *"You Have Stept Out of Your Place": A History of Women and Religion in America* detail the rich history of the often "invisible" women and their call to ministry.[3] The call, ordination, leadership, and lives of white women were addressed in such works as *Clergy Women: An Uphill Calling* and *A Still Small Voice: Women, Ordination, and the Church*. Similar issues in the lives of black women were in *Not Without a Struggle, A Time of Honor: A Portrait of African American Clergy Women*, and *Wrestling with the Patriarchs: Retrieving Women's Voices in Preaching*.[4] Cheryl Sanders's classic 1989 article, "The Woman as Preacher," was a comparative analysis of sermons of eighteen black women and eighteen black men. The research basis was three sermon anthologies in terms of language, form, texts, themes, and homiletical tasks. Christine Smith and Carol Noren analyzed the homiletical tasks of white women in their landmark works.[5] Ella Mitchell's sermon collections by contemporary black women and Bettye Collier Thomas's collection of sermons by black preaching women from 1850 to 1979 demonstrated the ability of black women to craft a sermon with different but effective voices.[6] This book will provide a brief review of the rich heritage of black female proclaimers and an analysis of the particularities of contemporary black women's call, models, sermon preparation, content, delivery, and personhood. I distinctly did not limit the classification to "preachers" because some sistahs see the term as not applicable to what they do. I realize there are thousands of African American women who "Say a Word" for God but are not ordained or operate under a different rubric. I define preaching as the verbal or nonverbal communication of the inward manifestation of a command by the Holy Spirit to relate to others something about God's presence, purpose, and power in one's life and in the lives of all humanity. To proclaim means to affirm, announce, declare, herald, profess, voice, illustrate, and inspire through articulating one's thoughts, beliefs, and feelings about God. Proclamation is sacred speech differentiated from public speaking. It centers on who God is, what God requires, when God acts, where God is, how God operates, and why God does what God does in the lives of all of God's people. The proclaimer is not operating on her own agenda but is empowered by the Spirit of God in prayer, preparation, composition, delivery, and feedback. The herald stands in the gap between God and the people to impart a healing, freeing, and life-giving word. The preaching moment can take place anytime, anyplace, anywhere, and by anyone regardless of age, gender, race, status, or ability. Central to the preaching event is the biblical text supported by images and illustrations that make the ancient word live in contemporary context. The purpose of preaching or proclaiming is transformation— internal and external moral ethical change in individual and group-lived faith. The centuries-old oral tradition, the homiletical task, the embodied hermeneutic is accomplished through conversational patterns of speaker/listener feedback, couched in sermon, song, testimony, writing, teaching, and action. Proclamation is a moment-by-moment, God-breathed, God-anointed, God-appointed, God-led, God-sanctioned, and God-controlled activity.

This study is not the definitive book on black women proclaimers, but the first attempt at a book about what black women do when they "say a word" about God. The intent is to provide a means of assessment for the distinctive nature of black women's proclamation. There are areas that some homileticians may think too obvious to omit and others that are seemingly unnecessary. The burden of undertaking this project is a desire not to cover too much, yet still to honor the persons evaluated and those elements that directly and consistently influence their proclamation. The onus of scholarly work is that one is vulnerable to critique, but that happens every time I preach. Somehow it seems appropriate for one in my social location—black female, ordained clergy, homiletics professor—to present a different perspective on the elements of the preaching moment. There is a familiar hymn that begins, "This is my story, this is my song." This project is about *living* testimonies, songs about what black women actually do in the preaching moment rather than what is theorized or assumed. No one else can tell it like they do. Although I affirm that there are general preaching templates, I also understand that ultimately no one can preach someone else's sermon or sing someone else's song. This book is the overture to a symphony of resultant texts on when, where, why, and how African American women tell others about God in spite of resistance (weary throats) and in the face of support (new songs) in religious and social communities.

Methodology

A fifteen-question survey was mailed to 485 ordained and nonordained black women in forty-one states and thirty denominations (Appendix, Chart 1). The list of names and contact information was initially compiled through a random search of denominational lists of women in ministry. Other sources included Internet webpages; commercial videotapes and audiotapes sold in churches and religious bookstores; television evangelists; seminary professors; other authors; seminary students; clergy spouses; business cards compiled over the past twenty years; recommendations from colleagues, bishops, and boards of ministry within varied denominations; women's religious group contacts; informal dinner conversation; classroom or church office discussions; and attendance at various worship services and conferences over the past ten years. Personal contact with women was accomplished as I traveled for teaching and preaching engagements. Surveys were also distributed in informal, incidental contacts.

A second mailing was sent three months later to ensure selected persons received the information. The first one had gone out shortly after the terrorist attacks of September 11, and mail service was disrupted. Follow-up E-mails, faxes, and telephone calls were made to a representative sample to ask additional questions and to answer inquiries concerning the research. Respondents were asked to complete the questions and forward an audiotape or videotape for analysis of homiletical task and voice and diction. Through preliminary research and teaching of preaching, I know that African American women usually do not tape themselves or are overly critical of their taped work. In order to lessen the stress, the women were asked to submit a tape only if they felt comfortable with my analysis of their work. I also pledged to use blind response information if the respondent wanted to remain anonymous. Reasons given for anonymity include apprehension about denominational alienation, feelings of worth, intense personal information, critiques of mentors or systemic prejudice, prior commercial contracts, or general reluctance to share based in cultural perspectives about boasting. Persons who made this request would be referenced without identifying information. A letter of consent was included to provide the use of names, responses, and sermonic materials.

Survey information requested included contact information, official titles, name of church and affiliation, denominational affiliation, status, highest level of education, proclamation history, how often and why the person proclaimed, primary location of proclamation, preparation process, biblical translations used, delivery style, mentors or models, attire, and the name of the first woman heard proclaiming God's word. A randomly selected group was asked three additional questions on avoidance of specific topics, themes, or texts. Answers to survey questions will be used as supportive information for the book premise in following chapters. Whenever possible, direct quotations from written and taped submissions will be used. This is to provide the women an opportunity to share in their own words and voices. Each chapter will include an ecumenical representation of nonordained and ordained women proclaiming God's word.

One hundred and sixteen women completed surveys, and eighty-nine videotapes and audiotapes were submitted for analysis. One hundred and two signed consent forms for use of their submissions and identifying information. There was some consternation about allowing persons to know about their work and exceeding joy that someone was writing about black women. A number of women called or sent E-mail to say that they did not have anything to say. They did not think that their work warranted evaluation or presentation. Others missed all the deadlines for submission due to hectic schedules or misplaced forms. One hundred and four forms were returned due to address errors and postal service delays.

Respondents were from twenty-four states: California (13), Connecticut (1), Mississippi (1), Georgia (34), Virginia (3), Texas (3), Massachusetts (6), Oklahoma (1), Tennessee (7), New Jersey (3), New York (10), Illinois (1), Florida (6), Maryland (5), Alabama (1), Arizona (1), Pennsylvania (1), Missouri (2), Michigan (3), South Carolina (2), North Carolina (1), Colorado (8), Iowa (1), and Delaware (1), and from the District of Columbia (1). My residency and ministry, face-to-face contact and follow-up, and the sheer number of women proclaimers may have contributed to the number of respondents from the forty surveys distributed in Georgia.

Black women are proclaiming in traditional black denominations as well as in mainline Protestant denominations. Black women often begin new denominations as a means of living out their call. Denominational affiliations reporting were National Baptist (15), Progressive Baptist (6), Full Gospel Baptist (1), American Baptist Churches (3), the African Methodist Episcopal Church (45), African Methodist Episcopal Zion Church (1), United Methodist (10), Presbyterian, U.S.A. (2), Cumberland Presbyterian Church in America (1), Catholic (1), Pentecostal (2), Church of God (1), Congregational (1), Apostolic (1), Pan African Orthodox Church (1), Church of God in Christ (1), Disciples of Christ (3) and Nondenominational churches (21). Seven women reported dual affiliations: Apostolic-Pentecostal, Pentecostal-Nondenominational, Disciples of Christ-National Baptist, None-Denominational-Full Gospel, Pan African Orthodox-United Church of Christ, Progressive Baptist-National Baptist, and Progressive Baptist-American Baptist. Two reported triple affiliations: Independent-Pentecostal-Presbyterian, U.S.A., and Nondenominational-Baptist-Episcopal.

The age of the proclaimer affects the relationship with the congregation, response to perceived wisdom, and validation of time in service to God. The survey age range was broken into seven categories: 18-30 years (5), 31-40 years (19), 41-55 years (56), 56-65 years (29), 66-77 years (5), and 78-85 years (2). Fourteen of the women reporting were nonordained. The remaining one hundred and two were in various ordination categories: seven women were bishops, sixteen served as pastors, five were assistant pastors, seven were copastors, five had held major denominational leadership positions, and four worked as university chaplains. The positions affect the opportunities to proclaim and visibility in ministry. The length of the proclamation journey indicated three had begun the ministry within the past year, while five had served for over fifty years. Statistically, the results of the surveys indicated: 0-5 years (14), 6-10 years (25), 11-15 years (28), 16-20 years (10), 21-25 years (11), 26-30 years (14), 31-35 years (2), 36-40 years (2), 41-50 years (3), and 51-55 years (7). Seven persons indicated that they had been called from their mothers' wombs and had been proclaiming their entire lives.

Charges of too much and too little education have been measuring tools for qualifying women to proclaim God's word. In some traditions, the preacher does not need to go to school, because if God called "him," that is sufficient. The rationale for the lack of encouragement for men to seek further education included men's responsibility to provide for their families or that God's work will never leave "the righteous forsaken or his seed begging bread" or that the Bible is the only tool necessary for study. I find it ironic that pastors are dependent on black women to finance and carry out church projects. Black women preachers are part of that economic base, yet their skills are often deferred. In determining women's ability to proclaim, boards often insist that women go to school and learn the "how tos" of ministry. Some women are even ordained to Christian education or women's ministry but not to pastoral roles. Education is viewed as both a vehicle for developing alternative ministries and professions and for economic survival and a means to avoid sanctioning women's ordination, particularly for women with children. Women are generally assigned smaller, economically struggling churches, are on circuits, or receive the societal standard of lower salaries than male proclaimers doing the same work. In my tenure as a seminary professor, I have found that the majority of women students are generally on their second or third careers and returning to school for ministry degrees. Survey respondents' highest degrees reported were: sixteen Doctor of Philosophy, two Doctor of Psychology, two Doctor of Education, fifteen Doctor of Ministry, thirty-eight Master of Divinity, five Master of Arts, two Master of Science, six Bachelor of Science, one Bachelor of Arts, six Bible college, twenty some college, and three secondary education. The sample included three pastoral counselors, three psychologists, three lawyers, one social worker, two accountants, a nurse, and several educators.

The format of the book will follow a general assessment I use in teaching a class on women and preaching. Factors that I believe influence sermonic moments are age, education, geographical location, personal experience, denomination, sense of call, authority issues, mentors, context, preparation, exegesis, organization, imagination and imagery, verbal and nonverbal language, recurrent themes, and preaching passion. In approaching the outline of the book, I chose to follow my homiletical composition procedure. I have been in constant prayer since God presented the project to me. I have exegeted the readers or potential market for such a work and determined that the book is written for all the named and unnamed women who have proclaimed God's word across the ages. It is also for homiletics professors, laywomen's groups, women's study departments, clergywomen's support and networking groups, Christian educators, seminarians, denominational boards, church history teachers, and communication specialists. I have determined that the behavioral purpose is to give voice to black women's homiletical process. I have asked the relevant questions through surveys and evaluations of audio and video submissions. I have called on my hermeneutic in repeated reading of the varied translations of information sent to me. I have considered both the historical text and the contemporary listener. The voices of the women will illustrate the purpose as I attempt to fill in the blanks. The application of the texts will be dependent on the reason the readers deem necessary. I celebrate the richness of black women's —my sistahs'— proclamation all the way through the book by verbatim quotations when possible. I intentionally use clergy titles, in the first mention of a name, as a matter of respect for the struggle and the office. I invite a continuation of the acknowledgment that black women possess powerful messages about God and seek to share them in a number of ways, whenever and wherever they can.

Chapter 1, "Weary Throats," briefly reviews the history of black women proclaiming the word from the 1800s to the present. The chapter frames the reality that black women proclaim God's word with or without institutional sanction. Black women's invisibility, movement to be heard, struggle to be affirmed, and results of or response to proclamation are critical elements. Remembrances of the first black woman respondents heard preach support the historical review.

Chapter 2, "Singing in the Key of G-O-D," analyzes black women's proclamation and affirmation of their call, authority issues, frequency of proclamation, mentors, role models, support systems, and navigation of ecclesial waters. Methods of escaping the "big chair syndrome" will be assessed. When denied opportunity or space to effect their call, black women formulate alternative pulpits such as missions, hospitals, mental health facilities, social outreach, or music.

Chapter 3, "Sight-Reading: Half Notes and Whole Notes," evaluates black women's modes of sermon preparation. Moving from the germination of an idea to text selection, preference for Old Testament or New Testament, choice of translations, exegesis, research methods, and use of related texts are discussed by selected women speakers or preachers.

Chapter 4, "Resting but Remaining in Tune," explores proclamation purpose, preaching passion, use or avoidance of particular texts or themes, sermon type or form, organization, illustrations, imagery, content, cultural relevance, and supportive materials such as songs, poetry, or testimony. Comparison and contrast of various proclaimers paint a picture of commonalities and differences based on age, geography, denomination, and training.

Chapter 5, "Singing the Song in a Strange Land," signifies the passage from weary throats, stifled voices, and ecclesiastical deferment to communicability. Orality, audibility, voice and diction, sermon introductions, delivery, idiosyncratic phrasing, call and response, hooping, celebration, and contextualization are reviewed. Selected videotape and audiotape presentations serve as resources.

Chapter 6, "Choir Robes and Choreography," delineates the diversity in black women preachers, teachers, and speakers. Using videotapes and survey information, this chapter evaluates mannerisms, posture, mobility, carriage, attire, appearance, and affect.

Chapter 7, "New Songs," details projections for black women proclaiming God's word based on the author's experience as a preacher and teacher of preaching, teaching, and writing. Research implications, similarities to methods of others, shifting ecclesial barriers, and future research are included here.

A significant number of people asked me to include myself in this research. I found that my response was similar to that of many women I asked to participate: "I do not have anything to say," or "People have heard enough about me." My sisters' responses included, "Your voice needs to be heard." "You represent us." "Teresa, you have done this preaching thing longer than us. At least include your sermons." So, I will follow my sisters' advice. My general response to the survey is that I am fifty-one years old. I have been in ministry all my life and ordained ministry for twenty years. I hold a Master of Divinity and a Doctor of Philosophy in Religious and Theological Studies. I am an ordained Itinerant Elder in the African Methodist Episcopal Church. I have been teaching homiletics since 1986. This book is about black women proclaimers. I believe it is important for each proclaimer to speak in her own voice. My voice will be heard on each page and in a sermon brief at the end of each chapter.[7]

CHAPTER ONE

WEARY THROATS

*You will not let what man may say or do, keep you from doing the will of the
Lord or using the gifts you have for the good of others. How much easier to
bear the reproach of men than to live at a distance from God.[1]*

*I proclaim the Word of God because God awakened me and in a still, small voice
declared, "You are to preach my Word." From that moment there has been a fire
in my bones to tell the old, old story of Jesus and his redeeming love. There are
too many people who have no hope and no help. I have a desire and a duty to
tell, to share with them, the story of salvation, but also the story of how Jesus can
give you peace everyday of your life.—LaTrelle Miller Easterling, 2002*

In the 116 years between the spiritual narrative of Julia Foote—an
ordained Deacon in the African Methodist Episcopal Zion Church—
and the survey response of LaTrelle Miller Easterling—an ordained
Elder in the African Methodist Episcopal Church—the way of black
women's proclamation has been of pressing on in spite of denominational
detours, unexpected road closures, and seemingly impassable routes. The
inner quest to answer the call of God is exemplified in the late Episcopal
priest, lawyer, and social activist Pauli Murray's statement, "Hope is a
song in a weary throat."[2] The call of God on the lives of named and
unnamed black women has been and still is stronger than the resistance
they have, do, or will encounter.

The excuses, charges, challenges, and barriers have become legend. Women are too weak. Preaching is hard work and women's menstrual cycles will cause them to cry or yell at the wrong time. Besides, the Bible says that the letting of blood will desecrate the temple. Families will fall apart. Their voices are too high. Their voices are too low. They don't sound like preachers. There were no female disciples. They are just trying to be men. It's really their husband's call. A woman caused Adam to sin, and that's why we're in the mess we're in now. A woman can't tell me nothing. Women's minds are not deep enough to understand the mysteries of the Bible. They are just trying to take power from men. They don't have the right credentials. There are too many qualified men waiting for pulpits, so why give one to a woman? It's all right for her to preach, but the Bible says she cannot pastor. No woman wants another woman to rule over her. Let's just create a separate women's ministry space and let them fight among themselves. Women ought to know their place. That's why the black family is falling apart, too many women out in the street instead of in the home.

These are just a few of the charges that can make one bone-tired. If one bought into the characterizations of humanity, she or he might not hear from God. On this side of twenty years, I choose not to respond to the minutia, but rather to look to what God has charged me to do. I do, however, raise responses as points of discussion. Is there a tape of Jesus' voice or even of Paul's depicting what a preacher sounds like? Did God leave a compact disc of the "voice of God"? Didn't Adam have a brain? How can one be a helper or helpmate if she is under someone's foot? How long have black women had the option to stay at home and not contribute to the support of the family? Have you ever given birth to a baby or endured the cramps of menstruation and still worked a full-time job, kept a house, and supported a church? If black women make up 75 to 95 percent of a congregation, why do so many churches reject leadership by women? Isn't it time for the debate to end? People are in need of a word from God. If you are going through a crisis, do you really care what a person is wearing, how she or he sounds, and what gender is represented, or do you just want comfort and support? Hope is a song in a weary throat. Many have sung even when their throats were so dry sound barely escaped. Somehow the groaning in their souls reached the ears of the people.

Though there are certainly women who encountered no resistance to preaching or proclaiming, thousands have affirmed the presence of God's Spirit in their lives and enunciated the word of God even with their last breath. Many have fallen by the wayside, left ordained and nonordained ministry, became disaffected with the faith and left the church, or decided that the detractors were right all along and women have no business in ministry. Many, however, such as the foremothers, affirm the "anyhowness" of God. It is the power of God to make space for life when all around us seems dead. It is the purpose of God to take the most unlikely person and help her sing praises in the middle of a prison. It is the presence of God that protects vessels of praise even when family and friends desert them. It is this "anyhowness" of God that enables black women to utter a word, annunciate who God is, declare saving works, and evidence that they are called by God and God alone.

Although there are those who believe they are the first to encounter religious restrictions, wrestle with calls, or have the most oppressive engagement in a church, history reverberates with stories of the foremothers. Pious women met in private homes and camp meetings during the nineteenth century. Spirit endowment served as the basis for their call to proclaim.[3] Often discounted by the religious bodies of their birth, they found places and people who would affirm their call. Their public conduct, out of their proper place, was the basis for contention. The socalled Cult of True Womanhood, developed in the nineteenth century, defined womanhood through our cardinal virtues. This emanated from Victorian standards and delineated the proper place of white women in society. Piety meant that women were naturally religious, moral, virtuous, and more open to the call of conversion and consolations of religion than men. It was a woman's duty to teach the children about God and ensure that her spouse was religious. This strengthened the family and protected the republic. Women were to be pure and asexual. Men, on the other hand, were sexually rampant and could not help themselves. They had to depend on women to assist them in denying their urges. Women were to be submissive, to accept subordination to their husbands who ruled by divine ordination. "Female influence" was to be exercised gently and subtly, or one was deemed unfeminine. Finally, a woman was to be domestic. Her sphere was her home, household tasks, and nurturing and bearing children.[4] The church was a desirable setting for men and women; however, men were rulers of public and private castles. These ideals were adopted by blacks and applied to black women as well, although black women's status was null and void. Even the Constitution of the United States stipulated that black men were three-fifths of a person while black women were not mentioned at all. Black women rarely had the privilege of remaining exclusively at home. In stark contrast, asserts sociologist Cheryl Townsend Gilkes, patriarchy was not present in the West African worldview. Women were not excluded from religious or political authority. Women were self-reliant, established their own identity, controlled marketplaces, served in religious ceremonies as priests, and gathered in their own secret societies.[5]

C. Eric Lincoln and Lawrence Mamiya concur with Townsend Gilkes. Women played major roles in African religion; however, in the United States Protestant Christianity, males led. In West African culture, storytelling and oration, exhibited by women and men, were highly valued. The ability to speak publicly was one of the highest levels of art. Charisma and the ability to preach appeared with the Protestant notion of a call as being endorsed by God. Models for black preaching for enslaved women were mainly black and white male preachers. Personal experience came into conflict with patriarchal values adopted from the larger society. In spite of numbers of black women in the late–nineteenth and the twentieth centuries who expressed a desire to preach, none were recognized as preachers or pastors in major denominations. Women affiliated with congregations of other faith systems or formed new denominations when they faced impenetrable walls blocking their calls. Black women were very active during the First Great Awakening and found creative ways of expressing themselves.[6] Black women's self-definition, speaking up for themselves, and beliefs contradicted the white/male hegemony of race and gender. Speaking in the public domain challenged the *Cult of True Womanhood* and was critiqued as unnatural.[7]

Historian Darlene Clark Hine describes a *culture of dissemblance* in which black women developed "the appearance of openness and disclosure but actually shield the truth of their inner lives and selves from oppressors" to counteract negative social and sexual images of their womanhood.[8] Women at times affected the domesticated, subservient, less intelligent demeanor while working out their calls.

The Second Great Awakening (Protestant revivalism) took place from 1795 to 1830. The movement prompted American women actively to evangelize families and neighbors. The primary outcome of the revivals was holiness as directly tied into charisma. This meant a new authoritative power in position and religion with one's personal access to the divine. The coupling of a women's call to proclaim and the Holy Spirit enabled women leaders to achieve self-empowerment and personal freedom autonomy. They were empowered to minister with the people by bringing a different perspective to God's word in house meetings and by speaking healing in the lives of the listeners. Charisma enabled women to found religious institutes and inspire movements and outside patriarchal mainstream religions. There was a social expectation of leadership due to the move of the Holy Spirit in the life of men and women.[9] The foremost preacher during this time was a Methodist, Phoebe Palmer. Beginning in 1839, she stimulated the Holiness movement, stressing conversion and sanctification. This movement gave rise to numerous traveling women preachers, including black women such as Jarena Lee and Amanda Berry Smith.[10]

Historian Bettye Collier-Thomas writes that the Holiness tradition is central to black women's preaching. It was the source of empowerment, rooted in African spirituality. Black women decided they did not need the sanction of the church because God had already authorized their ministry. They were sanctified and freed from sin and liberated through the indwelling of the Holy Spirit. Black women were empowered to act, think, speak, and be themselves in God. These reformist revolutionaries formed sects and participated in revivalism and camp meetings. As early as the 1700s, black women preachers wrote conversion accounts as their spiritual narratives or autobiographies. They chronicled their lives and experiences in sanctified churches, repudiated slavery, and disavowed any form of prejudice. Still, black churches in general, and black males in particular, disagreed with their interpretation of sanctification as authority to preach. The women led protests for opportunities to exhort, evangelize, and perform ex officio preaching roles. Many were afforded opportunities to lead house meetings and prayer meetings and to travel as unlicensed evangelists. Women preached to both black and white, male and female, old and young blended congregations.

A Word from the Foremothers

The earliest black female preacher recorded by Collier-Thomas was Elizabeth, age forty-two, in Baltimore, Maryland, in 1808. She preached for over fifty years in the Methodist Episcopal Church.[11] Elizabeth was born a slave in 1766. She began life as a Methodist. Her sermonic content was personal salvation and divine conversation with God. Sold to a Presbyterian family, she attended services in the neighborhood. At age thirty, she attended meetings in the vicinity of her home, and, though urged to speak, she "shrank from it" due to the reverence for the cross. She preached until she was ninety years old, when she settled in Philadelphia.[12] Elizabeth died at age 101.

> I did not speak much till I had reached my forty-second year, when it was revealed to me that the message which had been given to me I had not yet delivered, and the time had come. As I could read but little, I questioned within myself how it would be possible for me to deliver the message, when I did not understand the Scriptures. . . . Whilst I thus struggled, there seemed a light from heaven to fall upon me which banished all my desponding fears, and I was enabled to form a new resolution to go on to prison and to death.[13]

Elizabeth's struggle to believe that she was called to proclaim God's word foreshadowed testimonies of wrestling with personal and communal decisions calling from the lips and in the writing of countless black women.

In the spiritual autobiographies of the nineteenth century, women repeatedly used Joel 2:28-29 and 1 Corinthians 14:34-35 as support for their calls, defense to their opposition, and direction to spiritual egalitarianism. There was a strong relationship with biblical texts despite the oppressive use of some texts.[14] Their calls were manifest by the spiritual anointing and gifting. These texts about God's Spirit being poured on all humanity were perceived as a mandate from God to articulate and spread God's word in all societal spaces. Some left homes, families, children, husbands, churches, and friends to preach as directed by the Spirit.

Richard Douglass-Chin provides literary critiques of nineteenth-century spiritual narratives or autobiographies. He says that they are like the "double consciousness of DuBois"; that is, guarded black expressiveness written in vernacular. They contained challenges of patriarchal biblical interpretation, with veiled criticism of racism and blatant sexism as encountered in the black church. These self-portraits of women preachers, called metaperformance, resist objectification; they present the self as truth-telling by black women surrounded by the white establishment. He also charges that in narratives such as *Memoirs of the Life, Religious Experience, Ministerial Travels and Labours of Mrs. Zilpha Elaw, an American Female of Colour*, published in England in 1859, there are textual manipulation and at times emotional manipulation of the reader.[15] In reality, whites edited many of the narratives. In some instances, the voice of the woman is sanitized. Yet the narratives serve as a source of encouragement for modern-day proclaimers.

Julia Foote was born in 1823 in Schenectady, New York. Raised in the Methodist Episcopal Church, she could not understand how persons who said they believe in God could be against blacks.[16] Her religious instruction spoke of a loving God, but social barriers were ever present. In her spiritual narrative, *A Brand Plucked from the Fire*, she relates:

> When called of God, on a particular occasion, to a definite work, I said, "Lord, not me." Day by day I was more impressed that God would have me work in his vineyard. I thought it could not be that I was called to preach—I, so weak and ignorant. Still, I knew all things were possible with God, even to confounding the wise by foolish things of this earth. Yet in me there was a shrinking.

Her self-disqualification when faced with a call is present throughout the biblical text as well as in the lives of black women who wrestle with God and society at the same time:

> I took all my doubts and fears to the Lord in prayer, when, what seemed to be an angel, made his appearance. In his hand was a scroll, on which were these words: "Thee have I chosen to preach my Gospel without delay." The moment my eyes saw it, it appeared to be printed on my heart. The angel was gone in an instant, and I, in agony, cried out, "Lord, I cannot do it!" . . . The darkness was so great that I feared to stir. . . .
>
> I had always been opposed to the preaching of women, and had spoken against it, though, I acknowledge, without foundation. This rose before me like a mountain, and when I thought of the difficulties they had to encounter, both from professors and non-professors, I shrank back and cried, "Lord, I cannot go!"[17]

It is important to understand that opposition to women's proclamation arises from the most unexpected sources. The nay votes are often from other women. I remember when I answered my call, the first people to rise up and protest were women. It took about three years to gain their acceptance. They then became my most ardent supporters. There are contemporary testimonies of women who encounter resistance by both men and women.

One of my most virulent female critics answered the call to preach two and a half years after me. She was wrestling with her own life and focused on me so she would not have to face her own. Julia Foote's call story reflects the struggle many women face:

One night, as I lay weeping and beseeching the dear Lord to remove this burden from me, there appeared the same angel that came to me before, and on his breast were these words: "You are lost unless you obey God's righteous commands."[18]

Visitation by angelic beings to validate the call is a recurring motif in spiritual narratives. The messenger comes in visions and a variety of forms. In the end, the response and acceptance is one of spiritual obedience regardless of the world's standards. She says that the call will "certainly not be denied that women as well as men were at that time with the Holy Ghost." Referencing Joel 2:28, Foote says it is expressly stated that women were among those who continued in prayer and supplication: "Women and men are classed together, and if the power to preach the Gospel is short-lived and spasmodic in the case of women, it must be equally so in that of men; and if women have lost the gift of prophecy, so have men."[19] Foote stressed holiness, atonement, women as preachers, vivid descriptions and language usage, and inner purification.

Amanda Berry Smith's autobiography informs us that she was an itinerant preacher whose spiritual journey impelled her to preach in spite of place, time, and lack of ordination. Born in 1837, her initial religious education was in Methodist camp meetings. Her graphic 1870 call to preach at Fleet Street African Methodist Episcopal Church in Brooklyn parallels Foote's visionary call. As the pastor preached, Smith said she closed her eyes in prayer and, upon opening her eyes, saw a star that changed into a white tulip above the head of the preacher:

> And then I leaned back and closed my eyes. Just then I saw a large letter "G," and I said: "Lord, do you want me to read in Genesis, or in Galatians? Lord, what does this mean?" Just then I saw the letter "O." I said, "Why, that means go." And I said "What else?" And a voice distinctly said to me, "Go preach." . . .
>
> Oh! glory to God! How He put His seal on this first work to encourage my heart and establish my faith, that He indeed had chosen, and ordained and sent me. I did not know as I have ever seen anything to equal that first work, the first seal that God gave to His work at Salem.[20]

Smith held prayer meetings in Virginia and any place people let her speak. She did not have formal education, but that did not prevent her from challenging prevailing views of slavery. Her work eventually led to an eight-year missionary tour in Liberia. When her authority was questioned, she retorted, "God had ordained me, I needed nothing better."[21]

Maria Stewart was born in 1803 in Hartford, Connecticut. She worked as a lecturer and abolitionist primarily in Boston. Her mentor was David Walker. Her refrain was against slavery and empowerment for blacks. In 1832, she issued a call to the "daughters of Africa" for activism, self-improvement, and embracing whom God has made them.

> O, ye daughters of Africa, awake! awake! arise! no longer sleep nor slumber, but distinguish yourselves. Show forth to the world that ye are endowed with noble and exalted faculties. O, ye daughters of Africa! what have ye done to immortalize your names beyond the grave? what examples have ye set before the rising generation? what foundation have ye laid for generations yet unborn? where are our union and love? and where is our sympathy, that weeps at another's wo(e), and hides the faults we see?
>
> How long shall the fair daughters of Africa be compelled to bury their minds and talents beneath a load of iron pots and kettles? Until union, knowledge and love begin to flow among us. How long shall a mean set of men flatter us with their smiles, and enrich themselves with our hard earnings; their wives' fingers sparkling with rings, and they themselves laughing at our folly?[22]

This laywoman used the biblical text in all of her public speaking. Stewart was one of the earliest, if not the earliest, public speakers. The tradition of black women proclaiming in sacred and civic venues was continued in a number of black women's civic groups as part of the women's movement in the 1800s, which included the 1809 Africa Female Benevolent Society of Newport, Rhode Island; the 1818 Colored Female Religious and Moral Society of Salem, Massachusetts; the 1832 Colored Female's Charitable Society of Boston; and the 1837 Young Ladies Literary Society. The Daughters of Africa in Philadelphia were working women who pooled their resources for the benefit of the community.[23]

Struggle for Ordination

Women's ordination was and is a complex entity. Denominational polity may not sanction ordination of women or persons outside a particular church family. If women founded a denomination, or if at that founding women were included, then ordination is not a question for that denomination. Some women leave one denomination that refuses ordination and affiliate with one that does. At times, political pressure within denominations that historically ordain women leads to denial of ordination. Some women are ordained for a particular purpose other than pastoring. Many women operate without institutional ordination yet lead congregations. Some see no reason for ordination because of the restrictions that may overshadow their purpose, what God called them to do. Mark Chaves lists "merger of denominations" and "denominational rule changes" as opportunities for women's ordination.[24]

Congregationalists began ordaining women in 1853. Traditional black denominations were formed in a movement for civil and religious freedom. The ordination of women in these denominations spans seventy-one years. According to Mark Chaves in *Ordaining Women: Culture and Conflict in Religious Organizations*, the first groups to affirm women's calls were the National Baptist Convention in 1895 and Pentecostal Holiness in 1895. They were followed by the African Methodist Episcopal Zion Church (AMEZ) in 1898, the African Methodist Episcopal Church (AME) with deacons in 1948 and elders in 1960, and the Christian Methodist Episcopal Church (CME) in 1966.[25]

The Church of God in Christ (COGIC) did not ordain women as elders, pastors, or bishops. Men were to preach and women were to teach, although public speaking of prominent women in the denomination is indistinguishable from exemplary preaching. The most powerful women's department in traditional nineteenth-century black denominations was located in the Church of God in Christ. When denied pastoral positions, the women became evangelists. They led churches in the absence or death of the pastor and developed individual congregations. COGIC women who began churches were included in the church history. They assumed leadership in education, prayer, and Bible study and sustained the churches economically.[26]

Bettye Collier-Thomas lists the AME Church as first granting women the position of evangelist to avoid the ordination question. Sophie Murray was given that status at Mother Bethel AME in Philadelphia in 1816. Male clergy welcomed women evangelists because they built churches; raised funds; and ministered to membership through church revivals, camp meetings, and Women's Days beginning in 1904. The AMEZ, she writes, was the first black denomination to grant suffrage (the right to vote and hold office in the church) to women, in 1876. In 1894, Julia Foote and Mary Small were ordained deacons. However, when Mary J. Small was ordained an elder in 1898, she was a threat to male clergy because an elder can supervise other clergy and had both power and authority. Other denominations said that the AMEZ had challenged the natural order of life. Mary Small's husband, with whom she shared pastoral appointments, became a CME bishop. The African Methodist Episcopal Zion Church admitted Florence Spearing Randolph to full conference membership in 1898. She was assigned to a small congregation. She worked diligently, and the church grew. Thus, the denomination began a still popular tradition. Women were often assigned to a "dead" church, or at least to one on life support. They received little support. Through their efforts, the church became healthy. They were then replaced by a young man and sent to another "dying" place.[27]

The official debate on black women's ordination began in the AME Church in the 1880s. Bishop Henry McNeal Turner ordained Sarah Ann Hughes in 1884. Her ordination was revoked in 1885 when Bishop Turner was sanctioned. The CME ordained women between 1895 and 1960, but there are insufficient records on names and numbers. In 1897, Mary Mims was made a CME elder in Kentucky.[28] Florence Spearing Randolph was licensed to preach and was ordained a deacon and an elder in the late nineteenth century. She received appointments to several churches (against the wishes of her husband) between 1925 and 1946. She compiled one of the few sermon collections of a black woman preacher of that era. Her focus was sin, economic empowerment, racial discrimination, gender ideology, and women's capabilities in religious work. In 1948, Rebecca M. Glover was ordained a local deacon and served as Assistant Pastor of Metropolitan AME in Washington D.C. She received full ordination in the AME Church in 1956.[29]

"First Time Ever I Saw Your Face"

Black women sing of victory and testify about how they got over. Black women also have a plethora of firsts. Someone has to break the path. Someone has to stand all alone. Someone has to be the first to try, the first to cry, the first to speak, and the first to die trying so that others can live. There are hundreds of thousands of black women proclaimers whose names are contained in history books who many have come to know.

Mary Evans, pastor of St. John AME Church in Indianapolis, was the first black woman to obtain a Doctor of Divinity from Wilberforce

University, in 1924. The first black woman to celebrate Mass was Deacon and former Oblate Sister of Providence, Rose Marie Vernell. She was ordained a Catholic priest in the AACC in Washington D.C., in 1992 by Bishop George Stallings.[30] Mother Leafy Anderson founded the first African American spiritual church in the 1920s in New Orleans. She practiced a blend of Roman Catholicism, African American Protestantism, Holiness, Pentecostalism, nineteenth-century spiritualism, and African-based religion such as Voodoo. Spiritual churches in New Orleans offered ordination to women's leaders as evangelists, ministers, bishops, and even archbishops. Druecillar Fordham was the first ordained and first woman pastor in the Southern Baptist Convention, 1972. Leontine T. C. Kelly was elected United Methodist Bishop in 1984. Barbara C. Harris was consecrated as the first (suffragan) assistant Episcopal woman to bishop of Massachusetts, on February 11, 1989.[31]

Just as Roberta Flack was captivated by a life-changing view of a face, the survey respondents speak about the first time they saw the face of a woman proclaimer and how that proclaimer influenced their spiritual lives. In the tradition of black preaching, celebration may include a list or designation of heroes of the faith. Persons cited have evidenced in their lives that God led, guided, and protected them. The list is of not perfect, but rather faith-filled, people who serve as models for succeeding generations of the faithful. This is a means of connecting the listener to the content of the sermon. In this case, it is a means of connecting the past and the present and giving honor where honor is due. In their own words, pioneers and laywomen—those who have been in ministry in excess of twenty years and have significant experience—a middle generation of ministers—with ten to twenty years of experience—and those neophytes—who are at the initial stages of ministry—celebrate and lift up those who illuminated their paths. They call the roll in sistah fashion.

The first face I saw that confirmed my belief that "Yes I can preach!" was the Reverend Susie Whitman, an associate minister at Shorter AME Church in Denver, Colorado. Reverend Whitman was a mother, a singer, and a woman of God. She always wore a black robe and sometimes a collar. She was regal in her carriage and approached the podium with authority. Up until that point, I thought the women I saw were frightening. I grew up in a Baptist church and the evangelists literally scared the hell out of me. Reverend Whitman showed me a more excellent way of being a minister.

Pioneers

The Reverend Dr. Arlene Churn of Philadelphia, a child evangelist of the 1950s, has been proclaiming God's word for over fifty-five years. She calls the name of Bishop Ida Robinson, founder and pastor of the Mount Sinai Holy Church of America. Bishop Ida B. Robinson was born in 1891 in Hazlehurst, Georgia. In 1908, she joined the Church of God. Moving to Philadelphia in 1917, she affiliated with the United Holy Church of America and became a street evangelist. The focus of her ministry was women's full rights as clergy. In 1924, she founded the Mount Sinai Holy Church of America. The officers of the denomination were women. There were over five hundred churches designated in this denomination. She was consecrated as bishop in 1925.[32] Dr. Churn said that Bishop Robinson's congregation was the first black church to buy property on Broad Street in Philadelphia. Dr. Churn continues to call the names of other pioneers in the proclamation of God's word: Bishop Bessie Washington, Bishop Robinson's sister, also established a church; Bishop Lottie Miller, who was a pioneer in Christian education; and Mrs. Irene Gaffney, Church of God in Christ, who broadcast prayer services every Friday night. Her husband was a bishop in the Church of God in Christ.

The Reverend Dr. Barbara King, founder and pastor of the Hillside Chapel and Truth Center in Atlanta, Georgia, calls the name of the Reverend Dr. Johnnie Coleman. Dr. Coleman is the founder and minister of the Christ Universal Temple in Chicago, Illinois. It is the largest African American Unity Church in the world. Dr. King says:

> I joined her church in 1968. I was so thrilled when I attended her church on an invitation from a neighbor. Since my neighbor never mentioned that Johnnie was a female, I assumed by the name she was male. Imagine my surprise when I entered the sanctuary and saw the minister. Both she and her assistant were females. I was overwhelmed. This was my dream in total manifestation. I joined and she took me under her wing. Later, I met with her and shared my life dream of being a minister. This was my beginning. She sent me to Unity School of Christianity for two years of summer study.

Laywomen

Dr. Dorothy Adams Peck, president of the AME Church Women's Missionary Society, does not speak of being an ordained preacher;

however, since her teenage years, she has responded to the call to speak and make public declarations of God's word and what God means to her. She says that the first woman she heard was Reverend Stewart in a revival: "I was impressed with her intelligence, excellence of delivery, and spirit-filled presentation. Reverend Stewart's personal carriage and mannerisms, although expected, were associated with male characteristics and were to be avoided."

Mrs. Edwina Patrick of the AME Church is a retired schoolteacher and widow of an AME minister. She became a member of the AME church more than seventy years ago. Although she could not recall the first woman she heard, she did express remembrances of the Reverend E. R. Hooks, who was one of the earliest women preachers in Little Rock, Arkansas, during the 1940s. "Reverend Hooks was an evangelist then and was exciting. She never used notes. She was a gifted preacher. Reverend Hooks was a gifted preacher, fluid, sound in Scripture, and energetic."

Andrea Hassell, an AME pastor's spouse in Delaware, says, "I cannot remember anyone in particular because growing up there were several women preachers, especially on our annual Women's Day. If I have to state someone, I would have to say that my Sunday school teacher Mrs. Dismount was the first woman to introduce me to the Bible when I was about six years old."

Kim Martin, Pentecostal, a teacher and bookstore owner in Denver, reminisces,

> The first woman to preach and teach God's word to me would have to be my mother, at home, teaching the Bible to us. I liked when she used to read the Psalms. The first woman that I took real notice of in public preaching would have been Dr. Teresa Fry Brown at Shorter AME Church. I was young at the time, but I remember I could understand what she was talking about in her message.

Deborah Vanoy, Baptist, from Kansas City, Missouri, says, "My mother in 1977 at my church. She was the Women's Day speaker. I thought her message was very spirit-filled and informative. Her delivery was awesome."

Stephanie Thompson, a dynamic youth worker and pastor's spouse in Georgia, relates, "The first woman I heard preach was at St. Philip AME, the Reverend Karen Williams. My reaction was that I thoroughly enjoyed the word that was given."

Judith Tolbert, a Baptist woman from Florida, writes that the first woman she heard proclaim was Dr. Ann Davis, at St. John United Methodist Church in Fort Lauderdale, an official member of the ministry and pastor in the early 1990s.

> My reaction was, "About time they recognize women's ability to lead a congregation." I had heard other women proclaiming the gospel and teaching, but this was the first time I had an opportunity to be around a black female in the mainstream denomination as a pastor, not as an assistant pastor or just a special occasion speaker. I hoped this would be a wake-up call to the traditional black Baptist church—not yet.

Miriam Frye, a Baptist woman in Arizona, proclaims that her grandmother Tessie Parks is the first woman she remembers: "She was explaining Easter to us. I was maybe five or six. My reaction was, at that time, Jesus was a very nice and a special man. I still believe the same thing, but now I can add awesome."

Those with Significant Experience

Pastor Sylvia Penny, assistant pastor of a multicultural, nondenominational church in Denver, has been in ministry for more than forty years. She calls on three women: "I remember Katherine Kuhlman on a radio broadcast during the 1960s, and my reaction was shock. Marian Anderson, although not a preacher, was a woman activist and deeply impressed me. Finally, there was Mrs. R. V. Coger in Washington D.C. in 1962. That's when I knew I wanted to do this."

The Reverend Zina Jacque is an ordained American Baptist clergywoman in Cambridge, Massachusetts: "I have been preaching since I was a child, possibly eight years of age. I would say that I have been proclaiming God's word for thirty years." When asked about the first woman that she heard preach she responded:

> I cannot remember the first woman I heard preach, but the first who had an influence on me was the Reverend Dr. Brenda Williams Little. Brenda was the associate at Second Baptist Church in Evanston. Each summer the senior pastor would take his vacation from Father's Day through Labor Day. Each summer Brenda would take over. She was a *powerful* preacher and pastor. I was astonished to hear a woman powerfully handle the word of God and with unabashed clarity speak the word

of God truthfully, clearly, passionately, and with power. Brenda is currently the pastor of Bethany Baptist Church in Evanston. The preparation of this document makes me know I should call her and let her know how much of an influence she was more than twenty years ago.

The Reverend Mary Anne Bellinger, from First African Presbyterian Church in Lithonia, Georgia, was ordained Baptist and AME. She has been in ministry for twenty-six years. She writes:

> The first woman I heard preach when I was a child was Evangelist Sister Edith Randolph. She scared me to death. She was tall, had a mustache, and sounded like a man. At the time I was living with my grandmother, and Sister Randolph would come to conduct a revival in Cincinnati (my hometown). We were worshiping in a former home for unwed mothers (the city haven't taken over that responsibility), and we used the downstairs living room and parlor as our church sanctuary. For years Glad Tidings Tabernacle was a beacon of hope for the community. It was founded by my grandfather, who was the sweetest little black ex-slave I was ever to know.

The Reverend Rosetta DuBois Gadson remembers well the first woman she heard proclaim. She calls on the memory of Evangelist Mother Charlotte Long:

> Evangelist Long was one of my grandaunt's daughters, who helped "raise" me. I was about four or five years old, and she would take me to Father Divine's church and to Daddy Grace's church. She told me that I had actually preached at Father Divine's church what I was five! She had a storefront church in Detroit that was "nondenominational," and she was the first woman preacher I can remember "making a living" as a preacher, complete with having a devoted "following of believers," driving a Cadillac, dressing in beautiful clothes and fur! She would take me to her church in Detroit, and my mother would take me to the Seventh Day Adventist Church on Saturdays, when she went to church.
>
> My reaction was one of being mesmerized because she was a very powerful preacher. She was a large woman who commanded attention. She spoke loudly and used her hands a lot. Looking back, I'm not sure about her theological training, but she had studied the Bible a lot and could quote Scripture with the best of them! I vividly remember watching her read the Bible, which I'm assuming included her Bible study, and my sitting down to hear her reading it. She was instrumental in helping

me to learn how to read, and I thank God that it was from the Bible! She planted the seed of my desire to become a minister.

Middle Generation of Ministers

Bridgette Young, Associate Dean of the Chapel and Religious Life at Emory University in Atlanta, Georgia, has been proclaiming God's word for eleven years. She is an ordained elder in the United Methodist Church:

> The first woman I heard proclaim was a young woman who was not ordained but worked with my Associate Pastor who was also a campus Minister. I heard her preach at a gathering of college students—a student retreat worship service. At the time, I didn't think of her as a "preacher," but in retrospect, I know that she was proclaiming the word of God. I remember being impressed with how clear she was, and that she was an excellent teacher of the word. I don't think I was able to conceptualize women as preachers—definitely teachers, but not preachers. At that time in my life, there was something about the role of power and authority I associated with the preacher that I did not associate with women. Ironic, isn't it? Over the years, my faith experiences as a college student really formed my spiritual journey. That's why it is so important to me today to be in ministry with college students.

Minister Linda Richards, affiliated with the Church of God, shares that "the first woman" was Kay Arthur in Chattanooga, Tennessee, in 1990. Linda has been proclaiming for over ten years and says,

> My reaction was, "Lord, I wish I could make the word come alive for others as it is coming alive for me as I listen to Kay Arthur speak." I had no idea that that was where the Lord had me headed as I thought I was getting management/supervisor experience for the position I was seeking in the field of criminal justice.

The Reverend Zelia Brown-Harvey is an Assistant Pastor in Georgia and has been an AME Pastor in Ohio:

> The first woman I heard preach was my mother. My reaction was varied. Sometimes I wished she would hush and at others recognized the truth, passion, and relevance of her words and treasured them.

41

The first female preacher I heard was Vashti McKenzie (now an AME bishop). My reaction was twofold. One, her purple, straight dress with a split in the back, makeup, and attractive feminine presence affirmed me. This was a pivotal part of my ministry, for so many men looked at my physical attributes and saw me as a sexual object. Then, because of their natures, they would work to take away a part of who I was. Two, Reverend McKenzie's preaching style was a mixture of femininity as well as traditional preaching techniques and mannerisms. This cemented in me a determination to appreciate the style—if you can call it that—God had given me. To this day, I work at being me.

United Methodist Church Elder, "preacher's kid," and Chaplain of the Wesley-Westminster Campus Ministry at Norfolk State University in Virginia, the Reverend Jan Prentace reminds us of the importance of the teachings we received as children. She says, "It was probably my mother; however, she did not consider herself a preacher, but she proclaimed the gospel. The first woman may have been Katherine Kumer or a Pentecostal woman. I was Baptist, and the Baptists did not ordain women in the community where I grew up."

The Reverend Almella Starks-Umoja, the daughter of a preacher, relates her reaction to the first woman she heard, Evangelist Arniece Sayh at the St. James AME Church in Memphis, Tennessee, in 1960. She says, "I didn't think she knew how to preach. Compared to what I was accustomed the hearing, the sermon was more of a personal testimony."

Pastor Antoinette "Toni" Alvarado serves as copastor with her husband at a nondenominational, independent church in Decatur, Georgia. "The Reverend Priscilla Brady Lee was the first woman I heard proclaim. It was about twenty years ago at a women's retreat. My reaction was one of surprise because I did not realize that God could use a woman in that context."

The Reverend JoAnne Robertson, a member of the National Baptist Convention, USA, Inc., is affiliated with the Metropolitan Interdenominational Church in Nashville, Tennessee. The senior pastoral assistant reports that the first woman she heard preach was Chestina Mitchell Archibald, who was at the time Dean of Chapel at Fisk University: "It was a Martin Luther King Day worship service. I thought her sermon was hastily prepared, but too, she had so much power—I thought she was just raw. I was overwhelmed but also oddly affirmed. No one made any issue about this woman preaching, so neither did I."

Neophytes

Readorah Stewart-Dodd was raised Southern Baptist and National Baptist. She currently attends a nondenominational church, the Faithful Central Bible Church, and All Saints Episcopal in California.

> The first women I heard preach were actually the white wives of Christian televangelists on PTL and TBN (Tammie Faye Bakker, Gloria Copeland, Jan Crouch). I realized early that these women were preaching, but the men were calling it teaching and speaking. The first women I heard preach from the pulpit were at women's retreats when I first moved to Southern California (Evangelist Terri MacFadden and Pastor Juanda Green Peters). It was refreshing to hear women preach Jesus, but I still struggle with them today because of their resistance to use inclusive language and acknowledge feminine divine imagery in preaching and teaching (God is still da' Man!).

The Reverend Elizabeth E. Yates, an AME Itinerant Elder in Florida, has pastored for the past five years and has been in ordained ministry for ten years.

> The first woman was Reverend Lawrence. She was a local elder at St. Paul AME Church in Valdosta, Georgia, when I was eight years old. I thought that it was natural to see females in the pulpit. She wore dark clothes and high collar, no makeup, and had deep raspy voice. Looked and sounded like a man. I didn't look like that so I did not even think about preaching and women.
>
> The woman that most impressed me was the Reverend Shirley McCory Watson. When I first glimpsed her she had on a bright yellow suit jacket with black cuffs and a black skirt. She wore makeup and looked very feminine. This really helped me to know that women could be women, and still be preachers.

Telley Lynnette Gadson pastors two United Methodist churches in Sumter, South Carolina. She has been in ministry for ten years:

> The Reverend Angeline Jones Simmons was the first woman that I heard proclaim. She was the associate minister of my home church, Wesley United Methodist Church in Hollywood, South Carolina, during my early years. It was during the 1980s and because of her presence and her fortitude, I knew that I wanted to be "just like her."

This is the testimony of the Reverend Dr. Stephanie Crowder, who holds ministerial commissions in the National Baptist USA, Inc., and the Christian Church Disciples of Christ. She is a New Testament professor in Nashville, Tennessee:

> The first woman I heard proclaim was Gina Stewart, now the senior pastor at my home church, Christian Missionary Baptist Church in Memphis, Tennessee. She had not acknowledged her call to ministry when I first heard her in 1983 or 1984, but she did indeed preach. The "sermon" was given at my home on Youth Day. The first ordained woman I heard was Vashti McKenzie in 1987. She preached Women's Day at Metropolitan Baptist Church in Washington D.C.

Minister Helen Richmond serves in a nondenominational church where her pastor, the Reverend Arlene Robie, continues to model for her. She speaks about societal influences on our ability to pastor and to preach:

> I do not recall the name of the first woman I heard preach because I come from a Pentecostal background where it was not common for women to preach. However, the first woman that had an impact on my life was Missionary Johnson (I don't remember her first name) at the Temple of Faith Church of God in Christ in October of 1985. I was not saved at that time, but I gave my life to Christ that day.

Roslyn Satchel is an attorney and minister. She is an ordained elder in the African Methodist Episcopal Church. Her father is a minister. She says, "My mother, Dorothea Browning Satchel, was my first model of a woman proclaiming. She sang, played piano, and spoke on special days such as Women's Day or Mother's Day."

Minister Winona Drake serves as Minister to Singles at a nondenominational church in Denver. She also hosts a radio talk show for Christian singles. She says,

> As a young girl I heard a woman preacher who was actually a Pentecostal "fire and brimstone" preacher. I was impacted by the power with which she preached and quoted Scripture from memory. She was also a large woman with the charismatic presence. She was very intimidating. At that time, I had no idea I would one day proclaim the word of God myself.

The Reverend Dallasteen J. Yates is an AME Elder and a lawyer. She is also a consummate musician who works ecumenically:

My mother, Mrs. Jane D. Yates, was the first woman that I heard proclaim from birth at events, family reunions, and gatherings, and our local A.M.E. Church in Gifford, Florida. Other than my mother, another first woman proclaimer that I recall was Dr. Dorothy Peck at an A.M.E. Church Annual Conference worship service in Florida during the mid-1970s. I was inspired by and in awe of her manner, her presence, and her delivery. Everything about her portrayed intelligence, strength, confidence, boldness, power, grace, passion, and poise. My reaction was that I wanted to be like both of these women when I grew up.

I also remember that I saw Evangelist Shirley Caeser perform at the Gifford High School gymnasium in the early 1960s, when I was about five years old. There was a "power" in her singing and "preaching" that both mesmerized me and that commanded my respect. (I did not yet know that it was called "the anointing"). However, I was somewhat turned off at that time by her seemingly brash and unrefined style.

The vast majority of women proclaimers, exhorters, testifiers, missionaries, singers, etc., that I encountered as I grew up were predominantly from the holiness, Pentecostal, "the sanctified church" backgrounds. I had tremendous respect and reverence for the Christ content of their messages; but their styles were all consistently rough sounding, uneducated, and unrefined. And my reaction was consistently the same: I was not attracted to that style of delivery or their plain, drab appearance (usually all white, head-to-toe covering, and no makeup or well-groomed hair). Yet, their method of proclamation seemed to be deemed by the church and community as the "real thing." As an ingénue experiencing the early tuggings of a "call" of some sort to sing and/or to "speak" professionally (NEVER wanted to or considered that I'd become an ordained preacher), I often feared that the same manner of delivery and appearance would also be required of me. The presentation and affirmation of other voices and Christian witnesses like Dr. Peck's and my mother's was refreshing and encouraging.

The Reverend Jacqueline Rowland is an AME minister in Georgia. She calls the name of the Reverend Ruth Murray: " I grew up in the Church of God in Anderson, Indiana. It was quite frequent that I heard women preachers. Reverend Murray was an older woman who boldly proclaimed the word with enthusiasm and sound theology everywhere she walked. I was impressed."

Deborah Matthews preached her first sermon two years ago. She is a member of the Cumberland Presbyterian Church in America. She resides in Alabama:

> I am sure that I must have heard women proclaim the word, but I was profoundly affected when I head the Reverend Endia Scruggs proclaim the word a few months before I was to proclaim the word for the first time. It was at the July 2000 meeting of the Huntsville Presbytery where Rev. Scruggs is now the Moderator. That night I was convicted that I could proclaim the word. I am a Baptist-bred woman. Although I had publicly accepted God's call, I was in the "wilderness" about my "suitability" to proclaim the word. Reverend Scruggs was the instrument that God used to bring me out of the wilderness into the Promised Land.

When I worked as a speech and language pathologist, I learned and taught the power of voice. There were so many times that I felt the brand new words of a child or the relearning of an adult just beneath the surface, waiting to burst forth into the air. This is the process of women waiting to proclaim God's word. It is simmering just beneath the surface. The Reverend Dr. Prathia Hall said in my formative ministry years that if one is denied the call to preach, she or he is perpetually pregnant. Too many women are in labor and the pains will not go away. They need to be able to burst forth in song before the word is aborted. Their throats may get weary, but the air passage is still open. Black women continue to redefine their personhood and say a word in spite of social and ecclesiastical restrictions. In the genius that is black preaching, they continue to issue forth words that heal, help, transform, transcend, reconnect, and reconcile God's people in the midst of it all.

One of the foremothers whose spirit continues to light the way for women is Jarena Lee. She was a traveling AME evangelist in the 1800s, having requested permission to preach in 1809. I first delivered this mini sermon at the AME Women in Ministry Conference in 1999 in St. Louis, Missouri. In the mode of Jarena Lee, it was self-published so that black women could know about her call and ministry.[33]

"A Letter from Jarena Lee"

God sends messages to teach us. God commissions forerunners to break new paths. God sets aside peculiar people, women and men, to reveal a foretaste of glory divine. God created one such sister—a *sasa*, a trailblazer, a daughter, a wife, a mother, a prayer warrior, a preacher—whose life speaks across the ages to encourage us to keep on keeping on.

In that set-aside place in my mind, God has written a letter from our spiritual foremother Jarena Lee to remind us that who got ordained is not up for a vote. Her life reminds us that when God calls, sanctifies, and sets us aside, no weapon formed against us shall prosper. No mountain is too high and no valley is too low. And no situation is too hard for God to work out. When God ordains us, no human manipulation, mendacity, mismanagement, mean spiritedness, madness, mediocrity, or mess can mess up God's plan. So, go with me to our letter.

Our sister writes:

Dear Daughters,

As I sit here in the cloud of witnesses, God allows me to hear your words, sense your pain, share your joys, and watch your running of this Christian race. I thought a few words of encouragement were in order. I know the road has been rough, the going has been tough, and the hills are just beginning to get hard to climb. I will attempt to speak the truth in love, but remember that sometimes the truth hurts.

First of all, we need to share that this ministry is not about us. It is not about titles, robes, crosses, rings, collars, shoes, hair, fingernails, handkerchiefs, lap cloths, pulpits, or sermonic proficiency. Just like in my day, people are dying. Children are still being abused. People are locked up, locked out, and locked down. But let me get right to the point.

I was born 216 years ago in another social political climate. But the more things change, the more they remain the same. I was born at the time of slavery. My first career was as a servant. At the age of seven I was separated from my family. I realize that some of you are second or third career. Use what you have to the glory and honor of God. Although my mother and father would not be church-going, Bible-toting Christians, somehow God planted a spiritual seed within me that took root and grew until fire was shut up in my bones. I could not hold my peace. I felt the fist of God pressing into my backbone. Every time I wanted to bend under the pressure of the established church, I had to stand up a little bit taller. And ringing in my mind the edict from God saying "Go preach my gospel!" The urgent expression of the good news would make me wake up in the middle of the night. It had me crying when I didn't know why I was crying. It had me walking the floor. I couldn't keep food on my stomach. All I knew was that I had to say a word for my Master.

So, sometimes I walked. Didn't have cars, planes, or a train then. I walked. Remember one year when I walked 2,700 miles preaching a mere 138 sermons. Not just to people who looked like me, but to brown folks, red folks, and white folks as well. I preached with men and women, boys and girls, no respector of persons as God instructed me. I preached in private houses, higher houses, camp meetings, on the roadside, at the bedside, and despite what anything or anyone said that I could be or do.

You probably heard of my conversion at age twenty-four. Then there was my attempt to take my own life because I thought I was crazy and that no one would believe me. I know you heard that I was married to a preacher. Believe me, being a preacher spouse is not an easy thing to be. We had two sons. Then Joe died six years later. There I was a single mother. No property rights. I had to raise my children by myself. I had passion, however, to tell the world about Jesus.

You know my story. I went to Rev. Allen (he was not a bishop then) and said that God had a call on my life. But he said that the laws of the church do not allow for women to preach. And yes I waited, still doing what God told me to do. I went back ten years later and asked again because I believed a human "no" is never the final answer God's kingdom.

But I want you to know, my sisters, that you have to be persistent. When they turn you away, keep going back, and going back, and going back, and going back, and going back. Even when I was given a verbal license to exhort and hold prayer meetings it was clear that God's hand remained on my life.

When God calls you, when God anoints you, when God appoints you, when God puts words in your mouth, and sets you before the people, know that you have been set aside, sanctified, and ordained by God to do God's work. No need for human conversation, criticism, or committee. God said it and that settles it.

After I expressed my call again to Rev. Allen, I felt relieved at first because he said no. After all, I was living my life. I didn't have to get up in the middle of the night to visit with sick folks, preach with anyone, or constantly bury the dead. But in my dreams, God kept calling me. As I cooked my children's meals, God kept calling me. As I went to the grocer, God kept calling me. As I played with the boys, God kept calling me. As I lay in my bed, God kept calling me.

I didn't go before the church for a trial sermon (unless you count the one I did that day the Spirit led me to preach when that brother had not prepared himself). It was at that time the Bishop said he believed I was called. The Spirit had convicted him. I was allowed to go out to exhort. No piece of paper from a presiding elder because my name is written on the Lamb's Book of Life.

I did not attend an institute. I did not stand before the annual conference to explain God's conversation with me. I just lived out my call and followed the directions that God gave me. I know now that I was no less a minister than my brothers. I was just as much blood-bought and Spirit-covered as they were.

No, my sisters, I was never brought before a bishop as a candidate. I was not asked if I was apt or meet or if I exercised ministry to honor God and the church. I was not asked if there was an impediment against what I could do to set a good example. My character was never passed. I did not stand before sinners saved by grace who needed their own characters passed. I just ministered to God's sheep and proclaimed God's word in season and out of season. I ministered to mixed congregations, different faiths, and different traditions, and God kept on passing my character.

No one asked me if I would forsake the world, lay aside worldly cares, or frame my life with the Scriptures or get rid of strange doctrine. But I can tell you that I was guided by the indwelling of the Holy Spirit. That Spirit shed light on the word and led me in diligent prayer. God kept me moving, and God will keep you moving.

My sisters, I never wore a black robe. I never knelt at the altar with the hands of seven elders pressing down on my head until I thought my spine would snap. I never had the opportunity to hear the bishop invoke the words "Take thou authority." My face was never pushed into or held on the Holy Bible. I did not hear a sermon about the perils and promises of ministry. I never had the opportunity to wash my hands and serve communion to other ministers and family members gathered for the service. I never had that chance but I will witness that God robed me with spiritual light. God placed me on the altar of sacrifice. Got impregnated me with an unforgettable ungovernable Spirit. God pressed me

and molded me
and melted me
and filled me
and used me as an estimate of his holy word.

The communion of saints broke bread together by welcoming me into their homes, their churches, and their lives. God's hand rested on me throughout my entire ministry. The sweetness that the word talks about was the honey of God's love for me. I had to share it with others. The peace of God was there in the midst of the storms of illness, separation from my sons, and when my friends did not understand that I was a fool for Christ. I had to keep on going because I was working under the hand of God.

Daughters, love was there through the blood of Jesus the Christ. Love was given when I couldn't even love myself. Love was given as Christ carried my sins in his body.

I know that you are probably saying that Sister Jarena is a little long winded, but I need you to understand that God, God, God ordained in me in my mother's womb. I did not wait for legal process. I didn't have time. I had to go forward. I could not wait for society to change. I couldn't wait for human beings to validate what I know God had given me. I had to do what God told me to do.

Beloved children, as we consider the place in ministry or as we think about how women are demeaned, discounted, discouraged, disrespected, denied, and disenfranchised, often by our own churches, remember the faithful brothers and sisters who attended to God's voice and stood behind and beside us in the struggle. Think about brothers, like Bishop Henry McNeil Turner, who was chastised by the church for ordaining women. Think of Amanda Berry Smith who had to go elsewhere to have her call validated. Think of Zilpha Elaw who preached anyhow. Think of our grandmothers, mothers, and sisters. Think of our fathers and brothers and children who affirmed us as God's messenger in spite of pressure and pain.

My life was not lived in vain. God blessed my ministry in spite of what others said or did. Even today as I look over the precipice of heaven in this cloud of witnesses, God continues to remind me of the power of God's calling. Our souls and spirits are linked because we're the daughters of the most high God. Above him, there is no other. God's calling is a foundation of our ordination. No one can deny us what God has for us. Nothing and nobody can stop the move of God.

My sisters, please note that every time you pray—I'm ordained.

Every time you send a song—I'm ordained.

Every time you have a word of testimony—I'm ordained.

Every time you bring a word of hope even when they make you stand outside the door—I'm ordained.

Every time you take a stand for justice—I'm ordained.

Every time you give a cup of cold water in Jesus' name—I'm ordained.

Every time you refuse to give up on your call—I'm ordained.

Every time you take the assignment in that little church they said was about to die and God blesses the effort and it thrives—I'm ordained.

Every time, every time, every time you yield to God's indwelling spirit and instead of outside influences—I'm ordained.

Your lives today, my daughters, help affirm for me that God is still calling, ordaining, and blessing women with all kinds of gifts and graces. So just keep on daughters.

Keep on praying

and preaching

and teaching

and living

and loving

and ministering

and giving your lives to Christ.

I may have been a voice crying out in the wilderness over 200 years ago, but I can hear a multitude of voices crying out today. Remember it is not about us. It is about God. God will straighten out the crooked places in your ministry. God will lift up the valley experiences. God will put you on a mountaintop and make your enemies your footstool. God and God alone will put your ministry in place and preserve it to his glory. The gifts God has blessed you with will make a space for living out your call.

My prayer, daughters, is that you learn to hear God's call above the noise of this world.

Do not compromise your integrity regardless of what you are promised by humanity.

Remember you are a daughter of the King.

Do not sell your birthright for a cup of instant soup. God is rich in houses and lands.

Do not barter your soul for microwaved power. The Bible says that what we obtain is not by power or by might but by God's Spirit.

Keep in mind that every tear you shed on the journey,
every pain you feel on the journey,
every lonely night you spend on the journey,
every headache you experience on the journey,
every joy you share on the journey,
every victory you have on the journey
is all to the glory of God.

Love,
Your mother in the ministry and your sister in the faith,
Jarena Lee

SINGING IN THE KEY OF G-O-D

*Take a good look, friends, at who you were when you got called into this life. I
don't see many of "the brightest and the best" among you, not many influen-
tial, not many from high-society families. Isn't it obvious that God deliberately
chose men and women that the culture overlooks and exploits and abuses,
chose these "nobodies" to expose the hollow pretensions to the "somebodies"?
(1 Corinthians 1:26-31 The Message)*

For years I served as a choir, ensemble, and soloist director. On those
days when the musicians and the director were in one accord, the
music invigorated the hearts, souls, and minds of the pulpit staff,
congregation, and choir. There were, however, those occasions when one
section or voice was out of sync and nothing seemed to get us back in key.
No amount of flailing of arms, stomping of feet, shaking of heads, rolling
of eyes, or turning off of microphones seemed to diminish the discordant
sound. Someone or something was in the wrong key. Then there was the
perennial problem of the "star," who had to lead everything regardless of
genre or abilities of others. You know, the one who comes in late, never
rehearses, rushes to the microphone, and acts as if everyone is his or her

background singers. The one who tries to be Luther Vandross, Patti LaBelle, Shirley Caesar, Prince, Kirk Franklin, Yolanda Adams, and the entire Mississippi Mass Choir at one time. No hint of understanding that God, the Chief Maestro, selects particular, peculiar, specific instruments for particular songs and sounds. The "star" sings in the key of M-E. God's proclaimers sing in the key of G-O-D. These are the section leaders of God's choir. Sometimes it's the last person everyone would pick—the one who sings softly, the one whose voice sometimes cracks, the one who barely makes eye contact, the one who keeps a fire burning but rarely speaks up—who is enabled to sing the truth of God so passionately that lives are transformed. God calls for the one who, in spite of castigating cacophonous criticism, debilitating discordant disbelief, or virulent vibrating voices, is to impart the word of life. God calls—not stars, not directors, not boards, not institutions—but simply calls. God provides a symphony of support when all others turn deaf ears. God calls in tones no one else can hear. God calls above the noise. If there is no room for God in a choir, God will simply create another one to sing in the key of G-O-D.

I define a call as an irresistible conviction, urge, pull, command, motivation, or attraction toward a particular person, place, or thing. In terms of ministry, a call is a divine mandate imparted spiritually. It is God's command for a particular purpose. One may attempt to avoid the call. Others may try to abort the call. That "something within" will not leave. It tugs at the edge of dreams. It stares us in the face in the morning and walks with us throughout our day. Once the call is answered, there is an ongoing review of the aspects and responsibilities. Although there may be modifications, elaborations, transformations, and increasing clarity, the essence of the call never ends. Ultimately God's purpose is accomplished often in unexpected ways. Like gifts of the Spirit, a specific call is given to an individual for the benefit of the community. Answering, responding, yielding, and submitting to a call means giving up one's will for the ultimate reward of doing another's will. It means responding to humanity in both leadership and servanthood. More important, it means saying to God, "Here I am. I am ready to be prepared to do your work and stand in the gap with your people." It means recognizing, as Paul says, that God can use even our earthen vessels as instruments for kingdom-building in proclamation of who God is, how God works, and why God was willing to sacrifice Jesus for our lives. The fruition of the call is measured not in numbers or finances, but in changed lives. The lived experience of the preacher actualizes one's authority. The proclaimer embodies God's will and purpose before the people.

The late Samuel Proctor, homiletician extraordinaire, states that the call of the preacher is part of the mystery of God. Elements of the call include a sense of transcendence in God's word. The person connects to the eternal in the midst of the existential situation. Tranquillity, meaning, purpose, and encouragement support the call. There is an invitation to accept God's grace and experience restoration and renewal.[1]

In the black church, one hears that a preacher is "under the anointing." This further substantiates the priestly and prophetic abilities of the preacher. The anointing is a credential that is not given in seminary or by church officials. It is a gift from God, and one's ministry is blessed and will prosper if and when the anointing is present. The Holy Spirit is nondiscriminatory, so both men and women may be "under the anointing." Homiletics professor James Earle Massey depicts the relationship between call and anointing. He designates call as a conviction that God has a claim on one's life. This leads to a focused identity and a sense of purpose, action, energy, and creativity. Anointing, on the other hand, is a sense of being identified with God's will in relation to some need. There is assertiveness to action, a basic instinct about what needs to be done. Massey identifies three types of authority: authority derived from God, authority shared with the community, and experiential authority from the Holy Spirit.[2] Those called to preach function under God's authority. One does nothing by himself or herself. All empowerment, all words, all actions, and all spiritual manifestation come from God. The preacher, the proclaimer, is merely an instrument, a vessel through whom God chooses to share information with the community of faith.

William Meyers's typology of call in the black community fits the patterns discussed by women in the survey as well as those cited in spiritual narratives. The inner call comes from God. The only person who can validate this call is the one with whom God has conversed. The community call is validation of the divine call, often by an initial or trial sermon and a congregational or ecclesiastical board vote of one's authenticity and evidence of ministry potential. Calls develop in at least three different ways.[3] The *cataclysmic/reluctant* call stems from some momentous event, either natural or supernatural. Sensory phenomena—such as visions, dreams, and signs—are reported. Women's narratives and some respondents report a personal crisis—health, divorce, death, loss of job, visions, and voices. There is a resistance to the call and then a sense of relief, joy, and peace after surrender. The *call of destiny* means that one is born, groomed, or nurtured in to consciousness of vocation. Men are more likely to be groomed "from their mother's womb," particularly in faith systems that believe a parent who preaches must have at least one child who preaches. No other vocation is entered. Women, however, primarily enter ministry after one or two careers. Nurturing the call may change, may become more egalitarian with the increase in female mentors and models and the reformation of denominational restrictions of women preachers. Finally, the *gradual call* unfolds amidst reluctance. There is an internal (divine) struggle and an external (community sanction sought) struggle. Reluctance may stem from "old tapes" women hear (shouting they cannot preach because they are women), personal feelings of inadequacy ("Are you sure you mean me, Lord?"), calamitous history within church life, biblical imperatives and erroneous exegesis, theological grounding, denominational polity, fear of alienation, loss of status, age, sociopolitical views, loss of income, and nonbelief. Several of the survey answers alluded to initial reluctance to proclaim and eventual acquiescence over a period of time.

Sistah Responses

Sistah responses in this chapter stem from the answers to three requests: Describe your call and how often you proclaim; name your models/mentors; and describe your place of proclamation. Responses included here have been selected to reflect the variety of persons who participated in the study. Again, I seek to honor the voices and words of those called to proclaim. The responses, when permitted, are given verbatim. The questions answered in the first section were: Why do you proclaim God's word? How long have you been proclaiming? How often do you proclaim? An overview of the 116 surveys on the question of frequency of proclamation yielded a range from thirty persons who proclaim weekly (three of whom preach two to three times each Sunday) to one person who rarely proclaims. Opportunities varied according to ministerial status, denomination, position, and time in ministry.

Bishop Nellie Yarborough is the pastor and bishop of the International Mount Calvary Holy Church, Pentecostal, in Boston, Massachusetts. She is also the Director of Education (Principal) at the Brumfield Johnson Academy and Nellie C. Yarborough Bible Institute. Bishop Yarborough has been in ministry for fifty-two years and preaches weekly at both her church and elsewhere as a guest preacher. This pioneer proclaimer says that she proclaims because "my passion is to deliver people for the kingdom."

President of the AME Church Missionary Society, Dr. Dorothy Allen Peck proclaims two or more times per month in local churches, conferences, and in AME Episcopal District meetings. She has declared God's word since her teen years:

> God's word is a lamp unto my feet and a light unto my pathway. I feel called to study, teach, and "proclaim" his word for my own personal and spiritual growth and for the purpose of helping others to understand that, as Christian missionaries, we must intensify our faith and continue the ministry of Jesus Christ. Proclamation of the word is vital for those purposes and for the undergirding needed to carry out the mission and ministry of the church.

The Reverend Orellia Marshall was the only person from the African Methodist Episcopal Zion Church to respond to the project. Representing the first traditional black denomination to ordain women, she has served forty-four years as a "speaker, an exhorter, and an ordained preacher." She is presently at Little Mount Zion AME Zion Church in Pensacola, Florida. She preaches "once per month as copastor and once weekly as Bible teacher. Also on a daily basis in the marketplace and the workplace." This mother of the faith proudly heralds, "My proclamation is a calling from my mother's womb, whereas I was chosen by the Lord to proclaim his name holy before man, preaching the message of repentance unto beings born again."

The Reverend Dr. Addie June Hall describes herself as "Evangelist, Teacher, and Speaker." She is a United Methodist minister in Florida. She has been preaching for more than thirty years and does so at every opportunity:

> I have always worked within various ministries in my church. Many of the former pastors of my church proclaimed that I was anointed to carry the word of God at a very early age.
>
> In looking back, it is clear that God has been a part of my life from inception, leading and guiding me through times of joy and pain. I heard his call even though I didn't want to accept it. I hear him as he speaks to and through me, now. He has given me many spiritual gifts, including prophecy, and I am obliged to share these gifts with others. I have so much to thank God for. God told me to go and tell it, and he

would draw others unto him. In order to live, I must proclaim his word. I have a passion for Jesus.

The Reverend Betty Hanna-Witherspoon, D.Min., is pastor of an AME Church in California. "I have been preaching for thirty years," she says. She preaches weekly and is the only minister assigned to the church:

> I proclaim because I have chosen to accept my calling and challenge to say a word for God from the most unlikely of sources—a poor, middle-aged, divorced African American woman. I believe that I had a choice to preach or not to preach. I chose to preach. The world is filled with really great preachers. There is only need for one more voice if God has something different to say through me; my call is a testimony to the hope and healing that exists in Jesus for people like me. I proclaim because God continues to call the foolish, weak, base, despised, and things that are not to bring to naught things that are (1 Corinthians 1:27-28). My ministry is testimony to God's continuing miracle of bringing hope and healing to and through those who are not highly valued in this world. I preach to proclaim hope and healing. (Luke 4:16-19)

The Reverend Dr. Melinda Contreras-Byrd is an ordained AME elder in Trenton, New Jersey. She is a licensed psychologist and owner and director of The Generations Center—a unique mental health facility in Cherry Hill, New Jersey, that specializes in the treatment of all women and also men of color. This clergy spouse says, "I proclaim about once a month, sometimes twice."

> Why do I proclaim God's word? Can't help it! I have been proclaiming since I was in high school. At this time I was trained by several white evangelical groups—The Billy Graham Crusade, Youth for Christ, Africa Inland Mission, etc. I also worked with black evangelical groups—Newark Evangelistic Committee and The Tom Skinner Crusades. At this time I was a member of an integrated, nondenominational evangelical church in Newark that had a very active youth ministry. We were groomed to travel and proclaim. It was interesting for me to note at the time of entry into the conference of the AME Church that the reason that there was so much time in between my initial licensing and the time I sought entry was the lack of a model for female ministers/proclaimers in my life. I was groomed for evangelism and Christian Education—while the males were groomed for ordained min-

istry and proclamation. Only the males of our group could "preach" at events. Girls were free to give testimonies only.

The Reverend Ayanna Abi-Kyles is an ordained member of the Pan African Orthodox Christian Church/Shrine of the Black Madonna and has UCC affiliation and has been used as God's vessel of profession of faith for twenty-five years. She is afforded an opportunity to share the word once per month at the Shrine: "I proclaim God's word because I have witnessed God's word become flesh in my life, in my family, in community, and in the world."

The Reverend Detra Bishop of Hattiesburg, Mississippi, has been in ministry for twelve years. She is a Baptist minister who proclaims daily. She describes her nurtured, innate call: "God chose me from my mother's womb to be his servant. On March 23, 1989, God called me to 'preach the word.' I say with the apostle Paul, 'Woe unto me if I preach not the gospel.' I have been charged by the Lord to preach." Her call text is 2 Timothy 4:1-5.

The Reverend Gail Hayes lives in Durham, North Carolina. She is a minister in a nondenominational church. She has been enunciating for twelve years, primarily through the Daughters of the King Ministries, Inc., that she founded. She says she proclaims

> because I'm called to do so. To ignore this call would be like ignoring the cries of my children (I'm forty-six years old with a three-year-old daughter and five-year-old son; and yes, they are mine. I had a physically closed womb, according to doctors' reports, and God opened it at age forty). To do so would be like crawling through glass in a mummified state, leaving a trail of my life's blood and only seeing darkness on the brightest summer day.

The Reverend Ernestine Mathis is Local Elder in an AME Church in Columbus, Georgia. She exemplifies the women who work in the church for years as nonordained, faithful ministers and, through a gradual call, enter ordained ministry in their mature years. Reverend Mathis declares,

> I proclaimed the word for fourteen years before formally answering the call to preach (songs, talks, ministering by listening and referring to spiritual matters). I have a daily broadcast ministry of "sermonette" type pieces. I do a sermon approximately six to eight times per year.

There's a *spirit*, that *something within* that propels me to a life of service to my God, to share with others how he moved within and thorough
me. It seems natural. I proclaim the word in obedience to the voice asking me to *love* and *serve*. That obedience shows me that as I teach the
word, I learn. As I serve others, I serve my God. It's like that lyric, "It
just won't let me hold my peace." To know God is to *love* God and allow
the Spirit in and give the tools necessary to proclaim to people the word
of God! I proclaim because it makes me happy to tell of God's love. I
don't get tired and *I believe* that what moves me is God's will!

The Reverend Regina Groff, an AME minister in Colorado, tells of her
reluctant call. Professing her call for eleven years, she says that technically, she preaches daily. She formally preaches an average of once a
month:

At first, it was because I didn't have a choice. The urge was so strong
that it could not be ignored. Although, I did try. I just figured that I
would give in to the calling. I was mad about it for a long time. I had
great plans for myself and clearly, ministry was not in *my* plan. Now, the
"urge" is still present, but I have come to understand it as the Holy
Spirit. The Holy Spirit reminds me that God has done too much for me
that I can't hold my peace. God has called me, given me a word to
preach, and that's what I'm going to do. No questions asked—at least
not today.

Sister Deborah Matthews is the most recently called and confessed
preacher in the survey. She is a Presbyterian minister in Alabama. She
submitted her trial sermon and exhibits a bold presence and is a reassuring reminder that many will follow behind contemporary women. "I proclaim God's word because that is what I have been called to do. I accepted
my call in April of 2000. Opportunities to proclaim the word seem to
come in 'spells.' I would say that I have had the opportunity to preach
about twenty times since my introductory sermon."

The Reverend Dr. Claudette A. Copeland ministers at the nondenominational New Creation Christian Fellowship in Texas. She has preached
since age eighteen and was licensed as Evangelist in the Church of God
in Christ at age thirty. She preaches weekly at her home church and also
serves as guest preacher at conferences and in churches worldwide. She
tells of a call of destiny nurtured in the household of faith. "The sense of
the 'call' to preach has been evident in my heart since age fifteen. The

relentless knowing. It has been confirmed by the results in the community of faith through the years."

The Reverend Bridget Piggue is an ecumenical minister. She also works as Director of Pastoral Education. She explained that she has two denominational affiliations: Independent Pentecostal Church at the New Creation Christian Fellowship Church in San Antonio, Texas, with Pastor Claudette Copeland and Bishop David M. Copeland (they recently formed an endorsing body with the name The Kingdom Council of Interdependent Christian Churches) and Presbyterian Church, USA at the First African Presbyterian Church in Lithonia, Georgia, with Pastor Mark Lomax. Reverend Piggue has been declaring God's word for twelve years and preaches at least once a month:

> I am clear that I am called to proclaim God's word and that I have significant gifts to share with the body. My passion in ministry is to provide others with tools that will assist them in living life in as much health as possible, mentally, emotionally, physically, and spiritually. Proclaiming God's word is one of the vehicles through which this can happen.

The Reverend Veronice Miles has been a Baptist (National Baptist Convention, USA, Inc.) for eight years. Her primary focus is youth ministry and Christian education. She proclaims two to three times a month with youth and five to eight times a year in other Christian settings.

> I proclaim God's word because I believe that the Scripture and proclamation of God's word can offer the hope, encouragement, and power necessary to live in the presence of God as people created in God's image. Proclamation of God's word can empower persons to continue the work of liberation and salvation/rescue that Jesus began, deal with the struggle of life and the evils of the world, and to imagine and work toward realizing a world in which love is the principle of life.

Pastor Sylvia K. Penny is Assistant Pastor of Colorado Christian Fellowship in Aurora, Colorado. She describes the church as a nondenominational/multicultural congregation. Presenting her gradual call, she lets us know that when one is called of God, she preaches not only "in season and out of season," but also "without ceasing." She trumpets, "I preach every chance and opportunity that God allows me. I preach in my office, my community, and my church."

I've been in church all my life, from Holiness, Baptist, to Assemblies of God and nondenominational. I love the word. I live it the best of my ability. I proclaim to others as the Spirit leads me. I know the power of prevailing prayer. I do operate in the principles of divine healing, and I've learned how to face life's implications and complications and surrender and die to self. Most of all I've learned that when you're on assignment by God, man has no agenda other than to be used fully by him. I've been talking about preaching for about forty years. But I've only been actually living to the best of my potential and walking in faith, sharing with others what thus sayeth the Lord, being used fully, trusting and obeying, seeking his face, and going beyond the veil for twenty years.

The Reverend Lisa Rhodes is the Dean of the Chapel at Spelman College in Atlanta, Georgia. She is a member of the Progressive National Baptist Convention and is the former Assistant Pastor of Ebenezer Baptist Church in Atlanta, Georgia. Her call is also a gradual call. Her testimony is one of societal restrictions and conventions that impeded, but did not stop, her response:

Initially, I believed only men were called to "preach." In my church home, only men were nurtured in the preaching task. At the displeasure of my home pastor, I pursued seminary to prepare for ministry. My goals were limited to Christian Education, Evangelism, and Pastoral Counseling. I therefore have struggled with feeling free to preach, but I know I must proclaim God's word because he believed I have very specific and unique gifts of healing and facilitating wholeness and that God empowers and uses these gifts as instruments for spiritual, psychological, and emotional liberation. The people of God, particularly women, are in need of soft, emotionally engaging, and sensitive language and symbols that correlate the Bible story with current everyday issues that speak to the love, reconciliation, and hope of the Christian faith.

My trial sermon at Ebenezer Baptist Church was in May 1990. Opportunities to preach Ebenezer were limited to mainly twice a year. Beginning in 1998, and for the last two years, local and national preaching engagements, revivals, and women's workshops have significantly increased. I preach on average two times per month, at the Sisters Chapel in Spelman College.

Sister Miriam E. Frye, Baptist laywoman in Arizona, has been involved in ministry for forty years. She specializes in musical proclamation. She reports a call that was nurtured by her role models—her mother and grandmother—and by opportunities for specialized ministry in the church. Her artistic nature sings in the key of G-O-D:

> God is the source of my life, my strength, my salvation, my understanding friend, and will be there for me no matter what. I have always been an introvert. I mainly proclaim in my mind, heart, and my actions. I was youth choir director for sixteen years and wrote music. This was my way of "preaching" or "proclaiming God's word."

The Reverend Sheri Smith Clayborn is Itinerant Deacon in the African Methodist Episcopal Church. As a clergy spouse, she recently moved from California to Georgia. Her focus is congregational care. She enunciates a call of destiny, nourished in the Baptist church of her youth:

> I was licensed in 1999. However, I've been proclaiming God's word since I was a little girl. I could not have been more than six or seven years old. I believe I proclaim daily, at least I try to proclaim the gospel not only through what I say, but also by how I behave and treat others.
>
> My primary location of proclamation is through everyday conversation and interaction with people. I do receive opportunities to preach at the church where I serve, but I try not to depend on those opportunities. I believe the words I say from the pulpit will have no value if I don't treat my neighbor right. If I do not try to care for God's people on a regular basis then my getting in the pulpit is in vain. Therefore, I concentrate on preaching through my actions.

The Reverend Shermella Egson pastors an AME Church in Riverside, California. She has been in ministry for over twenty years, preaching three or more times a week. In answer to the question, "How and why do you proclaim God's word?" she said, "How else will they know God and his purpose?"

The Reverend Mary Anne Bellinger has been in ministry thirty-three years. "In 1969 I had a dream and in the dream God said to me, 'I have a preacher.' Two nights later the dream returned with the message, 'The preacher is you.'" She delivered her trial sermon in 1976.

The Reverend Kimberly Detherage has been preaching for eleven years about once every other month. She serves as Youth Minister at an AME Church in Brooklyn. She says, "I proclaim God's word because I have no other choice but to preach God's liberating gospel to the people. I have been called by God to proclaim God's word. I preach because I must. I preach because it is the power of God within me that compels me to do so."

Connectional President of AME Women in Ministry and Itinerant Elder the Reverend Sandra Blair lives in Oakland, California. She has been in ministry since the mid-1980s. Initially, she taught Sunday school, vacation Bible school, Bible study, and membership development classes. She acknowledged her call to preach in 1986. She preaches on average once a month and teaches weekly. This is a path walked by many black women. Although the field of Christian education is vital to the growth and development of churches, it is at times used to avoid ordination. Other times it is the seeding ground for proclamation.

> I proclaim God's word because God's yes is louder than my no. I confessed all of my feelings of unworthiness and inadequacy to be God's messenger on the occasion of accepting my call to ordained ministry. In a sermon entitled "Called but Not Ready," I explored the response of Moses, Jeremiah, and others who, when called by God, had to be convinced that God saw the possibilities beyond their human limitations and had a special purpose for which they were to be used.
>
> My journey of proclamation began when I became active in the Christian education ministry of my local church and my gifts and love for teaching were rekindled. When I acknowledged my call to ordained ministry, my teaching vocation was affirmed when, in prayer one morning, I was led to Psalm 78, which speaks of the importance of teaching God's word and passing on from generation to generation the story of what God has done and is doing for God's people. It has taken some time for me to feel as comfortable preaching as I do teaching and I believe that teaching must be an integral part of authentic preaching. For me, the act of proclamation means conveying with clarity and conviction God's transformative power.

The Reverend Raedorah Stewart-Dodd was raised in the Southern Baptist and National Baptist Conventions. She had an eclectic, ecumenical background. She affiliated with the American Baptist Church, USA, while in seminary. She attends a nondenominational church with former alliances with ABC-USA, National Baptist, Progressive Baptist, and the "undenominational" Full Gospel Baptist Church Fellowship. She also attends an Episcopal church. She founded the Proclaim and Publish Ministries three years ago. She, too, describes a nurtured call and several ways of living out that call:

I have a strong sense of calling and awareness of destiny. I'm moved by passion for study, art, and delivery of preaching. Always, even as a child, I wanted to "preach" regardless of what I was taught in the church and home; and as a part of whatever else I did as vocation.

When I "played church" as a child, I only played if I could be the "preacher"! And then, actually took my text from Scripture on the Sunday school cards and required memory verses.

I "jack-legged" (preached before being designated as a licentiate or ordained) for about a decade because of tradition and my husband's opposition to women preaching and pastoring, but with every opportunity offered to "speak" or "teach" I was keenly aware that the calling was preaching and the role as pastoring.

The Reverend Michelle R. Loyd-Paige, Ph.D., resides in Muskegon Heights, Michigan. She gives her affiliation as nondenominational, but ordained in the Church of the Living God (CWFF). "My present church does not recognize my previous ordination. I am licensed within my present church as an Associate Minister of the Gospel." She is the organizer and founder of PreachSista!, a ministry by and for women in ministry that meets monthly. She has a website with a weekly posting. She formally preaches quarterly in other churches and conferences.

Why do I proclaim God's word? Because he asked me to. I must preach. If I do not, I do not please my Father. It is my part to play in the body of Christ. I preached my first sermon in January of 1986 (I was pregnant with my first child and the word!!!). I accepted my call into ministry that Easter Sunday.

The Reverend Almella Starks Umoja is an ordained Elder in the African Methodist Episcopal Church in Memphis, Tennessee. She pastors Greater Payne Chapel AME Church. She has been preaching for nine years and preaches weekly. She answers, "I cannot resist the call to preach the gospel, but I preach in obedience to the Holy Spirit. I believe preaching is a voice of God, and it is not possible for me to refuse to give myself to God's voice."

Richelle Fry Skinner is a laywoman and youth ministry director in Denver. She states that she has been proclaiming God's word for about twenty-one years. She felt the urge to speak even as a young person:

I proclaim God's word because it is what I have been called to do—
to share the good news of what Christ has done, is doing, and will

continue to do, if we only believe. It is our "job description" as Christians to proclaim the goodness of the Lord to everyone.

I have probably been proclaiming God's word long before I knew that my life was a testimony and therefore a proclamation of the goodness, blessings, and love of Christ. I proclaim daily. It is my desire to live my life so that I will be able to show the love of Christ and keep my light shining for him.

Diana Branch is a pastor in a Pentecostal/Nondenominational church in Decatur, Georgia. Spreading the word of God since 1993, Pastor Branch listed Jackie McCullough and Joyce Meyers as her role models.

There are many reasons, but mainly because I am constrained to preach this gospel. Also, because hearing the gospel is essential to believing, and one cannot believe in whom they have not heard, and "how shall they hear without a preacher?" Furthermore, I believe that the answer to all of life's problems, issues, conditions, etc., is contained in the word of God, and everything else pales in comparison to the wisdom found therein.

Regardless of the type or timing of a call, when God speaks most of us listen. The struggle, doubts, and resistance experienced—self-inflicted or from some other source—is less painful when one has a mentor or a role model, one who has already done what a neophyte is trying to do. The journey toward the goal is infinitely lighter when others walk before you, beside you, and even after you. My mentors/role models along the way have been my grandmother, my mother, the Reverend Dr. Prathia Hall, the Reverend Dr. Katie G. Canon, the Reverend Dr. Cheryl Townsend Gilkes, the Reverend Dr. Jacquelyn Grant Collier, the Reverend Dr. Emilie Townes, Bishop Vinton Anderson, Bishop John Bryant, the Reverend Charles G. Adams, the late Reverend Dr. Frederick Sampson, the Reverend Jesse Boyd, and each and every woman who proclaims God's word with and without ordination.

Mentors and Role Models

The results of the question "Who are your preaching mentors/role models?" included a listing of internationally and nationally known preachers, local pastors, members of ministerial staffs, teachers, denominational leaders, local ministerial staff members, and family members (most often a mother or grandmother). Three people listed Jesus Christ as their proclamation role model, and one person listed the judge Deborah. There were no restrictions on the number of persons who could be listed and no need to justify them in any way. The names of fifty-six women and fifty-one men outside of the family were reported. Thirteen family members were listed as proclamation models. Access to mentors and models thorough media, conferences, websites, preaching engagements, geography, time in ministry, publicity, denominational information, and educational facilities was a contributing factor to the results.

In this particular sample of 116 women, the internationally and/or nationally known mentors/role models appearing at least twice are listed in order of frequency named.

Female Mentors/Role Models	Male Mentors/Role Models
Teresa Fry Brown (26)	Jeremiah Wright (7)
Vashti McKenzie (11)	T. D. Jakes (4)
Jackie McCullough (6)	J. Alfred Smith, Sr. (4)
Renita Weems (6)	John Bryant (3)
Claudette Copeland (3)	Jesse Boyd (2)
Ella Mitchell (3)	Charles Stanley (2)
Joyce Meyer (3)	Otis Moss (2)
Cecelia Williams Bryant (3)	Frank Thomas (2)
Cynthia Hale (2)	Kenneth Ulmer (2)
Prathia Hall (2)	William Watley (2)
Brenda Little (2)	Samuel Proctor (2)
Katie Cannon (2)	Alvan Johnson (2)

Other mentors or role models falling within this category were Anne Wimberley, Jessica Ingram, Beverly Crawford, T. Larry Kirkland, Yolanda Adams, Donnie McClurkin, Fred Hammond, Caesar Clark, Alvin O. Jackson, Carolyn Knight, Barbara King, H. Beecher Hicks, Charles Adams, Noel Jones, Leontine Kelly, William Parnell, Barbara Lucas, Frank M. Reid, James Forbes, A. Louis Patterson, Joe Ratliff, Cecil Murray, Iona Locke, Gardner Taylor, Joseph Lowery, Noel Erskine, Charles Sargent, Frederick Sampson, Juanita Bynum, Ernestine Reems, Shirley Caesar, and Barbara Amos.

Mentors and models may reinforce and support one's call and authority. Often the mentor/role model consciously or subconsciously becomes the proclamation style model particularly early in one's ministry. In time, stylistic differences lead to appreciation rather than to emulation of the mentor/role model. Occasionally one may be reminded of a mentor/role model when the protégée is preaching and proclaiming. The mentor/role model may be instrumental in encouragement in the continuation of ministry. It does not seem to matter if there is sustained physical contact with a mentor/role model. Rather, at some point the person filled a need, which enabled the proclaimer to find her voice. The next section contains testimonies of respondents regarding mentors/role models.

Singing in Harmony

Like gospel music on a Sunday morning praising the one who makes all things possible, selected women sing about the people God sent to influence their ministries and provide an impetus to go forward, expounding God's word.

Claudette Copeland's main mentor is the Reverend Ernestine C. Reems, a denominational pioneer for preaching women in the Church of God in Christ. Other mentors are preaching peers who made the journey with her. They are Dr. Renita Weems, the Reverend Jacqueline McCullough, Caesar Clark, Alvin O. Jackson, Cecelia Williams Bryant, and Bishop Thomas D. Jakes.

Veronice Miles speaks of role models and mentors. Singing in the Florida Mass Choir fifteen years before she answered the call to preach, she was influenced by the Reverend R. A. Williams, the Reverend James Forbes, the Reverend Jeremiah Wright, the Reverend A. Louis Patterson, and Reverend Jones.

In 1990–94, I was introduced to preachers like Rev. Brenda Little, Rev. Ann Lightner, Rev. (now Bishop) Vashti McKenzie and was extremely encouraged to have women role models and to hear women who had found their own voice in preaching. This was a very formative time for me. As a student at Emory, I have been strongly encouraged by the preaching of Rev. Dr. Teresa Fry Brown as both my teacher and an exemplar of strong preaching. All of these persons have been role models. I cannot truly say that I have had a mentor, or someone who has sought to help me grow as a preacher outside of classroom settings. The two male pastors in my life have given little attention to my growth and development in this area, though they have both been affirming in their responses to my preaching.

She describes her late father as an influence through his sermons and her memories of his preaching in her youth. Other role models are her mother, her aunt, and women of the "sanctified church."

Zina Jacque has been preaching for about thirty years. She began by being the Mistress of Ceremony for programs, "speaking" at children's church.

My role models are both great proclaimers and proclaimers that are technically proficient. I can learn as much from those who are not prepared or equipped as I can from those who are. I listen intently to both. I have been a parishioner under the great Rev. Dr. J. Alfred Smith of the Allen Temple Baptist Church in Oakland, California, and a beneficiary of the tape ministry of Dr. Jeremiah Wright of the Trinity UCC Church of Chicago. I have also benefited from attending a church served by Rev. Dr. Brenda Williams Little of Evanston, Illinois. These three people have had more impact on my preaching than all others.

Sandra Blair, as role model for women in ministry in the AME Church, distinguishes between role models and mentors in remembering those who have influenced her homiletical development:

My proclamation role models are those who combine a critical intellectual analysis with openness to the dynamic movement of the Holy Spirit. Renita Weems is such a role model. Personal mentors include Alvan Johnson's story telling, Felix Dancy's keen insight into the living application of Scripture, Teresa Fry Brown's use of literary techniques, Gloria Smallwood's guidance on sermon preparation, and Marsha Foster Boyd's clarity. I was awed by her ability to bring the text to life, by the power of her delivery, and by the relevance of her message. Taking her preaching class during my first year in seminary was a major formative influence for me.

Dallasteen Yates and Miriam Frye lift up their mothers as chief influences in how and why they enunciate God's word. Both are musicians. Reverend Yates's ministry is primarily with adult choirs. Sister Frye's ministry is primarily with children's and youth choirs. Both write and arrange gospel music. In answer to the question "Who are your proclamation mentors and role models?" Dallasteen Yates says,

> Mrs. Jane Eva Davis Yates—my mother; although she is not a "preacher" per se, my mother (a retired schoolteacher) is a great orator and singer. Throughout my childhood and formative years, churches and civic groups regularly invited her, locally and throughout the state, to give "recitations" of poems and inspirational writings. With dramatic, witty, and inspirational flair, my mother has virtually hundreds of *memorized* verse that she can call upon for any occasion and deliver eloquently on the spot. Rev. Dr. Teresa L. Fry Brown, my homiletics professor and advisor at Candler School of Theology, pulpit associate, preacher, singer, and teacher at New Bethel A.M.E. Church, Lithonia.

Miriam Frye answers,

> My mother, Naomi Frye, although she has been in somewhat ill health, remembers and reminds me how much God is her strength. She goes to church at the nursing home, is in the nursing home choir, plays her keyboard with her old *Gospel Pearl* hymnbook, listens to her Mahalia Jackson tapes or CDs, and whenever I talk to her she has something good to say about God or what he has done for her.

Raedorah Stewart-Dodd (Nondenominational), Melinda Contreras-Byrd (AME) and Stephanie Crowder (Baptist/Disciples of Christ), gave multiple mentors and were quite specific in their rationale. Steward-Dodd names

> Rev. Dr. Jeremiah A. Wright, Jr., for his unapologetic address of social justice in sermon content and unpretentious kindness; Rev. Dr. Gardner Taylor, for his eloquent delivery, sermon order, and liberality in sharing soul and practical tips for preaching; Bishop Vashti Murphy McKenzie, for her "old-school" delivery and sermon construction, and doing it in her ghetto-fabulous mannerisms; Bishop Kenneth C. Ulmer, for aspiring to be more than just one of the "good old boys," seeking academic

transformation, and modeling the discipline of study; and unnamed old women who hug life into me, palm me money on the sly, and whisper their teary-eyed gratitude to God and me for how I preached and because I ministered to them, for them!

Melinda Byrd's proclamation models are

Dr. LaFrancis Rodgers-Rose, a womanist, black Nationalist founder and director of The International Black Women's Conference; and the Reverend Rochelle Hendrix, an Ordained AME Elder. Both have served as role models and mentors. To my mentor list I add the Reverend Dr. Leonora Tubbs-Tisdale, a previous professor at Princeton Theological Seminary.

Stephanie Crowder says,

I enjoy Frank Thomas (Mississippi Boulevard, Memphis), Carolyn Knight (ITC), H. Beecher Hicks, Jr. (Metropolitan Baptist Church, Washington D.C.), Teresa Fry Brown (Emory), Charles Adams (Hartford Baptist Church, Detroit), Bishop Vashti McKenzie (AMEC), and Noel Jones (Los Angeles). Their styles are very unique, but I believe they all exegete the text exceptionally well. This is of utmost importance to me. I do not have a mentor per se.

Minister Carolyn DuBose is a minister in the National Baptist, USA, Inc., in Detroit. Licensed to preach for five years officially and for some time unofficially, she uses biblical mandate for her call: "I proclaim God's word first and foremost because he has told me to do so. I stand on the Messianic scripture of Isaiah 50:4 and know that he has given me the tongue of a teacher to speak a word to the weary." She reminds us of the wide age range in the time of answering that call. She preaches five to six times a year and teaches year round. "Unofficially I preach all the time to somebody on the job, in the store, or on the street."

I have no proclamation mentor. It is sad but true that most people think that older women don't need a mentor. Mentoring is usually reserved for the younger person, however, it is far from the truth that older individuals do not need a mentor. I pray that the Lord would send me a mentor before I finish my course with him. If I could choose a mentor today, it would be Carolyn Knight. While this sistah does not know me, I admire her from afar. Every time she comes to my city I try and go to hear her proclaim. Also of late, I discovered Linda Hollies, who has a gift of preaching a word to the weary. I use my pastor as a role model because I have no choice as he is anointed to preach the word of God.

Model mentors are located both within the walls of a church and out-side them. Over the years, women have expressed both the absence of models and the lack of preaching opportunities. I remember the advice I was given as a child about choosing one's friends wisely. I say to women in ministry, choose your model wisely. Often the most visible person is not the one who has the time or the desire to walk with you during your ministry maturation. One of the ways that women fill the gap in mentor-ing is to form support groups for women in ministry. I either seek out a women's networking or support group or begin one in every location I can. I unapologetically believe that women need safe spaces. I believe that women need a place to be private, to recharge, to grow, to download, to prepare, to share, and to steel themselves for work in the public arena. Preaching is one of the most personally vulnerable activities I know. Walking the path of ministry alone can prove to be deadly. Mentoring is not about women hating men or women trying to be men. It is about ensuring that God's work is done by healthy, ethically sound, and well-prepared individuals. There are issues that women need to discuss exclu-sively with other women. There are issues that men need to discuss exclusively with other men. Then there are issues that are genderless, that both men and women equally need to discuss. I recommend to stu-dents that they have at least one female and one male role model for bal-ance. I also suggest having preaching partners or groups. These are to bounce ideas off one another, tell the truth about the sermon, provide feedback, and assist when someone is in a dry spell. The mentors and role models are also necessary to assist women in navigating the ecclesial waters—spiritual, social, and political. As I read the survey responses, the number of mentors/role models and the breadth of their experiences and religious affiliation were reassuring.

There are denominational support groups for women. Laywomen often work in missionary departments or women's ministry groups. The leader of these groups is usually a woman—the pastor's spouse or an elected offi-cial. In some instances, the pastor or designated layman is the "overseer" of the group. This is done so that a report can be given to the pastor of any "subversive" activity and to ensure that the women do what the pas-tor has ordered. In some churches, the pastor's wife may be certified or ordained to women's ministry. Women in Ministry is a group of women who are either interested in ordination or who are ordained. These organizations assist women in preparation for ministry, understanding denominational polity, teaching the particularities of being a woman in ministry, and sustaining women throughout their tenure in ministry. I was able to locate lists of women ministers through denominational webpages and conference roles. Individual women create support groups and most black mainline denominations have women in ministry groups such as Daughters of the King, AME/WIM, Sister to Sister, Sisters in the Spirit, Sistah Circle, and Black Women in Church and Society.

I am aware that in my social location—the black church—the "big chair syndrome" often is a reality. There seems to be a supernatural or at least extraordinary power about the chair that the preacher sits on Sunday mornings. I have watched persons literally run to sit in the center chair, the "preacher's chair," when the senior pastor is out of town or immediately after ordination. I have talked with laywomen who will not sit in the chair for fear of being stuck down by God's wrath for not being "holy" or "clean" enough to sit down. I have been in churches where women were not allowed to sit in the pulpit, and God forbid they should *touch* the center chair. It is like the throne of the priest in many cultures, the king's throne, if you will. There is power ascribed to being selected to sit in the "big chair," to "stand in John's shoes" (Mary Magdalene apparently was shoeless. Maybe *that* is why I am compelled to remove my shoes when I preach.), "to be invited up," "to grace the podium" or "to mount the pulpit," or "to stand behind the sacred desk." The pulpit, in the black church, is usually reserved for God's called-out, anointed, and appointed vessels. In some denominations and locations, this means men only, regardless of preparation, age, experience, denomination, or call. Even laymen are invited into pulpit areas before preaching women. Laywomen are also invited on special days, even in the face of ordained women who must sit on the front row or in a chair at the side of the pulpit. Women are not deemed *clean* enough to stand in the pulpit, and they never get to the chair.

Over the years, I have had to rethink the "big chair syndrome." I now ask, "Where is holy ground?" If I believe that God created and owns everything, then all ground, every speck of dirt, every grain of sand, every plank of wood, every section of carpet, and every piece of furniture is God's space. Why give power to a big chair in the middle of a pulpit? Why do women need to lose their minds because another human being tells them they are not worthy to sit someplace? I believe in the power of prayer and that prayer sanctifies. I also believe that whatever word God has placed in me will go forth regardless of physical structures. I now simply preach wherever I have prayed, stood, sat, or lain down. When I am invited into a pulpit, I honor that sacred space and respect the person who pastors in that space. I will also continue to seek out other sacred spaces.

Black women have fashioned alternative places of proclamation for hundreds of years. The foremothers mentioned in chapter 1 each were "seeking for a city" where they could be free to work out their calls. The women in this project held different titles, functioned in different capacities, served in a variety of ministries, and even created new spaces to proclaim.

All but one of the women have proclaimed in church in Sunday worship, Bible study, Christian education, church schools, revivals, Women's Day, Sunday school, choirs, Good Friday services, women's ministry, missionary activities, and youth ministry. Other places given were prisons, detention centers, television, radio, websites, hospitals, university chaplains' offices, seminaries, hospices, community activism, mission fields, women's conferences, hotels, civic functions, corporate workshops and retreats, retreat centers, workshops and seminars, and pastoral care centers.

The Reverend Dr. Melinda Contreras-Byrd, the Reverend Bridget Piggue, and the Reverend Margie C. Smith, D.Min., are pastoral counselors. Reverend Smith is a Baptist minister and licensed pastoral counselor in Richmond, Virginia. She says, "I know my calling is pastoral counseling. When I started in seminary I knew my call and I was and am pretty clear that my call is in counseling people. I have been doing counseling at my church for ten plus years." Although the field of pastoral counseling is relatively new in the black church, Reverend Smith provides counseling for the membership four days a week. She is paid staff and has an office at the church.

Detra Bishop, Ernestine Mathis, Winona Drake, and Gail Hayes proclaim on radio programs. Detra Bishop has a weekly radio broadcast called "It's in the WORD" in Hattiesburg, Mississippi. She is the founder of Women of God United, which operates a website and various women's conferences. Ernestine Mathis has a Monday-to-Friday broadcast called "Keys to Heaven" in Columbus, Georgia. Winona Drake hosts a one-hour talk show, "Singles Celebration," each Saturday in Denver, Colorado. She has written several articles for Denver newspapers and magazines. She recently developed Winona Drake Ministries. Her passion is to help Christian single adults. Gail Hayes produces a weekly online devotion, *In the Royal Court*. She is the religious columnist for the *Triangle Tribune*, an area African American-owned and operated newspaper. She also has had a weekly radio ministry. In addition, she serves as a columnist for several print and online publications. In her spare time, she hosts Christian Communicators Gatherings, which helps women (and men) publish and proclaim their God-given word of power, and quarterly meetings of the Alliance of Women Leaders, which is a gathering for women in leadership.

The call to preach is both individual and collective. Each person experiences the call of God in unique ways. Sometimes when institutions attempt to know all the details and intrusively press for a theological description, or a board decides to invalidate something so personal, the pain can last a lifetime. I appreciate the willingness of the respondents to step out on faith, face the pain, and in turn mentor those who are still struggling with the decision, "Lord, do you mean me?" When one has a mentor or role model, she is able to see what proclamation accomplishes and how difficult it is and to watch what happens when it is well done. If one is denied a place at the table with all the other preachers, she must decide whether to stay on the outside and play power games or survey the land and locate another sacred space. Moving from history to answering the call, the next chapter addresses how women prepare to preach and proclaim the word of God.

"Then Say So"

This sermon brief was originally written for a service following Thanksgiving 2001.

Old Testament Reading: Psalm 107:1-3

> 1 O give thanks to the LORD, for he is good; for his steadfast love endures forever.
> 2 Let the redeemed of the LORD say so, those he redeemed from trouble
> 3 and gathered in from the lands, from the east and from the west, from the north and from the south.

New Testament Reading: Revelation 7:9-10

> 9 After this I looked, and there was a great multitude that no one could count, from every nation, from all tribes and peoples and

languages, standing before the throne and before the Lamb, robed in white, with palm branches in their hands.

10 They cried out in a loud voice, saying, "Salvation belongs to our God who is seated on the throne, and to the Lamb!"

In my prayer and study of this theme, I went to that set-aside place in my mind and connected with how much God has done, is doing, and will do in my life and in the lives of all believers.

I lay that next to the contemporary tendency of what Dr. James Abbington calls charismania—the group, choreographed, directed, high-five, turn to your neighbor, get lost in the crowd, routinized, and ritualized praise.

I began to wonder how many of us give sincere thanks to God for the battles we have already come through, the storms that are currently raging and yet in which we live, and the struggles on the horizon that God has already laid the path for us to walk.

How many of us sit on the seat of sorrow?

Cower on the couch of complaint?

Hide under the hedge of hostility?

Or plod along the path toward a pity party because we do not recognize the plan God has for victory?

How many of us testify about the victory in our lives?

How do we remain anchored in the Lord when all around us seems to be in turmoil?

Walk with me for a little while through the words of the Psalmist.

Psalm 107 begins the fifth division of the book of Psalms.

A psalm of thanksgiving (congregational liturgy)

A sermon of God's steadfast love for us

Compassion for all people in need

God's forgiveness

God's deliverance in the midst of our distress

Song about a change agent

Let's know our current situation is not the end of our destiny.

Verse 1: *O give thanks*

Command, instruction

response to something received, courteous, reply

taught early—*tata, muchus gracias, danke, bene*—

in all languages and cultures

acknowledgment of something or someone that enhances our situation

76

Why? *Because God is good.*
   His mercy [unmerited love, grace] endures forever.
The sermon introduction says that in spite of our situation we—
   those from the entire earth—north, south, east, and west—
   are to recognize God for whom God is and for what God continues
      to do in our lives.

Let

   Who?

The redeemed

   Changed, covered, purchased, ransomed, reclaimed, reinstated,
      reconciled, repossessed, restored, retrieved

Of the LORD

   Not just the Baptist, Methodist, Episcopalian, Catholic, Lutheran,
      Presbyterian, Muslim, Jew, Nondenominational, Full Gospel,
      Interdenominational, Pentecostal, Apostolic, Jehovah Witness,
      Seventh Day, Quaker, UCC, Universalist, Congregationalists—
      but all of God's creation

Of the LORD

   The Most High God, the Sanctifier

Say so

   Confess, proclaim, tell, witness, recognize, state, testify
   Admit it

   The command is that those who have experienced any benefit or
      blessing from God say so—openly, spontaneously, without
      dependence on someone else.
   There should be some recognition within each of us that says, "God
      loves even me,
   I believe in God,

77

God has promised me that I will have victory. I will overcome.
I have already seen the promised land and know God has a place for
me.
My current situation is not the end of my journey.
I don't have to wait until this battle is over. I can shout now."
Perhaps there are those who remain silent, those who barely eke out
energy in response to God's benefits because of custom or fear
or because they are reticent of being charged with religious fanati-
cism. Perhaps there are those who believe that faith is determined by
how bad off one has been. Perhaps there are those who say, "I have
never had a bad thing happen to me so I don't see the need to say
anything."
Look at the Psalm

Verses 4-9: *Some wandered for years in the desert looking for, but not finding,*
a good place to live
Moving from place to place,
Church to church
Relationship to relationship
Job to job
Couldn't find a good life
No home
No purpose for life
Wandering without roots
Trying this and that
Sense of hollowness
Disconnected
Fragmented
Forgot what they learned from their parents
Denied their heritage
Hungry, half starved
Thirsty
Body and soul weak
Thought they would faint
In desperation they called out to God
Just when they were about to give in, to give up
Then they remembered who they were, whose they were
They cried to the Lord
"God we submit ourselves.
We are tired,

Our souls need resting.
Lord, we are ready to stop traveling and need to, want to, come
back home."
Prayed to God out of the depths of confusion and fatigue
Bible says in verse 6: *Then God*
At the right time
In the fullness of time
Then God *heard and delivered them from their distress*
God snatched them out of the grips of certain death
Raised them up on a rock higher than themselves
Redeemed them, gathered them from exile
Delivered what was distressed, disgusted, disappointed, dishonest,
disenfranchised, disgruntled, disrespected
Then God made paths straight
No more going this way and that
No more running back and forth
No more going in circles
God gave directions to the homeland of the soul
Led them to an inhabited town, community of saints
If that is your story . . .
Verse 8 says *Thank God for his marvelous love*
For his miracle mercy to the children he loves
For his steadfast (hesed) love even when we leave the paths of right
relationship God has marked with his blood
You see, God satisfies the thirsty souls and fills the hungry with good
things
He pours great water in our dry places
God provides wells of salvation
Out of our bellies God sends springs of living water
Nourishes our parched, arid souls with the water of the Holy
Spirit
God satisfies our hunger with the bread of heaven
Have you ever been in that group?
Then say so
Verse 10: *Some of you were locked in a dark cell, cruelly confined behind bars,*
prisoners in misery
Have you ever been walking around in broad daylight, bright sun-
shine, but couldn't see the light?
Clouds wouldn't lift

Fog had you locked in
No light, no vision
Prisoners in misery, in irons,
 Shackled to something or someone that bound you head to toe
 Eyes impaired with selective vision
 Hands cuffed with frustration
 Feet chained to weight of the world
 Hearts shackled to emotion you still can't identify
According to the word, we sometimes create our own prisons—physical, emotional, psychological, and spiritual
When we rebel against God's word—regardless of the translation we read, God's word is our reference for living a full, blessed life
When God tells us to do one thing and we do another
Make up excuses that someone else gave us poor advice
 We didn't know any better
Hearts burdened, heavy sentence, can't find anyone
Any human to help our case
 Go to daddy, he can't help us
 Go to mama, she can't help us
 Go to brother or sister, they can't help
 Go to friends, they have problems, too
Verse 13: **Then** *they cried out to the Lord in their troubles*
 In their desperate situation
God led them out of the darkness into the marvelous light
 God broke open the jail and led them out
 Pardoned the sins
 No parole board
 Said, "Start your life again"
Thank God for his marvelous, soul-changing, life-giving love
For his miracle mercy to the children God loves
If this is your group
Then say so
For God—not mother, not father, not sister, not brother, not grandmama, not granddaddy, not child, not spouse, not friend, not employer, not teacher, not preacher, not bank, not mortgage company, not fraternity, not sorority, not church, not bartender, not drug dealer, not lottery, not restaurant, not ego, not self—God shatters the doors, bonds, prison bars, chains

"Well, preacher, I have never wandered in the desert or been a
prisoner."
Verse 17: *Some of you were sick because you'd lived a bad life, your bodies
feeling the effects of your sin*
> Some were sick, not well
>> Life-threatening situation
>> Overindulgence
>> Ignoring common sense
>> Conspicuous consumption
>> Symptoms indicated some disease
> Every sick person doesn't go to the right doctor
>> Haven't been to an emergency room
> Some of you were sick, sick, sick, sick, sin-sick
>> Taking the wrong medicine
>> Refused treatment
> Going from doctor to doctor
>> Dr. Chocolate
>> Dr. Credit Card
>> Dr. Crank
>> Dr. Cocaine
>> Dr. Car
>> Dr. Courvosier
>> Dr. Cristal
>> Dr. Cheating
>> Dr. Cholesterol
>> Dr. Criticism
>> Dr. Career
>> Dr. Can't Do Ministry or Mission
>> Dr. Cute
> So miserable thought you would be better off dead
> Couldn't stand the sight of the food of life
> Got so bad couldn't eat, sleep, speak
> Cut off from God
> Beloved God places before us life and death
> Which one will we choose?
>> Choose life—choose death
>> Decide to follow God—decide to follow Satan
>> Raise hell or raise praise
> Some were sick, spiritually sick

Some were physically sick
Some were sick
But one day they called on Dr. Christ
Heard the question, "Do you want to get well?"
Verse 19: **Then** *they cried out to the Lord in their troubles and God saved them from their distress*
    God stepped in in the nick of time
        God spoke the word that healed you
        Pulled you back from the brink of death
        He sent his miracle mercy to the children he loves
    If this is your group
    Then say so
    Offer thanksgiving sacrifices,
        Tell the world what God has done for you each day
        Not the same tired testimony of what God used to do for you
    The Bible says that each day his mercies are new
    What has God done for you today?
        Sing it
        Shout it
    "Well Dr. T. you still have not included me,
        I have never wandered any place,
        I haven't been imprisoned,
        I have never been sick in body or soul."
    Well, my friends, God never leaves anyone out of the word
    There is one more group in the psalm
Verse 23: *Some went down to the sea in big ships, doing business on mighty waters*
    Knew of God's plan
    Saw the great things that God had done
        How God acts in breathtaking ways
    Felt God's presence
    Knew that each day as your career, relationship, life bloomed that
        God was in charge
    Little bumps along the way; God calmed the seas of life
    You shot high into the sky
    Then the bottom dropped out
        Your hearts were in your throats
        You were spun like a top
        You reeled like you were drunk

You didn't know which end was up
You went to Bible study
    Showed up on time for choir rehearsal
    You tithed
    You prayed without ceasing
    You raised your children responsibly
Then all hell breaks loose
    That promotion was one review away and someone else got the
        job
    Just about cleared up your credit and your house catches on fire
    Thought your relationship was improving, spouse asks for a
        divorce
    Finished a year of faithful exercise then find out you have cancer
    Began a new business and the economy slides into recession and
        bankruptcy looms
    Church began growing then members who were there in the
        beginning decide they don't like the new members
Heard about wars and death in other parts of the world and usually
    ignored them
Didn't even read the global news, didn't seek to know what others
    believed
Didn't think about the rest of creation since you lived in the land of
    the free and the home of the brave
Knew that God was on your side
Then your land is attacked and it is too close to home to ignore; fear
    abounds
Out on the mighty seas of life, rocking and reeling
    Tossed back and forth
    Courage melted
    Hostile forces seem to be taking over life as you knew it
Then you called out to God in your desperate condition
    He got to you in the nick of time
    He quieted the wind to a whisper
    He put a muzzle on the big waves
    God made the storm stand still
You were so glad that the storm died down
If this is your group
    Then say so
God is our shelter in the time of storm

God led you safely back to the harbor
So thank God for his marvelous miracle mercies
Lift high your praises when the people assemble
Shout Hallelujah!
The Psalmist concludes the song of thanksgiving
God turns rivers into deserts, deserts into rivers
He makes life grow where no one thinks it will last
He lets the hungry live and gives them places to live
Through oppression and trouble and sorrow, he blesses
God pours contempt on the haughty
God raises the needy out of distress
He allows the children of God to see the blessing of life
He makes the wicked, the evil, the busybodies shut up and sit down
God gives love to those who seem all alone
God blesses the faithful
God takes sure destruction and turns it into deliverance
Let the redeemed
Let the saved
Let the grateful
Let the thankful
Say so
If God has done anything for you
If God has blessed your life in any way
Then say so
That's why John's Revelation echoes the Psalm
John knew about the promise of victory
He saw a number that no one could number
Coming from the north, south, east, and west
Every nation
Every tribe
Every language
Every nationality
Every race
Every ethnicity
Some bearing the marks of Jesus in their bodies
Some running
Some walking
Some marching
Some crawling

Some leaping
Some limping
But all praising
Coming in gratitude, coming in thanks
Robed in white, waving palm branches
Praising God, not because someone told them it was the right thing
    to do
Some had been wandering but were found
Some had been in prison—some self-made, some mental, some emo-
    tional, some physical, some spiritual—but by God's grace were set
    free
Some had been sick but were healed, cleaned up, made whole
Some had been out on the sea, tossed about, but now stood in the
    present shalom of God
John lets us know that praising is not just for church services
He writes that
They cried in loud voices
We are here today because God saved us
Our God is seated on the throne and he loved us enough to send the
    Lamb to provide for our deliverance and the Spirit to lead and
    guide us to this place
They are led in the sevenfold praise of God
    Blessing
    Glory
    Wisdom
    Thanksgiving
    Honor
    Power
    Might all belong to God forever
Who are they?
    Who are they?
    These are they who have come out of great ordeal
        They have washed their robes in the blood of the lamb
        These are they who know how to say so
    They worship God before the throne day and night
        They have no more hunger
        They have no more thirst
        They have no more pain
        They have no more fear

They have no more darkness
They have no more trials
They have no more tears
In my sanctified imagination I can see people going up the rough side of
the mountain, going up toward the New Jerusalem
Praising God for the victory through Jesus
Shouting, singing, rejoicing
Can you hear them?
Thank you, Lord
For binding up our hurts
For feeding us when we were hungry
For hearing our cries above the noise
For forgiving our faults
For holding us when we were lonely
For comfort when we were grieving
For teaching us when we didn't know a thing
For keeping us safe when we were out there doing anything we
thought we were big enough to do
Not ashamed to praise God, to say so
For loving us in spite of ourselves
For knowing what we need before we ask
For being our shelter in the time of storm
For carrying us through the valley of the shadow of death
For preventing sickness when we did not care for our temples
Boldly singing on key and off key, some with sign language, some with
many languages, if they had ten thousand tongues they wouldn't have
enough to fully say so
For that job they said we were underqualified for
For that scholarship that allowed us to go to the school of our choice
For the family that you arranged for us
For the airplane that hit a turbulence but did not hit the ground
Say so
For leading us beside still waters
Around the edge of despair
Over waves of destruction
Above the canopy of disappointment
Under the weight of disrespect
For restoring our souls
If you want to be in this group *then say so*

Say so
> Witness it
> Shout it
> Enunciate it
> Proclaim it
> Speak it
> Sign it
> Sing it
> Tell it
> Talk about God
> Speak a word
> Hum if you have to
> Cry
> Pray
> Minister

Say so
> Don't wait until Sunday morning, *say so*
> Don't wait for someone to lead the praise, *say so*
> Don't wait for the choir, *say so*
> Don't wait for the worship leader, *say so*
> Don't wait for another blessing, *say so*
> Don't wait for the end of the battle, *say so*
> Don't wait for your friends, *say so*

I can't tell you what to say, why to say it, when to say it, or how to say it
> It's your story
> Only you know what God has done for you

Has God made a way for you? *Then say so.*
> Has God taught you how to live? *Then say so.*
> Has God brought you out of darkness into the marvelous light?
>   *Then say so.*
> Has God healed you? *Then say so.*
> Has God kept you? *Then say so.*
> Has God blessed you? *Then say so.*
> Has God rescued you? *Then say so.*
> Has God raised you? *Then say so.*
> Has God loved you? *Then say so.*
> Has God provided for you? *Then say so.*
> Did God send Jesus to redeem your soul? *Then say so.*

Say so with your

Tears rolling
Nose running
Face contorting
Sweat pouring
Makeup streaking
Head bobbing
Pulse racing
Chest heaving
Foot tapping
Shoulders moving
Leg swinging
Body rocking
Knee knocking
Neck snapping
Arm waving
Throat clearing
Muscle tensing
Bible reading
Tithe giving
Handkerchief waving
Paper fanning
Amen saying
Hallelujah shouting
Holy dancing
God loving
Self
Say so.

CHAPTER THREE

SIGHT-READING: HALF NOTES AND WHOLE NOTES

My mother, Naomi Parks Fry, was a Baptist church choir director and musician. She played piano and organ and had a beautiful second alto/baritone voice. Although she could play by just listening to a tune and "picking out" the parts, she usually used sheet music, hymnals, or special gospel music books when playing or teaching a song. Each of her seven children, at one time or another, played an instrument (piano, organ, trombone, trumpet, clarinet, violin, drums) or sang in a choir. She insisted that each of us learn to sight-read. Although the ability to "play by ear" was a coveted gift in the black church, she wanted us to understand the derivation of a song, learn the creative intent of the lyrics, and appreciate how the author originally intended the piece to sound. She warmed up our voices, and we went through repetitious vocal drills and scales for about fifteen minutes. Next, she would have us read over the music as she played it in its fullness. Then she would break down each line, so we could hear the parts, recognize the key changes, and know when to pause or rest for effect. Next, she would explain the rhythm or tempo, pitch, mood, and chord progression of the text. She made sure we knew the differences between a whole note, half note, quarter note, sixteenth note, and thirty-second note. She would remind us, "Stay in major key. Don't slide into that minor key." My siblings and I even learned to pronounce a few words in another language, words that felt musical on the tongue such as *obligato, fine, allegro,* or *pianissimo.* Some of us would infuse our conversations with these melodious words just to impress our friends. After we could sight-read well enough to understand the text and give honor to the original work, we could improvise. We would rearrange the music to fit our voices, transform it into our context, and translate it into our style of worship. Even though the form of the original was modified, the intent always shown through the new interpretive phrasing and personal, extemporaneous runs and riffs. In my mind, sermon preparation and presentation are reminiscent of the task of sight-reading whole notes and half notes.

When teaching homiletics classes and presenting at seminars, I ask persons to consider seventeen factors that may influence their approach to the preaching moment. This preparation assessment paradigm serves as initial consideration for entering the preparation. It led to the development of questions presented in this research project. The students are asked to do a personal evaluation of their preaching experience (estimated number of sermons preached); the frequency of preaching; the denominational affiliation of preacher and listener; role models; sermon styles; textual translations; number of tests to be included in the sermon and their placement; preaching passion; their hermeneutical process; how they begin a sermon; the behavioral purpose of the sermon (what the listener is to get out of moment); how the sermon is to end; supportive sermon/homiletical resources; sermon files and form—manuscript, notes, outline, extemporaneous—expected or average length of sermon preparation and delivery; and the individual's process of self-critique. This chapter will assess black women's sermon preparation. Do black women have a preference between Old Testament and New Testament texts? How do black women read and exegete biblical texts? What translations are preferred in the preaching moment? What steps are followed in sermon preparation? The respondents' answers are randomly selected. Some of the submissions are paraphrased. Others are direct quotations.

Text Selection

Determination of the text is a foundational stage in proclamation. The biblical text, the King James Version, was used for teaching reading to enslaved persons. There is an undying attachment and reverence for the "real Bible" in numerous black churches. Some prefer to use the Old Testament for the stories, while others like the "Jesus" aspect of the New Testament. Occasion, assignment, and Holy Spirit direction form the basis of text selection in the black preaching tradition.[1] The Bible is "God's word," and one must handle it in such a way that the listener knows that the preacher, regardless of "name, rank, or serial number," has been sent by God, knows Jesus for herself, and evidences being under Spirit anointing to "say a word." There are particular stories (Daniel in the lion's den, "These Are They," the woman with the issue of blood, the crossing of the Jordan), texts (Hebrews 11:1-2, Luke 4:18-19, Micah 6:6-8, Psalm 23, Ezekiel 37), and subjects (sin, salvation, favor, liberation, resurrection) that are known in black congregations regardless of theology, denomination, size, or location.

James Earle Massey says that selection and interpretation of biblical text depends largely on the social location and worldview of the interpreter. He describes the "community-situation approach" employed by persons with a history of oppression and social deprivation.[2] It is interpretation from lived experience and a need to experience and witness the possibility of freedom, justice, and God's deliverance. Black women certainly fit into this group historically, both in society and in the church. Reading from a marginalized perspective, black women read between the lines, behind the textual surface, through memories of demeaning and oppressive text use, past social hermeneutics, and around accepted interpretations and, at times, on the fringes of isogesis, find themselves in the text. They are able to proclaim affirmation of their own personhood without excluding others. Their individual lenses peruse the text as only a black woman's experiential base can. Hans Baer adds that blacks paraphrase the text to fit their social reality. Black Baptist men are described as the most literal translators, but other Baptists are more allegorical. Black women, in his research, are said to advocate cautious translations though those in the sanctified churches are "more Bible centered and literalist."[3] Carolyn Osiek posits that women read the Bible from a distinctive, feminist perspective. The historical, androcentric interpretation and language, the centrality of male-dominated texts, the women as submissive slaves, and the absence of women's voice in the use of the biblical text necessitated formation of new theological voices and interpretations. She concurs with both Massey and Baer when she says that there is no "value free exegesis."[4] People read the biblical text based on whom they are and where they are.

Whether announcing God's word in song, testimony, teaching, service, or sermon, the biblical text is the basis for expression of God's love, grace, and mercy. There are passages that black women avoid that, to them, seem too painful to discuss. The reality is that occasionally texts are misinterpreted, ignored, overused, and finessed to fit a particular agenda or theme. At the end of the day, the word of God is just that—the word of God.

One option for submission of materials was E-mail response. I responded to the thirty-three sistahs in order of appearance in the "old mail" file and requested additional information. In listening to sermons and public presentations and talking with male and female preachers for the past forty years or so, I became curious about their preference for one testament over the other. In the classroom, I have to insist that persons who preach only from the Old Testament use a New Testament text from time to time and vice versa. I realize that there are faith systems founded on one particular testament. I also know that many black preachers enjoy the narratives in the Old Testament over those located in the New Testament. There are those who love to tell the "Jesus stories," particularly the parables, miracles, and healing texts, and Paul's writings and adventures. There is a curious avoidance of most of Revelation—one of my favorite New Testament texts. There are, of course, the Revelation 3 Laodicea "hot or cold" prophecies, the Revelation 7 "these are they" sermons, and the Revelation 21 "new heaven and new earth" hoops; but the sermonic wrestling with the entire book, in my experience, is rare. The Old Testament stories almost "preach themselves." The information requested and answered by nineteen women was, "Do you use the Old Testament or New Testament equally or one more than the other? Why?" Responses depended on the type of ministry in which one was engaged, denomination, personal experience, and subject matter. Five used the testaments equally, eight primarily used the New Testament, and six primarily used the Old Testament. Other participants in the study incorporated their answers in other questions. This sampling is representative of distribution of those answers.

Sandra Blair (AME) draws equally from the Old and New Testaments. She uses the Revised Common Lectionary as a resource, and this process leads her to passages of Scripture from both testaments as well as passages she would not otherwise select. She says, "I love to incorporate stories in sermons both to illustrate the message and to add interest in my delivery. For this reason, I do have a preference for the Old Testament because of the narratives inherent to too much text."

Kim Martin (Pentecostal) uses the testaments equally. She teaches Bible study classes. "The Old Testament is the New Testament concealed and the New Testament is the Old Testament revealed. Combined, they give the fullness to God's spoken word."

Lisa Rhodes (Baptist) noted a shift in text usage within the past two years based on the work she does as the Dean of the Chapel at Spelman College. She previously focused on New Testament narratives.

> Since the start of my Women's Bible Study, workshops, and retreats, my preaching has reflected a balance between the two testaments. There are a number of women in the Old Testament, gender and family issues, personal struggles, etc., that are not found in the New Testament.

Telley Gadson (UMC) pastors two churches in South Carolina. She uses the testaments equally: "I challenge myself to always find a parallel in meaning or theme between an Old Testament and New Testament text in a effort to put the writers in conversation with each other." She says that it makes a good blend in preaching and allows the congregation to reflect on both testaments.

Kimberly Detherage uses the Old Testament most. She is an attorney with a passion for religious and social justice. "I find the Old Testament resonates with themes of justice, fairness, mercy, and God's redemption and love of a people, despite sin. The Old Testament has a multitude of stories of human frailties and God's willingness to listen to those [who] cry out to God." Reverend Detherage says that the language of the Old Testament is poetic, beautiful, and harsh. She mentions, "When I use the Old Testament, I always end with the cross and Jesus." This is classic in black preaching: the celebration of God's grace in spite of the judgment ends with Jesus, the cross, and resurrection.

Arlene Churn (Baptist) gave a similar reply and also speaks of grace. She prefers the Old Testament. Dr. Churn was a child evangelist, and she has been in the ministry over fifty years and has traveled across the United States and around the world. She preaches ecumenically and mentors wherever she goes.

I feel drawn to the stories of strength and struggle to do the will of God, and often at such a personal cost. I love the preparation that leads up to their use of God and the sacrifices made. I love their cries and pleas to God and even the conversations they had with God. I thrill at their form of praise and, above all, obedience to his bidding.

Zina Jacque (Baptist) tends to use the Old Testament more: "The stories of struggle over mighty obstacles are so applicable to black folk. However, most of my sermons have a CTJ ("Come to Jesus") ending, and that has a decided New Testament orientation."

LaTrelle Miller Easterling (AME), a pastor in Massachusetts, said that in the initial stages of her preaching ministry she used both an Old and New Testament passage. "I thought it was important to keep the Old Testament alive in the hearing of the congregants. However, now I find myself preaching more from the New Testament."

Dallasteen Yates (AME) primarily uses the New Testament with supplementary Old Testament passage. "I like to focus the hearer's attention upon the good news as realized in the new, while supporting it with the foundational, historical, prophetic word, pointing to that good news in the old."

Women in specialized ministries are more likely to use the New Testament. Mary Anne Bellinger (Presbyterian) is partial to the New Testament because of its theme of change. "The person of Jesus is such a strong representation of support and love. Both themes (change and love) so often are missing in our communities of fixed incomes and senior citizens, where they place women as pastors only in "certain denominations." Reverend Bellinger is in a seminary program for black women in ministry. Helen Richmond (Nondenominational) usually teaches women's ministry classes from the New Testament. "I try to encourage people and teach people, especially women, how to enjoy the benefits of being part of the Body of Christ." She says she refers to the Old Testament for background information or when she is actually teaching an introduction to the Old Testament. "For a long time, though, until I took Old Testament [classes] in seminary, I did avoid the Old Testament. It seemed so *long* and filled with violence, I couldn't understand the concept." Winona Drake (Nondenominational) tries to use both the testaments. When ministering with singles, women, and youth groups, she uses the New Testament more often, "with the exception of the book of Ruth, which is excellent for women, married and single. First Corinthians 6:14 is used a lot in singles ministry messages, or even Philippians 3:13 and 4:6-8. All are empowering scriptures to use when ministering healing, forgiveness, and holiness for singles." Judith Tolbert's (Baptist) focus is children and youth. She states, "I use the New Testament more often because the lessons from the Sunday school and children's worship guides are taken from there. The emphasis is generally the application of Christian principles."

Richelle Fry Skinner (AME) serves in youth ministry. She uses the Old Testament for background when working with the New Testament topics. "I use the New Testament more often; however, I really enjoy the book of Proverbs (Proverbs 22:6). The New Testament parables are easier to understand and apply as I work with young people."

Prior to sermon composition is translation usage. I emphasize usage of the New Revised Standard Version (NRSV) in preaching classes, much to the dismay of about one-third of the students each semester. I intone the seminary policy about inclusive language and imagery for God. I talk about the justice issues that are close to my heart and how oppressive texts can be for some people, especially women. I testify of my first theology paper, which was returned to me so red-marked that I thought something had been spilled on it. The professor said that I would have to change my exclusive theology or fail the course. I had grown up reading the King James Version as the only Bible. God was Father. I had never considered that the "mother to the motherless, father to the fatherless" saying in my community was deemed exclusive. I knew that women were seldom mentioned and that "man" was supposed to mean men and women, unless, of course, there was praise for the real heroes of the faith. The professor was insistent and I did not want to fail, so I began to read about inclusive language. I had found ways to read around the text and find myself in God's plan. In seminary, I began to use new translations and found new ways of reading the text. The KJV became my source for poetic readings in the Psalms or Proverbs, and the NRSV was my primary translation for sermons. Surely these seminary students felt the same way. Certainly black women would understand the importance of using a more inclusive translation. Couldn't they hear themselves talk using only male imagery for God? There they are, black women, in seminary, preaching, and working in ministry, yet using KJV and arguing against any other translation. I am aware that many students use NRSV because I require it but revert to KJV as soon as they leave seminary. In this project, the top four translations used are King James Version (KJV), New International Version (NIV), New Revised Standard Version (NRSV) and New King James Version (NKJV). Translation preferences were appraised according to number of times listed (Chart 2). The majority of respondents listed more than one translation. Other categories were: What translation according to time in ministry? (Chart 3); what was used according to age? (Chart 4); and usage by education level? (Chart 5). Fifteen translations of study Bibles were listed. The most surprising statistic was the overall usage of the NIV over the NRSV. Those women holding Master of Divinity degrees and above used the NRSV, NIV, KJV, and NKJV, in that order. In the age category, the order of use was KJV, NRSV, NIV, and NKJV and Amplified Bible (tied) in the 41 to 55 years group. The sisters in ministry for 21 to 30 years, for example, were more likely to use the NIV, KJV, NRSV, and Amplified Bible.

Numerical responses to translation usage question

King James Version (KJV)	60	Life Application	1
New King James Version (NKJV)	23	Contemporary English	
New Revised Standard Version (NRSV)	51	Version (CEV)	7
Revised Standard Version (RSV)	3	Today's English	
New American Standard Version		Version (TEV)	2
(NASV)	7	Living Bible (LB)	8
Amplified	9	New International	
Peterson Translation (The Message)	4	Version (NIV)	55
New Jerusalem	3	New Living	
Hebrew/Greek (H/G)	3	Translation (NLT)	1
Good News Bible	2	Phillips	1
Study	1		

Other factors, such as denomination, geography, senior pastor preference, congregation willing to use a different translation, exposure, habit, comprehension level, theology, and aesthetics, need research and analysis but are outside the scope of this project.

The Reverend Lenora Nicholas Welch, Progressive Baptist from Oakland, has been proclaiming most of her adult life as a speaker. She has been in ordained ministry for five years. In her writing, teaching, and preaching, she uses the New King James Version. "At times I will use the Contemporary English Version. The CEV gives me a more contemporary bridge into the application. The NKJV is a personal favorite and is used by most African American churches in this area."

Leah Gunning, a United Methodist Associate Pastor in Evanston, Illinois, has been in ministry for four years. She proclaims once a month in response to God's call to "proclaim God's word in sermon form, lecture, and acts of service." Leah tends to use the NIV most often, followed by the NRSV. "I find both of these translations to be more gender inclusive than some of the older translations and easier to understand. Also, most United Methodist churches have NRSVs in the pews. My hope is people will use them to follow along with the sermon."

Richelle Fry Skinner (AME) uses the New International Version because she finds it an easier translation for working with children and adolescents and young adults. The comprehension is markedly improved than when using the King James Version.

The Reverend Tracy Leggins Brown (AME Itinerant Elder from Los Angeles) uses the KJV because of tradition and familiarity. She has memorized particular scriptures in that translation and finds them easier to retrieve. Reverend Leggins Brown prefers the "style of the NKJV and the closeness to the KJV without the old, outdated language. I use NIV to help the proclamation [become] easier to digest and comprehend."

The Reverend Rosetta DuBois Gadson (AME) uses "the New International Version because of its closeness to the original Aramaic, which Jesus spoke, and the language flows easily." She uses the KJV for passage such as the Lord's Prayer. She prefers the NRSV, TEV, and CEV for the language flow and modernity. "I also use the Jerusalem Bible, the Oxford Annotated, the Thompson Chain Study Bible, Life Application Bible, and the Message because of "the ease of language, especially preaching to young people and adults who are new to Bible study."

The Reverend Eunice Shaw (Baptist) uses the New American Standard, Good News, KJV, Amplified, NIV, and The Message. "My goal is to provide the clearest understanding to the listener; therefore, I examine all of the translations for clarity."

Lois Clayborn (AME) is a musician and teacher from Memphis, Tennessee. This PK (preacher's kid) says that the contemporary versions of the Bible offer a clearer explanation of the word. She uses the King James Version, a study Bible, and the Contemporary English Version. She lists her research tools as "the Internet, newspapers (news items/comics, etc.), historical textbooks, personal experiences (mine or others), and my son, the Reverend Patrick Clayborn." Her presentations are organized in both notes and extemporaneous approaches.

The next stage in sermon development is exegesis. In composing a sermon, a lesson, a speech, or musical presentations, is biblical research evident, background given, language considered, definitions given, cultural perspective respected, related texts read, or supportive materials consulted? Biblical scholar Cain Hope Felder conveys that biblical usage in black churches is diverse. He identifies three tendencies within the black church tradition. The first one is *biblical literalism*, which leaves no room for any interpretation other that what is on paper. This generally means there is no room for any social, cultural, or denominational inter-pretation because the "my Bible says" mentality reigns. The second is *iso-gesis*. This is the process of leading or reading our own ideas into the text. This is a hallmark of some forms of black preaching. At times, the cre-ative edge and even the manipulative urge get the best of the proclaimer, and she or he leaves the root meaning of the text and ventures precari-ously toward a distinctively unsettling interpretation. Felder's third ten-dency is *conscientious exegesis*, which I believe is indispensable in proclamation. The preacher attempts to bridge the gap between the con-temporary environment and the ancient context through careful research and interpretation. At its finest, he says, black preaching takes the text seriously.[5] At its worst, I say, black preaching uses the text as a prop or pretext for congregational castigation, a series of stories, and vapid celebration.

Elizabeth Achtemeier says that sermons must logically center around one principal subject. She calls the preparatory communicative channel among the preacher, congregation, and God "priestly listenings."[6] Homiletics professor Thomas Long views exegesis as "a systematic plan for coming to an understanding of the biblical text." He says that the exegetical process involves distinctive steps for interpreting a biblical passage. "How one enters a text, listens, hears, processes, understands, explores, in relation to context, theme, genre, personal experience" is essential to the homiletical event.[7] Richard Hays stipulates that exege-sis is foundational to Christian preaching. He advocates careful study of the text, unfolding the message of the Scripture through close reading, poring over text, and understanding the history, context, literary genre, stimulation of the imagination, and basic language (Hebrew or Greek). He stresses the individuality of homiletical method.[8] Essential to the exegetical process is living in the text. The person who is to "say a word" should become a part of the text. Exegesis is a multisensory activity. One should become so familiar with the text that the Holy Spirit speaks not only to the preacher, but also to the needs of the congregation.

Watching the Director:
Steps to Sermon Preparation

Even before the inception of the black church, black women have been known as prayer warriors. The spiritual grounding of the black family, black church, and black community was centered in black women's relationship with God. Before any decision was made, any project undertaken, any word said, or any travel begun, prayer was uttered. Prayer prior to reading the Bible and preparing a sermon is critical to the spirituality of the preacher. Seeking guidance on what to say and how and when to say God's message is undeniably the most important feature of black women's preparation. The consequences of prayer are purification, direction, illumination, clarity, interpretation, and knowledge of what God expects in the preaching moment. Prayer infuses the entire preparation process. Prayer is not a last minute precautionary procedure, but integral to daily devotion, textual engagement, and lived experience. In review of the preparatory steps given by the research group, prayer was the common element.

New Testament scholar Raquel St. Clair works from the NRSV because of the use of contemporary English and inclusive language. "Texts usually 'present themselves' during my devotional time." She prays over the texts and journals a draft. She then types out a full manuscript, blocked to follow her speech patterns. She reviews the manuscript "with a colored pen to underline or circle important phrases and to add words and thoughts and examples that come as I mediate on it." She preaches from this manuscript.

The Reverend Dr. Bernadette Glover-Williams serves as Executive Pastor at The Cathedral Second Baptist Church in Perth Amboy, New Jersey. She preaches weekly from the NIV because, "There's a fire within that won't go out. I can do nothing else!" Using an outline format, Reverend Glover-Williams says that she begins her work with the prayer, "Lord, prepare me to stand before your people. Give me a transforming word that will lodge in the spirit of the people." The next step is to read the text as directed by the Holy Spirit. She then takes notes on verses or thoughts that "snag" her as she is reading. The next step is to brainstorm on themes of special events, listing the assumptions and thoughts that first come to mind. She then completes her notes, prays, and waits for the preaching moment.

Telley Gadson likes the language in the NIV translation but also uses the NRSV and recently began consulting The Message in preparation. "I grew up on the King James, so when I read these other versions, it makes it plain for me." She relates that prayer frames her preparation. She believes prayer is an opportunity to communicate with God. "I must hear God's voice and be a willing instrument that has not only heard but also listened. My prayer is always that God gives a fresh word for his people, which is what he always does." She also reads about modern issues and concerns so that the sermon is applicable to life. Occasionally, she consults commentaries and mentors. Her form has shifted over the years: "In the beginning, I was strictly a manuscript preacher, but now that I preach so often, I have moved to outlines and sometimes extemporaneous. Above all else, I let go and let God."

Antoinette "Toni" G. Alvarado enjoys the common vernacular of the day in the New King James Version. "Preparation for ministry begins with prayer to hear the message that God wants to convey during the time of ministry." Her text selection comes from the message she senses God wants to convey. Sometimes a text is taken from a specific theme (such as worship, prayer, marriage, and so on). Her supportive materials include Bible commentaries, Bible dictionaries, and lexicons. The liturgical calendar, church calendar, or type of meeting sometimes determines topic selections. Manuscripts and outlines are often used.

Sheranda Allen generally uses the KJV because "it's what I grew up on as a young saint." She also values prayer in preparation: "When I am seeking a word from the Lord, I pray and wait for God's direction. Once I know what the subject is, I begin to do research. Sometimes the Lord gives me the scripture he wants me to use." She then goes through the Bible for related topics and subject matter. Resources include a concordance and a bible dictionary, Webster's dictionary, pertinent material from the newspaper, and magazines. She uses all forms of expression, manuscripts, outlines, notes, and extemporaneous. It all depends on the leading of the Lord.

In answer to the question, "What Bible translations do you use?" Diana Branch said, "I am a lover of the King James Version of the Bible, for no other reason than that I love the sound of the King's English and probably because it is the text that I have memorized scriptures from all my life." In her homiletical process, she finds the KJV makes it easier for her to find words in the concordance and conduct word searches. However, in preaching, she often refers to the NIV or Amplified Bible because she finds they bring a greater level of understanding to the congregation. Her methodology differs from time to time: "I pray and seek the Lord as to the message for his people. Oftentimes, he gives me an issue or topic." Her next step is a concordance search of related scriptures. She chooses one scripture verse, from which she draws a subject, and then uses the others as points of reference throughout her discourse. She employs notes and bullets, with her main thoughts in bold print, to remind her of practical application or to further expound on a certain thought.

Regina Daniels, an AME laywoman in Georgia, uses the Life Application Study Bible and the New King James Version because, she says, they are very explicit. "I like the commentaries after key scriptures, which [give] you, I think, a closer insight into the Scripture." Her first step is to use the Bible. "Sometimes God will lead me to a particular scripture, and I'll build on it from there. I like to hear what others have to say about the subject. I have a girlfriend who is a Lutheran minister living in Minneapolis, so I'll call her and we'll talk it out." She says that the entire proclamation process is immersed in prayer. After the reading, after the consulting, she says that all she does is "pray and pray and pray." She works with notes and a manuscript in presentation.

Jan Prentace's primary location of proclamation is on the campus of Norfolk State University. She uses the New International Version and New Revised Standard Version translations. However, when exegeting more formal manuscripts, she consults the New Jerusalem, Harper Bible Dictionary, Oxford Annotated Bible, and study Bibles such as the HarperCollins Study Bible. She provided an outline of her preaching process.

1. I follow these steps to preach/proclaim
(a) Mostly look at what is going on in my life and the lives of people around me. I try to look at what and how the Scripture is speaking to this situation and what I can glean and impart as God's wisdom.
(b) I try to give it a catchy title since I am preaching to a hip-hop congregation.
(c) Sometimes I use current events such as 9/11 and what is going on in the world. I'll use newspaper articles, magazine articles.
(d) My style with young adults is very relaxed; it is almost in the form of a Bible study. I find that this works best for me in a college setting. However, when preparing for a church, I will be formal in my preaching style.
2. I will exegete the passage as much as possible.

She uses an expository style on the campus and a combination of manuscript and narrative expository style in the church setting. The college setting is the venue for a much more extemporaneous delivery.

Mary Anne Bellinger uses all translations except the King James Version. The only time she consults the KJV is when she is "looking for a particular poetic expression." Beginning with prayer, she questions what God wants or needs people to receive. She then reads the Bible, "and that—together with conversations, events of the day, and renewed energy—helps to determine where I might begin to put together a word." She is a full manuscript preacher, combined with extemporaneous input.

Leah Gunning tries to "correlate my test selection with the liturgical season, lectionary, or wherever God may lead me on a particular occasions." Supportive materials include newspapers, magazine articles, music lyrics, websites, television programs, and books. Her topic selection is centered on the text and the context. Pastor Gunning's form is usually expository, and she most often preaches with notes (in churches), a manuscript (in severely constrained environments), and extemporaneously. "I try to communicate God's word in a manner that is faithful to the leading of the Holy Spirit while relevant and appropriate to the context."

Veronice Miles reads from a variety of translations. She appreciates the NRSV and made a conscious decision during seminary to read from a less archaic translation on most occasions, so that the congregation could hear the text in a language that is easier to understand. She also likes the scholarship behind the NRSV and the efforts made to correct or highlight translation errors and inconsistencies in the KJV. "There are certainly very familiar phrases that I retain from the KJV because of their traditional familiarity in the black church. I also use the KJV for most of the poetic books and passages because it has a more palatable poetic rhythm and sound."

She most often selects the text through prayer and meditation. She, at times, adopts the lectionary. She reads and works through the text, reading from the Greek of Hebrew texts, before consulting commentaries. She then does a word/phrase study using a Greek or Hebrew concordance, trying to understand the text within the context of the specific book, historical setting, and surrounding passages. Prior to writing, she identifies the text's claim "about God within its ancient context, what the text wants to say to us today, the focus of the sermon, and what I hope the sermon will accomplish" (Tom Long's claim, focus, and function). The topic emerges when the sermon is complete. She most often preaches from a manuscript, "on occasion from a thick outline, and almost never extemporaneously."

Kim Detherage reads through the New Revised Standard Version, New International Version, King James Version, Jerusalem Bible, and sometimes the Hebrew and Greek translations of the text. She posits that this process yields accuracy, understanding, and meaning.

> The steps that I follow depend on whether the sermon is for a special occasion or a particular theme. If it is for a special occasion, I focus on potential texts that are geared toward that occasion. I look to see whether there are any specific issues/concerns. The following applies to all preparation: Then I pray about the text. I select a text. I read the text many times and the chapter the text is in. I ask myself what is going on in the text? What is the author trying to convey? How does the text speak to me? What is the text saying to my audience? How can I best convey the message?

In the process of asking the relevant questions, Detherage underlines words in the text and looks them up for clarity and meaning in the particular context. The next step is exploring the "historical background, time period, and so on. I will read various commentaries and different translations of the text. Then I will try and clarify a proposition: for example, "I propose to show that _____ to the end that the hearers will/may ___." She outlines the content and preaches from the resultant manuscript.

Dallasteen Yates is an ordained AME Elder. She peruses various translations, including NRSV, KJV, Amplified, and NIV, and reads them together to detect nuances, subtleties, and variances in the content and meaning of the texts for proper interpretation. Her preparation is "always preceded by, intertwined with, and enveloped in prayer. I am in constant conversation with the Holy Spirit." She searches the scriptures exhaustively (using a concordance and Hebrew/Greek key study Bible), and any other relevant texts, books, publications, or writings (sacred or secular). After making copious notes using and drawing upon any and all available resources—media (radio, television, newspaper, magazines); the arts (theater, music); academia (the law, sciences, math, history, civics, languages); current events; sociopolitical, sociocultural, socioeconomic phenomena; areas of special interest; and just everyday life experiences— she develops the sermon. During preparation, she reads and studies the key scriptural text in at least four to six translations to detect nuances, subtleties, and variances in textual content and meaning for interpretation. The scriptural text is generally the heart of her sermon. She usually prepares and preaches from a manuscript, but she is currently in transition. "Lately, however, my preaching is becoming more extemporaneous or from notes or an outline."

Sermon preparation is neither static nor monolithic. Claudette Copeland uses both the NIV and KJV. "The NIV translation is accurate and understandable. The KJV is used for its tradition, poetry, and connection to the pew for those who are KJV readers." Her preparatory stages have changed with the "seasons of my preaching life." For more formal occasions, she uses a strict manuscript, written but not necessarily used verbatim. For normal Sunday preparation, she uses an outline for extemporaneous delivery, preaching points from the text itself. Topics are selected sometimes seasonally by the Christian calendar or are "life-led" topics through prayer and observation of the lives of our people.

The Reverend T. Renée Crutcher, a Baptist minister in Georgia, has been preaching for four years. She has been proclaiming God's word in song since she was a child. Preaching three to six times a year, she prefers the NRSV and NIV but consults many different translations when writing a sermon. "There are times when I choose based on the poetic style that I feel will have the kind of impact on the ears that will draw a hearer to the text. I take liberties with the gender if necessary and make that known." As a rule, she meditates and prays for a revelation of a text. She may choose a text heard or read during study or in song that moves her and sticks with her. The next step is to pray and mediate on the text without going to any source but the Bible to glean an understanding of the text, to see how God wants the text to be used, and how she is to use the text. There is also consideration of how the text applies to relevant life circumstances. She customarily writes a full manuscript using the oral/aural form.

Cynthia Vaughn is a lectionary preacher. She says the NRSV is most often used because it is "the one my seminary recommended and is recognized by the church as an appropriate translation." Her process also begins with prayer: "I read it and meditate on it for several days (if possible) to see what insights God will reveal to me before reviewing commentaries, homiletic magazines, and articles and sermons published on text. I like to get the topic from the text, but if that does not happen, it may be determined after the sermon is prepared." She prepares a full manuscript and uses it almost exactly during delivery. She is an associate at a predominantly white church in Atlanta.

Sylvia Penny's textual choices are the KJV, NIV, Amplified Life, Key Hebrew/Greek Expository of the Bible, Bible dictionary, Thompson Chain, and a Hebrew/Greek Bible (for accuracy and clarification). Her procedure begins with "prayer to hear from God and to cleanse my vessel." Her research on the text begins with study of the Hebrew/Greek for clarity and its life application, focusing on customs, habits, rituals, and beliefs. She "unpacks the word as the Spirit leads." Her preaching form is narrative. She manages either with minimal notes or extemporaneously.

Cynthia Hale preaches sermon series before her congregation. She prefers the NIV and KJV. She says, "I pray and stay before the Lord, listen for his leading, and develop a series in keeping with where I am trying to take the congregation." In the process she selects texts and accomplishes exegesis using commentaries, a Bible dictionary, and other materials read or studied. Before writing, she reads for a day and prays. She writes a full manuscript each time.

Almella Starks-Umoja is at times a lectionary preacher. She uses the KJV or NRSV. She maintains that most people know Scripture by the King James words, but she thinks the NRSV is a better, less biased version. "My African Methodist Episcopal Church does not emphasize the use of the lectionary. However, I exclusively use the lectionary to preach during Advent and Lent. Generally, sermons are based on themes that are relevant to the spiritual growth and development of the church. Certainly major social and political events—as well as the dominant events of the church's calendar—influence the selection of sermons." The scriptural passage is identified through prayer and meditation. She writes the entire passage in longhand, examining other senses in the text that allow her to experience the text more deeply. She uses an interesting process for composition of the sermon:

> Next I use a technique called *mind mapping* to visually map the content. In this mapping process I focus on identifying the underlying relationships of the text, how the text is connected, patterns of usage and style, comparative and contrasting issues, analogies, and so on. I ask the conventional questions posed by an exegesis, but I also search the "mapped" test to explore how these answers fit within the "whole" of the text. At various times I review the map and attempt to summarize the intent or critical message of the passage. Once I have completed the mind map, I have a good sense of what issues are addressed in the text. After I have identified these issues, I then question their relevance for the audience I am addressing.

She predominantly reads the NRSV and the NIV, preferring the language style, limited gender bias, and the integrity of the texts. These translations are easier for most people in her congregation to understand. She describes her delivery style as charismatic, engaging in typical elements of preaching from the African American tradition such as celebration, call, and response.

Stephanie Buckhanon Crowder principally uses the NRSV but may consult other translations if there are particular words in a text that draw her attention. She also likes to use Greek and Hebrew. Following prayer for guidance and discernment, she reflects on the theme (if one), purpose, audience, and nature of event. She spends days writing notes centered on a particular theme or ideas. The notes become an outline, and the outline becomes a full eight- to ten-page manuscript. For the most part, there is an introduction, two to three points, and a conclusion. Form and style depend on the nature of the sermon or on church composition (racial, ethnic makeup). This varies as the Spirit and occasion direct.

Extensive responses came from the Reverend Dr. Betty Hanna-Witherspoon (AME). She divided her preaching into regular Sunday morning opportunities with her congregation and sermons for special days such as Martin Luther King Jr.'s birthday and Founder's Day:

> For pastoral preaching relying upon the Spirit, I choose an overall theme for the year, and then I explore the Bible books that speak to that theme. This keeps me from bouncing all over the place and gives me and the congregation a chance to grow by exploring books that we might not explore and by approaching books in a systematic way. After the books are chosen, I do research for supportive material, stats and stories, and then I go to the writing. For most weekly preaching, there is time only for a first and revised draft, if that. I preach from a manuscript, but depart from it often.

On special days, Reverend Hanna-Witherspoon preaches topically. She follows the lectionary for high holy days, Advent, Christmas, Lent, Holy Week, and Easter. Sometimes she preaches in response to particular congregational issues that arise, such as violence among young people.

Raedorah Stewart-Dodd not only prays for herself and illumination of a text, but also requests that the pastor and congregation (specifically women) pray for her. If preaching for a special event, she uses the assigned test. If a church uses a lectionary, so does she. When no text is assigned, she says, "I discovered that texts and notes that had emerged from casual or meditative Bible reading emerge as the necessary word for the occasion. I tend to keep preaching notebooks and journals of sermons in process." She prefers the "NRSV for its inclusive pronouns; NIV for its language and cadence; [and] NKJV for congregational reading and responses." She finds it to be a sufficient bridge between the still popular KJV as pew and personal Bible.

Her supportive materials include current events, actual historical data, and psychosocial interpretations from field experts. "I absolutely abhor 'feel good' or 'guilt trip' or 'chicken soup' illustrations." In addition to selecting readings of seminary-approved commentaries and references (mostly those of dead white men and reformed), she intentionally consults commentaries and biblical studies books by contemporary scholars (such as C. Keener, M. Jacobs); Catholic commentaries (valuable in broadening knowledge and practice of mysticism); and the Women's Bible Commentary, which she finds is a useful guide to filling in the blanks where other commentaries fail to count the women.

She is emphatic regarding her preaching preferences. She remarks that her form and style depends most on context (or, audience, occasion, familiarity).

> At my home church, preaching is central to worship. I am a "daughter" of the house, with a shared expectation to teach, preach, and celebrate. (The altar ministry following the sermon is as integral to worship as the preaching moment and takes up to an hour or more.) Pulpit supply preaching is often the necessary role left unassigned in the pastor's absence; sermons tend to be more aesthetically pure to task of teaching, preaching, and sitting down within the half hour! When preaching at a white church, there is often the expectation for me to "entertain" them with black preaching, while adhering to the proscribed fifteen- to twenty-minute preaching time slot. This expectation is not hard to resist, as I am gravely offended by it, and respond by crafting a theologically sound sermon suitable for this usually cerebral crowd.

She opines one of the difficulties in preaching in a variety of settings. Preaching in a different cultural venue may "straitjacket" the preacher.

> I have watched and heard a preacher so free and engaging in a his or her own racial/ethnic/denominational setting become imprisoned in political correctness, fear of critique, the inability to find a rhythm, dependency on the call and response or lack thereof, or by having

flashbacks of old tapes mask the effectiveness of the message. I recommend preaching universals and being one's self.

Diverse text preferences, distinct translations, dissimilar styles, and disparate support materials result in prayerful homiletical delivery. Black women take care in "handling" God's word. They strive to honor God by giving their best during study, composition, and presentation. They do not take the task of preaching lightly. They hear the music, learn the original score, seek means of deepening their knowledge of the author's intent, and, after entering the text, begin to formulate their own ways to present it in the most harmonious manner possible. They learn to sight-read whole notes and half notes. This chapter has reviewed the preliminary steps to proclamation prayer, text preference, translations, and exegesis. It also included steps in sermon preparation and form for delivery. The next chapter will review homiletical purpose, themes, passion, imagery, illustrations, and content.

"But What Do You See?"

This sermon was preached at the New Bethel AME Church in Lithonia, Georgia, on Palm Sunday, March 24, 2002. It has also been used to encourage people to use their own insight to interpret their beliefs.

Old Testament Reading: Psalm 40:1-5

> 1 I waited patiently for the LORD; he inclined to me and heard my cry.
> 2 He drew me up from the desolate pit, out of the miry bog [NKJV clay] and set my feet upon a rock, making my steps secure.
> 3 He put a new song in my mouth, a song of praise to our God. Many will see and fear, and put their trust in the LORD.
> 4 Happy are those who make the LORD their trust, who do not turn to the proud, to those who go astray after false gods [NKJV turn to lies].
> 5 You have multiplied, O LORD my God, your wondrous deeds and your thoughts toward us; none can compare with you. Were I to proclaim and tell of them, they would be more than can be counted.

New Testament Reading: Luke 19:37

> 37 As he was now approaching the path down from the Mount of Olives, the whole multitude of the disciples began to praise God joyfully with a loud voice for all the deeds of power that they had seen.

Today is Passion or Palm Sunday.

The beginning of a journey of teaching, betrayal, injustice, prayers, commandments, suffering, death, and resurrection. It is a day for reflection on the meaning of Jesus in our individual and collective lives.

As I read the four Gospel accounts of this day, I was struck by the Lukan passage. It had a focus that the others lacked. It revealed the actions of believers each and every day, not just once a year.

As we walk back through our focus text:

It has been thirty-three years since a baby was born in a manger in Bethlehem to a fifteen-year-old girl and a much older carpenter.

Heaven and nature rejoiced while earthbound kings sought to kill the newborn hope of the world.

It has been twenty-one years since a boy of twelve taught elders in the temple as his parents searched frantically for him, only to be told he had to be about his father's business.

It has been three years since he was tempted on Quarantania in the wilderness by an egotistical fallen angel trying to use food, identity, and power to abort his ministry and mission.

It is seven days before his mission on earth is complete

Seven days before he gives himself for generations born and unborn

Seven days before the greatest gift ever created is unwrapped.

Jesus is on his fourth and final trip to Jerusalem

It had been a long journey from Caesarea Philippi, to Galilee, to Cana, to Judea, to the region beyond the Jordan, to Jericho and back

A long journey through Jericho, the stopping place for Galilean pilgrims going to Jerusalem

A trip on a donkey that had never before been ridden by a human

A jaunt down the slope from Jericho, the city of Palms

Up the twenty-mile ascent toward Jerusalem

A stop in Bethphage and Bethany

And a short descent of the Mount of Olives about a half-mile to Jerusalem

It is Passover
>Passover, the mandatory feast in remembrance of Israel's deliverance from captivity in Egypt
>March or April, beginnings of spring
>Old things were passing away,
>New life was celebrated

Every adult male over twelve is required to travel to Jerusalem for the Passover at least once before he dies

All lodging was free in Jerusalem and in the surrounding towns of Bethphage and Bethany, some even in Jericho fifteen or twenty miles away

There were over three million pilgrims from around the world in Jerusalem
>Parthians, Medes, Elamites, residents of Mesopotamia, Judea, Cappadocia, Pontus, Asia, Phrygia, Pamphylia, Egypt, Libya, Cyrene, Crete, Arabia
>Worshiping God for deliverance for physical slavery

It was seven days before deliverance from the slavery of sin.

Verse 37 says: *As he was approaching the path down from the Mount of Olives*

It is the day of the parade
>No floats, no marching bands, no queens, no elephants, no white horses, no clowns, no balloons, no flags

You know how it is at a parade
>Some arrive early
>Some late
>Some anticipate of colors, sights, and sounds
>Some excited
>Some just there

It was the custom to have parades, processions, and public victory parties when a conquering king returned from battle.

This parade had one focus, a man on a borrowed donkey
>Facing the rising sun

Jesus never says a word in this entire passage.
>He just rides on the donkey, past the multitude facing his destiny

Jesus doesn't have to tell everyone he is present. They just know it

Do you know someone that can just walk in the room and the entire atmosphere changes? That's Jesus

Brother just riding on the donkey, rocking back and forth as he made the ascent to Jerusalem

Book says *the whole multitude of disciples* had followed Jesus from Galilee
    Numbers were added along the way
    The group that began with Jesus and four called from their fishing
        boats increased as Jesus' ministry grew.
    I imagine in the multitude were Simon Peter, Andrew, Zebedee's and
        Mary's sons James and John, Phillip, Bartholomew, Thomas,
        Matthew, Alphaeus's son James, Thaddeus, Simon the Cananean,
        and Judas Iscariot,
    Mary from Magdalene, Joanna, Suzanna
    Mary, mother of James and Joseph
    Salome, married to Zebedee, mother of James and John
    Mary, the mother of Jesus
    Elizabeth, Zechariah
    Mary, Martha, and Lazarus
    Zacchaeus
    Woman found in adultery
    Jarius and his daughter
    Those who had followed John the Baptist
    The widow with the mite
    The former paralytic and his friends
    The thankful former leper
    The centurion and his son
    The Syrophonecian woman and her daughter
    Some of the four thousand who ate from the multiplied seven
        loaves and a few fish
    Some of the priests from the Temple
    Even those who followed Jesus far off because they did not want
        their friends, family, or boss to know they were beginning to
        believe this man's teachings
    Just to name a few
They had seen and heard Jesus in Galilee
They welcomed the opportunity during his ministry
Some had been directly touched by Jesus' ministry and had to pro-
    claim him the Messiah
Some had merely heard about this man who had done great things
The crowd swelling as Jesus went toward Jerusalem
    Getting progressively larger, like people following the sound of
    sirens to see whose house is on fire

Like rubbernecks bottling up traffic to see an accident

Like the wait line in a new restaurant on Friday night

Like the numbers in churches following a national tragedy, natural disaster, or personal trauma

Look at this crowd:

True disciples [churched] I imagine included

Some looking for a prophet

Some, a king to destroy their oppressors

Some, not sure what happened in their lives but following anyway seeking to learn more each day

Seekers, the Unchurched [nonbelievers, seeking], no home temple,

Going from place to place, looking for something but not knowing what,

Club one day, store the next, church sometimes,

Worshiping in the stadium or before the television but never in the minds of God's house

Sometimes the unchurched are in church—plotting

Trying to find fault

Seeking to kill and destroy

Embarrassed by the noise

Wanting power without any investment

Teaching what they don't know and leading where they won't go

Negative about anything they did not think of

So caught up being believers they can't explain what they believe

Good-time folk [Any excuse for a gathering folk, seeking entertainment, a date]

Just there to see what was going on, no allegiance to anything or anybody

Carrying a Bible but never going to Bible study

Quoting Scripture but mixing it up with the word on the street

Hiding talent so no one will ask them to work for the church

Dechurched [those who were once believers but lost faith]

Began to question what was happening

Will the Messiah ever come?

Used to attend temple regularly but had a disagreement and stopped going except on special days—funeral, Mother's Day, Christmas, Easter, or family reunion

The me, mine, and my crowd [Pray for self, only they've forgotten about the model prayer that begins "Our Father"]

Want to keep these newcomers out

"How dare she think she can come in here and run something."

"Doesn't he know this is my territory?"

"Nothing happens unless I say so."

"We were here when he got here and we will be here when he's gone."

"Let me go report this to the authorities [pastor] even if I have to lie so I can have my spot back."

Remember not everyone who praises God believes what they are saying.

Bible says the whole multitude began to praise God joyfully

Can you imagine a great multitude like the multitude that sang when Christ was born?

Like the multitude that listened to the Sermon on the Mount?

Like the multitude gathering in Jerusalem?

Like the multitude that will watch the Final Four next weekend?

Like the multitude no one could number in John's Revelation?

Matthew and Mark report the people spread their cloaks on the road

Others spread branches from olive, myrtle, and palm trees from Jericho on the road

John says they waved palm branches as they went out to meet Jesus and shouted, "Hosanna! Save us now!"

Luke says as he rode along, people kept spreading their coats on the road

Whether it was with branches or fabric, the multitude recognizes the entrance of their king.

Most followed out of gratitude

Some even came from Jerusalem to join the parade

They were willing to tell the world that this solitary figure riding on a donkey was their king

Didn't care who saw them

Didn't care when someone critiqued how he or she praised

Didn't need to be told to praise

They were willing participants in this procession toward eternal life

They praised their king, the one they saw before them, in their midst

Not a soon-coming king

Not a sweet by-and-by king

But the here and now king

The reach out and touch king, ·

The one who walked among the people without bodyguards
The homeless king
The king without purchased political clout but with the clout to
    purchase all humanity
Their leader
Their deliverer
Their friend
The God with us, not the "get back to you later" voicemail God
    But one who hears and answers all prayers
    The living, breathing, presence of God who knew their sorrows
      and their victories
    The power that ruled all nature
    The "I love you more than my own life" kind of king
They praised God [natural response for gratitude]
Praised in a loud voice
    Some sang
    Some prayed
    Some waved the palms
    Some shouted, "Hosanna!"
    Some ran back and forth
    Some cried
    Some clapped
    Some probably remembered David's song
      I waited and waited and waited for God
      He looked
      God listened
      Lifted me out of the ditch
      Pulled me from deep mud.
      Set me up on a solid rock
      Made sure I wouldn't slip
      Taught me how to sing the latest God-song
      A praise song to our God (The Message)
    More and more people are seeing this
    They enter the mystery, abandoning themselves to God
      I start talking about God
      Telling what I know
      What I have seen
      I run out of words.
This multitude praised God in a loud voice for they had seen

Seen—perceived with their eyes, comprehended, witnessed

Not everyone in the multitude, in the crowd, saw the same things

> They had different experiences with Jesus so they had different visual perception

In my sanctified imagination I see the multitude, the crowd of pilgrims on the road: all races, all colors, all heights, all ages, all manner of dress, all kinds of occupations,

> All levels of faith and spirituality
>
> Some *Nearsighted*—remembering the last thing Jesus did but not seeing all the blessings of life
>
> Some *Farsighted*—overlooking present blessings, too busy looking for the next one
>
> Some *Astigmatism*—too busy looking at what God has done for others missed what God was doing for them
>
> Some *Blurred vision*—detached from presence of God by focusing on other things
>
> Some *Tunnel vision*—thought Jesus only blessed them
>
> Some *Vanity vision*—changing the description of the blessing so they will look holier than others
>
> Some with *Conjunctivitis*—contagious gossip. Malice, envy, sin—wanting to stop the parade, had to do things in a group to ensure power, like the Pharisees who stood back watching, plotting to kill Jesus, eaten up by envy, trying to please the Romans
>
> Some with *20/20 vision*—know who they are and whose they are, only God could have brought them to this parade and kept them, recognize the king of life, worshiping him out of gratitude and not because someone told them to
>
> All looking for, looking at, looking to Jesus

What do you see?

Whatever their visual acuity, they praised Jesus

> [NRSV]   *For all the deeds of power;*
>
> [NIV]   *for all the miracles they had seen;*
>
> [KJV]   *all the mighty works that they had seen*
>
> [CEV]   *for all the miracles they had seen*

The multitude followed and praised Jesus for the miracles they had seen

> Miracles *[dunamis, doo-nam-is]*
>
> God's strength, power, ability
>
> Inherent power residing in or exerted through an individual or thing

Biblical miracles, great works [erga], signs [semeion], wonders [terata
    L. thauma] requiring direct causal agency of a supernatural being
New and higher power
Extraordinary event, inexplicable by ordinary forces
    Indicative of something larger than the direct event
Not magic
Signs for nonbelievers to change ways
Miracles teach a lesson
Miracles are given by God when God sees fit, not when we call for
    one
Miracles are not "name it and claim it"
There are requirements and order about the miracles in the Bible
Some of us have changed the biblical definition to fit our need to
    boast about what we have.
Look at Jesus' forty miracles recorded in the biblical text (there were
    many others, but not all of them made this edition of the book).
    Someone had seen or heard about Jesus
    Someone approached Jesus
    They requested something of Jesus
    Jesus called on something inside the person to change
    Jesus showed them a more excellent way
    "Faith has made you whole."
Miracles are essential to Christianity
    Produces astonishment in the observer
    Discerned through senses
    Authenticates or seals divine mission
    Competent witnesses required
    Results in trustworthy testimonies
Miracles are the result of "faithing" that God can do all things
Jesus worked miracles to demonstrate that the kingdom of God had
      been inaugurated
    The messianic age had arrived
    He is the Christ who will fulfill God's word
The crowd began praising Jesus joyfully with a loud voice for all the
    deeds of power, miracles, and great works that they had seen,
    experienced,
For something that they could not fully explain but knew it did not
      come from the Roman or Bush government,
    The temple or faith system

The job or
Themselves
They praised in a joyful, in a loud voice for all the miracles they had
    seen
    Some recognized Jesus as amazing when demon-filled pigs jumped
        off the cliff and a man regained his sanity.
    Some identified Jesus as extraordinary as seven demons left Mary
        Magdalene
    Some looked at Jesus as the deaf began to hear
What do you see?
    Some noticed Jesus as he took a coin out of the mouth of a fish.
    Some saw Jesus turn six stone jars of purified ritual water into 180
        gallons of wedding wine.
    Some witnessed Jesus as a healer when Bartimaeus received his
        sight
    Some envisioned Jesus as sent from God as Lazarus walked out of
        the grave.
What do you see?
    Some realized it was Jesus who got up out of his bed and com-
        manded the wind and the waves to stop making so much noise.
    Some perceived Jesus as ecumenical when he stepped across cul-
        ture and spoke with the woman at the well.
    Some recognized Jesus as the one who walked on the water early
        in the morning
What do you see?
    Some glimpsed the divinity of Jesus when a woman merely
        reached out to the bottom of his robe and her bleeding stopped
    Some attended to Jesus when a bent-over woman stood up
        straight
    Some discovered Jesus when the man who had lain by the pool for
        thirty-eight years got up and walked into the water.
What do you see?
    Some comprehended the power of Jesus when he stopped the
        funeral procession outside of Nain and a son was returned to
        his mother
    Some watched Jesus feed five thousand with two fish and five
        loaves of bread and have leftovers.
All the multitude of disciples—named and unnamed—
    Saw Jesus, the greatest miracle of all—

Riding on the donkey toward an even greater miracle in
Jerusalem and on to Calvary.
What do you see?
What has Jesus done for you?
I see Jesus repairing the breach of covenant relationship
I see Jesus refinancing the mortgage of bankrupt spirituality
What do you see?
Have you counted your blessings lately?
I see Jesus reorienting the minds of objectified humanity
I see Jesus re-keying the doors of obstructed opportunity
What do you see?
Do you have a personal relationship with Jesus?
I see Jesus releasing the captives of self-initiated addictions
I see Jesus replenishing the landscape of polluted creation
What do you see?
Is Jesus the king of your life?
Are you still looking for love in all the wrong places?
I see Jesus riding the donkey of humble submission
Pressing his way through the crowd for you and for me
Eyes on the prize
Have you looked to the hills for help lately?
Knowing that if he turns back, our souls would be lost.
Knowing that even as they praised him on Sunday, he had to endure
the pain and the shame of Monday to Friday, the darkness of
Saturday, to get to the joy of Sunday.
Do we see all that God in Jesus has done to keep us in his care?
Do we see new possibilities for life, or are we stuck in the grave?
Do we see Jesus in our brothers and sisters, no matter who they are
or where they live?
On this Passion Sunday, let's do more than wave palms in order to rush
to resurrection.
Let's see Jesus, as he is a living servant who wants us to live.
Let's lift joyful praise in loud voices for the one whose miracles we
have seen.
What do you see? What do you see? What do you see?
I once was blind
I once was nearsighted
Once farsighted
Once blurred vision

Once astigmatism
Once double vision
Once vanity vision
Now I see with 20/20 vision
You see, I had a visit to the divine ophthalmologist
Opened my blind, weak, feeble eyes
So I would stop looking at the problems and start looking toward the
solution
Gave me
New eyes, new vision, new trust, new faith, new belief, new courage,
new sight of the one who is able to do all things well
Helps, restores, saves to the utmost
One who lets us live from glory to glory
Can you hear the Psalmist?
Mine eyes have seen the glory, not of some human pretend god, but
of the coming of the Lord
God is tramping out the vintage, those hidden places, where the
grapes of wrath were stored
God has loosed the fateful lightning of his terrible, his terrible, his
terrible swift sword
(Oh beloved, it doesn't take God long when God begins to move)
God truth, God's truth, God's truth, God's truth, God's truth is
marching on
I see God. *What do you see?*
Glory, glory Hallelujah
Glory, glory Hallelujah
Glory, glory, glory, glory, glory Hallelujah
God's truth is marching on
What do you see?

Resting but Remaining in Tune

A rest is a rhythmic silence, a pause in reading, a momentary hiatus, and a succession of pleasing musical tonality. It is that period of adjustment for more effective production. The transition following a rest may result in key changes, tempo augmentation, or volume modification. In singing, it is a time to gather one's energy or emotion. These moves add flavor, dimension, emotion, and meaning. The intent of the song does not change, and eventually there is a refrain that is still true to the original intent of the piece. The harmony, the attitude, the resonance are in sync even though in places on either side of the rest they appear discordant.

There are parallels in the process of sermon preparation. I begin with an idea or premise. I seek God's face for direction. I wait (rest) on spiritual intervention to gain understanding of what is to be done. I may listen to a number of tunes (texts) until one begins to stand out in the midst of the cacophony of ideas, issues, and agendas. I rest and meditate on the text and begin to read over the passage several times and read aloud so I can sense the feel of the text in my mouth, my ears, and my eyes. I search for how the text is written and why it is important to the concerto of

God's commands and instruction. I rest again and then begin to write, subconsciously aware that my passion for justice and social transformation is subtext playing throughout the process. The rests help in deliberation of relevant questions: Why do we preach? Where is God in the process? Where does proclamation fit in the life of the church? What is the context of the sermon? How is the text used? Elements of preparations discussed in this chapter are sermon purpose, preaching passion, theme selection, sermon types, illustrations and images, and content. They are the rests, notes, key changes, modulations, and rhythms of God's saving song. The irreplaceable elements in proclamation preparation are the rests, those places where preachers hear from God. They allow us to remain in tune by following God's direction.

Olin Moyd maintains that the preacher needs to ask a basic question prior to sermon preparation: "What is my theology of preaching?" or "Why am I doing this?" He says that a theology of preaching is "acknowledgment and affirmation that preaching is the primary, divine mandate and medium for communicating, elucidating, and illuminating God's revelation for God's people."[1] The authority to preach is established by God through revelation of the Holy Spirit. The preacher addresses what happens between God and the people by wrestling with the text, knowing the people, and being in a position to hear from God.

The role of the black preacher is to assist the listeners in the identification of spiritual, social, cultural, psychological, and economical issues that affect daily life. The sense of disenfranchisement stagnates personal pursuit of relationships, goals, and objectives. The preacher presents the realities of black life through a hermeneutics of suspicion, or examination of the status quo. James Harris, noted homiletics professor, states:

> There are enough—indeed, too many—proponents of the status quo. This is why there is an urgent need for effective preaching that is truthful, indicting, confrontational, straightforward—a radically simple strategy that will be heard and acted upon rather than alienating—preaching that will challenge and transform the prevailing.[2]

In a summer school preaching class fifteen years ago, Dr. Charles G. Adams, Senior Pastor of Hartford Memorial Baptist Church in Detroit, taught us that action-oriented preaching averts the annihilation of humanity. The possibility of silence in the pulpit is a travesty. The preacher must place himself or herself in the position of the congregation. The preacher must be aware of the lives of the listeners. Needs cannot be met through mute, glib, or trite persons and sermons from pulpits. I find myself telling students that preachers too often leave the congregation wounded, bleeding, and lying in a bed of "why try?" The challenge of addressing social issues is absent in many contemporary black pulpits. I believe that part of the problem is the transitory nature of congregants, the distance between the preacher and the people, fear of confrontation, separation of the secular and sacred, and belief that there is no need to address injustice, just the spiritual.

The true personality of the congregation is often overlooked. At times the preacher believes that everyone is at the same level, going through the same problems, achieving the same levels of "success," and that "isms," such as ageism, sexism, racism, exist only in the church down the street. The hoped-filled events of the individual members, the tragic events that affect everyone, the life passages, the celebrations, and the day-to-day living of the membership must be diligently addressed or the sermon is irrelevant. This is not to say that one must always address an "issue" or "problem." The preacher is, however, obligated to understand evil in all its forms and power. Dignity of the individual must be preserved. The listeners should have some insight of self-empowerment.

Ethicist Katie Cannon reminds us that the African American sermon is the earliest form of spoken religious art in the black community. It wrestles with how evil can occur in a world that a loving God created. The messenger considers domination, subordination, and the constraints of the world resultant from moral evil. She continues, it is essential for those interested in liberation to "debunk, unmask, and disentangle" the messages of marginalization that hang over the word like smog over any major city in the country. The preacher should seek to unearth images that dehumanize others. The continued self-inventiveness of the black preacher leads to a running commentary on not only scriptural passages, but also how the Bible speaks to alleviating oppression in the form of "emancipatory praxis."[3] The preacher's challenge, according to H. Beecher Hicks Jr., is to face evil head-on and engage it, realize the depths of pain, and remain empathetic in addressing the congregation.[4] The content of black preaching has historically involved critiques of individuals, church, and society. The prophetic nature of black preaching meant to address what was deemed not of God and to point persons toward life-changing decisions that were said to meet God's standards of behavior as recorded in the biblical text and as revealed to the preacher. The preacher must realize that we often see only the surface issues. The preacher must *mine the deep*. Knowledge of the congregation is enhanced when preachers spend time listening to the levels of conversation. What appears to be the real problem is, at times, really a secondary concern. African Americans may relate one event but are troubled about another. There is a cultural understanding that one does not divulge the full extent of one's concern. There is a certain embarrassment or question of the depths of faith when one is going through stress. Some issues are too painful to recall or discuss. It is up to the preacher to frame the issue in such a manner that the listener can identify it, understand its effect, and seek transformation. The black preacher utilizes lived experience to relate to the congregation. The preacher should be well-read in areas that affect the congregation. The preacher should empathetically reference the concerns of the congregation with care, yet challenge the congregation to look past the present circumstance to a God-ordained end. Combining my studies in individual and social transformation with homiletics, I encourage preachers to be aware of the context before assigning a text and a particular social issue to it.

Preaching Passion and Themes

C. Kirk Hadaway speaks of sermon purpose in transformation of communities of faith. He says that the purpose of the sermon or proclamation is to educate the listener about God's transcendent and transforming presence (I believe the process also educates the speaker), motivate action and change, alleviate oppressive constraints regardless of their origin, and liberate (save from a deluded life).[5] Past President of the Academy of Homiletics Christine Smith remarks that preachers are to face the world with truth. We are called on to confess our own complicity as well as that of others in the injustice. She implores the preacher to name evil and to seek to verbally transform it.[6] Choice or avoidance of themes is a common occurrence. Even lectionary preachers have an option to use a particular text and may be able to brush by the assigned theme. Themes are usually assigned for special days in the black church. Women's Day themes are notorious for length, complexity, and creativity. Preaching passion is that underlying theme that seems to characterize most of our discourse. Regardless of where we begin, that passion steps from the corners of the mind into the midst of the conversation. It may be subtle or pronounced, smoldering or blazing, soft or loud, but the passion is ever present. It is the lens that overlays each text. The questions for this section were: "Are there themes or topics you find yourself using often or avoiding? What is your passion in this ministry?" They were sent to a group of thirty-three women. Twenty-two responded. A representative number of the sistah proclaimers talk about wrestling with themes or topics as part of their preparation and their preaching passion. The information is divided into themes about women and general Christian principles, which are age-specific, occasion-driven and ministry-focused.

I believe that a significant number of black women evangelists have received opportunities to preach because of Women's Days and missionary society programs. Although there are now local and international women's conferences, women's ministries, televangelists, "teaching" ministries, and independent pastoral assignments and ministries, the starting place in the local church is in part due to Nannie Helen Burroughs, a Baptist laywoman who organized the Women's Convention of the National Baptist Convention. Isn't it ironic that women will spend thousands to hear a man tell women how to be women but will listen to women only on special days or if the (male) leader validates their gift. This will have to be addressed in another book. The first group of pulpiteers has a passion for ministry with women.

The Reverend Gail Hayes, Nondenominational, speaks of personal identity as her primary focus:

> I often speak on image, purpose, and destiny. I can't think of any topic I would avoid. My passion is helping others (especially women) discover, accept, embrace, and walk in their God-given purpose and identity. Once they do these things, they become dangerous to the enemy and can then pursue destiny with passion. If a person does not understand who [she is], then the freedom the Lord purchased for [her] on Calvary has no real meaning. If a person does not grasp [her] identity and walk in [her] purpose, then [she] [becomes] like a prisoner, who, once released from prison, goes back to the only life [she has] known; heartache and bondage.

Liberation is the chief theme of the Baptist preacher and College Chaplain Reverend Lisa Rhodes:

> I use themes that parallel women's issues, social and political oppression, and God's grace, favor, deliverance, healing, value, and purpose for women. My passion is emotional, psychological, and spiritual liberation for all of God's people, but especially women—healing and community

among and between women. People, particularly women, need to hear about God's love, God's purpose and value for women, and the power and grace God provides for women to live to the fullness of life with and among each other as Sista girls . . . and friends.

The Reverend Helen Richmond, Nondenominational, is also a pastor's spouse. Her themes are prayer and empowerment:

> I don't believe I avoid topics. But again many of my sermons and teachings involve benefits of being a part of the Body of Christ. That involves subjects such as believing you can receive what you pray for, how to pray to get results, walking in love; not having a spirit of fear, being more than conquerors, doing all things thru Christ, and so on. Again, I especially focus on women. My passion in ministry is getting women to empower themselves with the word. The benefits are there. We just need to take advantage of them. Women need to see themselves as powerful agents for Christ in all areas, whether in pastoring, teaching, preaching, evangelizing, prophesying, or whatever. My job at Women of Divine Destiny Bible School is to aid them in becoming empowered to evangelize, not just the world, but the Body of Christ. My curriculum is geared toward doing just that. Not only do I offer foundational courses, but also I offer spiritual courses, too—such as "Walking in Love" and "Prayer, Praise, and Worship."

Women understand women's issues best because of their social location. They are black women in America. Their souls inhabit female bodies with associated physical abilities and issues. They live inside and outside social constrictions specific only to black women. They survive and thrive in spite of what others say or do about their personhood. This is not to say that men cannot speak about women. It is merely to reiterate that women are able to tell their own story. Black women are not unidimensional however. They are responsible to God for their actions and communicate basic Christian principles with passion also.

Pioneering Baptist preacher and grief counselor, the Reverend Arlene Churn voices her passion for the local church:

> I avoid preaching about women in ministry or attempting to justify preachers who are women. I found that anointed preaching and proclamation is proof of the call on the part of any preacher. My passion is for souls and the strengthening of the saints. People need to hear the truth about God, his mercy, his anger, and things are as they are, and why people act and react to the problems we all face in these trying

times. My passion is for the local church to serve the people in the midst of their needs, both spiritual and temporal. I have a burning passion for a denominational statement of faith and for the people to be governed accordingly by that stated belief and faith. I see the need for restoration of ritual and respect for the house of God and the Body of Christ and for verbal witness of our faith. I am concerned about the fad of programmed testimonies that only relate to financial blessings. We need to hear overcoming witnesses and testimonies to the power of God in one's personal life [now] more than ever before.

The Reverend Jacqueline Rowland, AME Itinerant Deacon, preaches topics about God's grace:

One of the themes that is consistently woven throughout my sermons and teachings is, "Now that you are a Christian, does your life reflect your Christ?" I avoid the scripture that is frequently quoted, "I'm just a sinner saved by grace." I believe the statement to be accurate. However, I am personally concerned that often it is utilized to give license to those who want to continue in sin. So that I am not mistaken or misunderstood typically, I reserve comment when this scripture is quoted. I prefer to quote, "Shall we continue in sin that grace may abound, God forbid."

The Reverend Sandra Blair, AME Itinerant Elder, preaches themes of sin and wholeness:

I have heard Renita Weems say that, out of the context of our individual life experience, we each have a recurring theme in our preaching and that it shapes our sermons regardless of the Scripture text used or the sermon topic. I have found mine to be that of acceptance— coming to the awareness that God accepts us as we are, growing into self-acceptance, and learning to accept others as well as to find acceptance in others. I wrestle with the fundamentalist notion of sin as an inherent and condemnable corruption in human nature and instead try to convey the understanding of sin as those aspects of our humanity that cause us to feel separation from God but are overridden by God's love and grace. Mine is an unusual ministry of comfort and strength to quiet, silent sufferers and troubled souls. This captures my passion to share a message of assurance that each of us is loved and valued by God and that, because Jesus shared our human experience, we can find, through His grace, reconciliation, healing, and wholeness, with God, within ourselves, and with others.

127

Kim Martin, Pentecostal laywoman, focuses on God's love and judgment:

> Topics I use often are guidance, faith, and overcoming obstacles. I don't avoid anything in the word of God because it is the truth and all of God's word leads and guides into greater understanding of the world we live in and the things that shall come to pass. My passion in ministry is just to know God trusts me to be his vessel of honor and not dishonor, to proclaim the word of God, and to be his servant. In my heart, I believe people need to hear the truth that God is love but also that God is a God of judgment. God is consistent—he's the same yesterday, today, and forever—and his desire is to reconcile [everyone] unto himself [or herself]. That no man should be lost but all should come to repentance and salvation.

Andrea Hassell, AME laywoman and pastor's spouse, speaks of individual responsibility and spiritual growth:

> I like to speak on the love of God, oneself, and others. It is important that we study God and Jesus because they introduced love to us, and once we have a clear understanding of them, it is easy to love our neighbors and ourselves. My passion is to see people develop a personal relationship with Christ. Too often we depend on the preacher on Sunday to teach us about the Bible [but] never take the time to learn it for ourselves. We all have the ability to listen to God and allow him to minister to us through our prayers, studies, music, or devotional, but we do not know it. For example, I should not depend on the pastor to pray for a healing in my life but should know without a shadow of doubt that the Lord hears my prayers as well. Too many Christians are babies in Christ [even though they have] been in the church all their lives. Thus, people need to be taught how to be disciples of Christ through personal studies and prayers.

The Reverend Telley Gadson, United Methodist pastor, speaks of God as a loving parent:

> I often preach about forgiveness and God's redemptive power. I spend a lot of time letting the congregation know that no one is perfect and those who claim perfection are "perfectly inaccurate" of whose they are. I also talk a lot about God's love, grace, mercy, power, and graciousness. I make every effort to present God as the loving parent and compassionate guide that God is. My passion in ministry is preaching, teaching, and learning. In these regards, I am purposed to be real with

the people so that the gospel becomes real to them. The church, as a human-made institution (not as the Body of Christ), has failed the people of God, because so much of what is real has been lost in people trying to be who they are not. In the final analysis, people leave the church, leave their relationship with God, and develop spiritual comas. It is the responsibility of the proclaimer to be real and allow God to be God. I believe without a shadow of a doubt that people need to hear more and more of God's love in spite of humanity's sin.

Hope is the major theme of the Reverend Regina Groff, AME Itinerant Elder:

I preach mostly about hope. I avoid being too condemning. That no matter where they've come from or what they've been through, God is a redeeming, merciful, graceful, and loving God who never gives up on us. We have to trust him and accept his most precious gift—Jesus—in order to maintain hope in the midst of the most hopeless situations.

The Reverend LaTrelle Miller Easterling, AME Itinerant Elder, reflects on God's purpose and presence in individual lives:

As I began to look back over my sermons, I found that I often talked about individuals knowing their purpose. Without knowing our purpose in God's kingdom, we cannot fully complete the task God has given us to do. I also believe this brings ultimate fulfillment. I don't think I consciously avoid any topics, although I do tend to speak of sin more in the existential sense than in the personal sense because the latter is often used to degrade or alienate people. My passion is bringing souls to Christ. To help facilitate that process, I often preach about forgiveness, healing, and acceptance. I find all too often that sermons don't preach enough about God's love and acceptance of us and the fact that Christ can meet us wherever we are. Also, to become the disciples that we are called to be, we first need to love ourselves; once that is accomplished, we can genuinely love others.

Some of the sistahs worked in age-designated or special interest ministries. Their thematic emphasis and passion underscored their situation. The Reverend Sandra Blair, AME minister, works with women's ministries and youth. Life themes are the focus of her youth sermons.

Since I teach young people, the common topics are salvation, life after death, what the Bible says about sex and relationships, who God is, . . . the Trinity, and cults and other religions. No subjects are avoided.

Richelle Fry Skinner, AME laywoman and youth worker, speaks of God's promises:

> My passion is to introduce God and Jesus to young people as a God for all ages and every time period in your life. People need to hear that God is real and has made promises to give you joy and peace and that he will keep them.

The Reverend Cynthia Vaughn, United Methodist minister, has an interest in pastoral care and focuses on God's love.

> No, [I do not avoid topics] except that I have to be careful not to chastise too much. Some people are more used to the "love" aspects of the New Testament that when you preach the Old Testament text more often than the New Testament, people tend to think you can be abusive. My passion, if I have one, is pastoral care. I believe people need healing: physical, mental, emotional, and spiritual. There is probably more need for emotional and spiritual healing than for anything. Many of us need to learn to forgive ourselves and to love ourselves.

Minister Winona Drake, Nondenominational, focuses on grace and mercy in her singles ministry.

> The only topics I usually try to avoid when preparing messages, especially for singles ministry, is fornication. This is only because, I believe, singles ministry leaders and pastors have beat singles over the head on this topic over and over again. Singles need a new word, a revelation, fresh oil, new wine. I have however, tackled this issue head-on numerous times, especially on the radio broadcast. Most recent, the Lord has opened the door for me to minister on the subject of severing sexual soul ties. This topic is very touchy, and the message gets real graphic; but in the end, healing, forgiveness, and deliverance is the message I try to get across. My passion in ministry is to see God's people set free. My passion is also to deliver God's word as His vessel in such a way that someone gets delivered. I believe the only way to "get real" and minister deliverance and healing is by being transparent. No one ever got saved by us "playing church." God's people need to hear more about His grace and mercy. God wants His people to be free, and the message of freedom rarely comes across the pulpits of our churches. I believe the Lord is moving His church into more of the Prophetic and the Apostolic.

The Reverend Mary Anne Bellinger, Presbyterian, focuses on inner feelings:

> In the few times I have been free to preach open sermons—not Women's Day and such—I work with scriptures that can help open the hearts and minds of the congregation to the very real possibility of change in their [lives]. Also I tend to be a teaching preacher—what is the lesson I feel led to share this day?

Six people spoke of avoiding particular books of the Bible. Others used exclusively one testament or the other. Two persons agreed that the book of Revelation may prove daunting.

Miriam Frye, Baptist laywoman and music director, speaks of God's love:

> I avoid Revelation because it is so descriptive it frightens me because I could "visibly" see it as I read it. Too deep for me. Music is my passion. God is there if you trust and believe, and God loves us no matter what.

Carrie Dunson, Baptist, says that the manner in which ordained clergy speak of topics affect the use of those themes by laypersons.

> I am beginning to use topics that refer to how one should be faithful and treat others and the life we will have when Christ comes again. I have avoided the entire book of Revelation because I have not had many teachers [or] preachers to speak from it. I guess I am doing the same. I have attempted to read it for the first time, but it is still a struggle. My passion is to tell the story [of] how Jesus wants us to live without all the added rhetoric one gets from false leaders. People need to hear that Jesus loves us, wants us to prosper and do good and, that if we get off track and take a detour, we are not doomed to hell for it. He is a forgiving God and he loves us and he understands that as human beings with flaws, we are going to err. I believe too much emphasis is put on how people ought to live based on man's interpreting God's word to make others feel small and doomed.

The Reverend Lonzie Symonette, AME, is a certified ecumenical hospice chaplain.

> My topics include God's love, death as a part of the living process, spiritual healing, and finding one's life purpose. Everyone is equal before God. I am honored to walk with them as they face their final hours.

The occasion affects the preaching moment. In the liturgical year, specified topics are preached. Funerals, weddings, baptisms, and Communions require particular topics. In the black church, there are also other special days that drive the sermon theme or topic. Among them are Founder's Day, Church Anniversary, Mother's Day, Father's Day, Pastor's Anniversary, Pastor's Appreciation, Pastor's Birthday, Marriage Emphasis, Laity Sunday, Choir Anniversary, Ushers' Anniversary, Seven Last Words or Women at the Cross (Good Friday Services), Heritage Sunday, Missionary Sunday, Roots Day, Elders Sunday, Martin Luther King Jr.'s birthday, Kwanzaa, Juneteenth, Thanksgiving, Watch Night, Annual Conference, Convocation, Graduation Sunday, Men's Day, Mortgage Burning, Church Dedication, Youth Day, Women's Day, Homecoming, Friends and Family Day, Voter Registration Sunday, and revivals.

The Reverend Dallasteen Yates, AME Itinerant Elder, chooses themes based on the occasion:

> My themes vary according to the occasion and the current word that God wants to get across. I draw heavily from the vast legal references and implications in the text. Because the Bible is a book of "laws" (covenants) both old and new, the legal concepts and inferences are immediately apparent to me. My passion is encouraging people [toward] excellence and the fulfillment of their divine purposes in life. There is so much MORE in life that we can realize and experience and that God has for us—especially as people of color in this world. More love, more compassion, more hope, more power, more peace, more joy, more life, a MORE EXCELLENT WAY. I believe that we live beneath our means, or only scratch the surface of life and living. I sometimes call this the perfecting or maturing of the saints, as opposed to stopping with the initial call to salvation. It's the working out of that salvation. It's about the "greater things" that Jesus said we would and could do. The multiplied loaves and fishes that meet the peoples' needs, with something leftover. Ever coming to know God even as we are known. And it comes through a more intimate relationship with God in Christ Jesus through the power of the Holy Spirit. Jesus said, "I came that they may have life, and have it [more] abundantly" (John 10:10).

The Reverend Zina Jacque, Baptist, speaks of our unique relationship with God:

> This is embarrassing but I did not have a good Pauline background before seminary and it is still shaky. I push myself to check out how

often I avoid Paul and make myself go there. Last week, I preached an entire revival from his letters and was blessed by it. But it was a struggle to be obedient to the call to turn to his letters for my material. There are two answers to this question for me. The first response speaks to our individual selves. We are unique, special, created and beloved by God, equipped for his work and the building of his kingdom. God loves us, and we are worthy of all that is accorded to his children. AND we are part of the body that must seek social and moral justice for the body. We cannot be limited to an individualistic, pietistic response (I got mine, you just keep on till you get yours).

One sistah fit into a number of categories. Her spiritual narrative exemplifies a passion for the entire life of the church. Black women proclaimers may have relatively few opportunities to sing their song, but during the rest period, they remain in tune.

I find that I often use themes of justice, mercy, God's love, and grace in my sermons. When I listen to parents, children, and individuals in the church and the community and see what is happening politically, socially, and economically, these issues have a continuous refrain in my sermons. I am sure that also growing up in the 60s and being around members of my extended family who were in the Black Panther Party and listening in on meetings have had an effect on the themes I use often. I was preaching about women because the only themes my brother heard me preach were on Women's Day or Missionary Sunday. Another reason is, I thought the congregation, women in particular, needed to hear the stories of women in the Bible, which were often left out of typical Sunday sermons. If women were mentioned, they were Jezebels and [were given] other negative images. . . . I can't stand the "Virtuous Woman" text of Proverbs 31. I don't think that there are themes that I avoid. I find that I don't often use topics on sin, the devil, stewardship, and sanctification, although they may broadly be in my sermon or different terminology [is] used. My passion is justice, fairness, mercy, and God's abiding love. SALVA-TION . . . I know in my heart that people need to hear more [about salvation] than [about] anything else: God loves us. God forgives us. We have first to forgive ourselves. We must love ourselves. We have to stop abusing our bodies and being in relationships that are destructive. We are unique, special. We don't have to be like anyone else. We have the opportunity or ability to be all that God has called for us to be. "It does not yet appear . . . what we shall be. We must not fear or let others tell us what we can/cannot do. . . . With God all things are possible." Trust and [do] not fear. As [we are] Christians and children of God, God requires more from us. We must be involved. We must be responsible Christians and stewards to self, community, nation, and world. We cannot sit back and let the school system miseducate our children. We cannot let our government roll back the law and violate the civil rights of our nation and community and other privileges and rights we should hold dear. We must not sanction police brutality or the death penalty. [We must] be more attentive to our children, not just materially, but [also] emotionally and spiritually. Be parents and not best friends. Young teenage girls are sexually more active and damn the consequences. I have a few youth that I know are dating men eighteen and above. One . . . has lost her virginity by a man from England whom she met on the Internet, and the man came to the U.S., met her in a hotel, and took several rolls of film. We must not be too quick to sing "God Bless America." (I'm not sure if this is what I think the people want to hear or what I think God is telling me the people ought to hear.) We must love and respect one another. We must be in the ark of safety. God and Christ gave up so much for us that we might have life and have it more abundantly. His death, and the manner in which he was killed, was the ultimate sacrifice—the depth of God's love for us. We should not abuse it. Kingdom of God is at hand. Here on earth. Don't have to wait to get to heaven.

African Americans in general, and black women in particular, face a myriad of difficulties based an age-old stereotypes, institutional injustices, racial segregation, social stigma based on skin tone, assumptions about intelligence, private and public addictions, and the struggle to survive or live above the stuff of the world. African Americans have a rich legacy of God's presence in all they do and are and will become. It is the knowledge of the faith history that continues to inspire the black preacher to "Say a Word" about the pregnant possibilities of God's presence, even in human suffering. Black preachers articulated hope as the sacred oil that heals brokenness. Black preachers speak of hope in the affirmative. In black preaching, the question of the existence of a "balm in Gilead" is answered, "Yes, there is a balm." Hope springing from the lips of black preachers is the alleviation of impending spiritual death. In the context of black preaching, hope becomes the sustaining force, excruciating cry, the fertile expectation, or the blessed assurance that God is moving in the midst of the people.[7]

The black preacher midwifes deep faith, entrepreneurial talents, personhood, family values, a sense of being and belongingness, creativity, intelligence, stick-to-it-tiveness, and hope for the black church. Black preaching, at its best, preaches hope with the intention of liberation, connectedness, imagination, and as a corrective for those things, those people, those places, and those things that are not of God. Black preaching is open-ended. It is the not yet, but soon, of black faith.

In articulating themes or topics, development of a sermon topic is a common practice in black preaching. Some people compose titles before they pray. Other preachers compose titles before preparation. Still other heralds move through a series of thoughts during composition as a title evolves. Yet, other pulpiteers think of a title after the sermon is noted, outlined, or written. There is even a group of proclaimers who do not receive a topic until the preaching moment. Those working through a sermon series may have a theme for the entire series and subtitles. Some denominations do not use titles. Just as special days produce definite topics, they also yield unique sermon topics. Titles function as recurring thoughts that support the sermonic purpose. If not carefully used, however, the title can distract from the sermon purpose, especially if there is no connection between the text, content, and title. The following is a selected list of videotaped and audiotaped sermon topics submitted for review.

Preacher	Sermon Title	Text
1. Rev. Ida Kenner Presiding Elder, AME	Lord, Please Show Me Your Glory AMEC Planning Meeting	Exodus 33:18-22
2. Rev. Suzan Johnson Cook Baptist	All or Nothing at All, Great Preachers' Series (commercial tape)	Proverbs 3:5-6
3. Rev. Dr. Millicent Thompson Hunter, Baptist	You've Got to Be Crazy (commercial tape)	1 Samuel 1:12-19
4. Rev. Lisa Rhodes Baptist, assistant pastor	A Test of Faith Sunday Morning Service	Matthew 12:22-30
5. Rev. Dr. Claudette Copeland Nondenominational	Seek My Face Woman Thou Art Loose Conference	Psalm 27:1, 7-9
6. Rev. Michelle Loyd-Paige Nondenominational	An Inside Job	Isaiah 60:1

7. Rev. Tracy Leggins Brown AME	Staying on the Right Path	Psalm 25:1-5
8. Rev. Bernadette Glover-Williams, American Baptist	It's Time to Believe, Wednesday Night Post Resurrection	Luke 24:1-11
9. Richelle Fry Skinner, AME	God's Construction Crew Youth Day	Nehemiah 4:1-6
10. Rev. Dr. Anne Lightner-Fuller AME	Making It Through Your Night Season United We Stand [9/11 service] 9-16-02	Psalm 77:10-12
11. Rev. Detra Bishop, Baptist	Follow Me	Luke 5:1-11
12. Rev. Dr. Cynthia Hale, DOC	How Much Is Enough?	Philippians 4:10-19
13. Rev. Stephanie Crowder, DOC	The Burden of a Bent Back Women's Day	Luke 13:10-17
14. Rev. Sheri Smith Clayborn AME	Answering the Call Trial sermon	Psalm 118:17
15. Minister Debra Matthews Presbyterian	Mission Unstoppable Initial Sermon	Matthew 28:6
16. Pastor Diana Branch Nondenominational	Hungry Hearts with a Passion for His Presence Women's Revival	Luke 7:36-50
17. Pastor Toni Alvarado Nondenominational	The Power of Prayer and Praise	Acts 16:11-27
18. Rev. LaTrelle Miller-Easterling, AME	Keep Your Mission: You Are Saved with a Purpose in Mind, Women's Day	Judges 4:1-8
19. Rev. T. Renée Crutcher Baptist	Thank God for the Midwives	Exodus 1:15-22
20. Dr. Thelma Chambers-Young, President, Progressive Baptist Women's Department	Proceed and Possess the Land Church Anniversary	Deuteronomy 2:24
21. Rev. Valentine Royal Director, American Baptist, WIM	Choosing the Best Part AME/ Women In Ministry (WIM) Conference	Luke 10:38-42
22. Rev. Sandra Blair, President, AME, AME/WIM	Cracked Cisterns and Watertight Wells AMEC Minsters' Spouses Conference	Jeremiah 2:13
23. Dr. Dorothy Adams Peck, President, AME Women's Missionary Society	GO! GO! GO! Missionary Sunday	Matthew 28:16-20

24. Rev. Telley Gadson UMC	Who Do You Think You Are? Youth Sunday	1 Peter 2:9-10
25. Rev. Joanne Robertson Baptist	Heaven's Human Resource Department	John 21:1-19
26. Rev. Darlene Marshall Smith AME	What Does the Lord Require of You? Sunday School Revival	Micah 6:6-10
27. Rev. Kimberley Detherage AME	It's Midnight Law Day	Acts 16:16-17, 25
28. Minister Carolyn DuBose Baptist	That God Is at Work	Philippians 1:3-7
29. Rev. Marie Davis AME	The Cross, the Cost, and the Crown Class Leaders' Day	Luke 9:23; 14:27
30. Rev. Zelia Brown-Harvey AME	Rules of Engagement	Ephesians 6:12
31. Rev. Eunice Shaw, Baptist	Community: Keeping It Real	Acts 2:43-44
32. Minister Carolyn DuBose Baptist	Getting Up and Moving On in the Face of Adversity	Acts 14:19-22
33. Rev. Bridget Piggue Presbyterian	What Is Your Excuse?	Exodus 3:1-11
34. Rev. Bridgette Young, UMC	Don't Make Me Come Down There!	Psalm 137:1-4
35. Rev. Melinda Contreras-Byrd AME International Black Women's Congress	It Don't Hold Water	Jeremiah 2:1-13
36. Stephanie Thompson AME	Lighten Up!	Ephesians 5:8-14
37. Rev. Addie June Hall UMC	Phenomenal Women Using Their Talents for God, Women's Conference	1 Samuel 1:21-28; Esther 4:13-15
38. Rev. Raquel St. Clair AME	Things That Money Can't Buy	Isaiah 55:1-5
39. Rev. Jan Prentace UMC	Ordinary People, Extraordinary God Campus Chapel Service	Matthew 1:1-17
40. Rev. Veronice Miles Baptist	God Is Doing a New Thing Sister to Sister Weekend	Numbers 26:1-2; 27:1-10

Titles may be taken from the scriptural text, popular movies, television programs, all forms of music, art, difficulty, social events, athletics, community sayings, poetry, novels, magazines, billboards, universal experiences, life notes, and advertisements. There is a wealth of homiletical resources available. The memorable titles stem from the connection of the text, listener, Spirit, and the preacher's creativity.

Sermon Form or Type

The form or type of sermon varies by proclaimer also. In analysis of the forty tapes listed above, the narrative style (biblical or extrabiblical story) predominated. Twenty-one were expository, narrative (detailed explanation of facts in text, exegetical, point by point) sermons. Seventeen were topical and thematic (highlighting the importance of theme with logical points and facets) sermons with varying degrees of exposition. Three employed a rhetorical (application of reason through questions) pattern. Thirty-two outlined the content in an introduction, three to nine points, and a conclusion.[8]

Melinda Contreras-Byrd preached a topical sermon called "It Don't Hold Water" from the text Jeremiah 2:1-13. She was preaching at the International Black Women's Congress and began with a six-point introduction.

1. There is power, presence, and individuality of Spirit in your life.
2. We are a mighty people with a holy inheritance.
3. The race is not always swift but to that person who endures to the end, as the scripture says; so if you are involved in a struggle, you have to hold on.
4. Know no matter how dire or negative, the race is not in vain; even a struggle that seems negative in the end will be positive.
5. We come from a long tradition of faith.
6. The challenge is to be a sister to someone, not believe the hype, believe what someone says. To be a sister, one must believe what another sister has said, given the fact that many times a sister's statement is deferred just because she is a woman.

She spent almost four minutes on the explanation of call-and-response definitions and spoke of the specificity of the sermon. "I see no use in preaching a sermon for just anybody. A sermon should be relevant to the context." The sermon content was a combination of elements of sister-hood, Afrocentricism, and self-improvement. She challenged the women to avoid a life that "revolves around a man." "If you don't have a man, have a sister." The behavioral purpose was how not to become compla-cent with historical and contemporary achievements because all of "our stuff don't hold water" in relation to what God does and is in our lives. The sermon title was laced throughout the sermon. She celebrated throughout the sermon, usually following one of eight points in the body of the sermon. Each point was developed and referred back to the title and text.

1. We no longer remember our songs of freedom.
2. We have left the streams of liberation charted by our fore-fathers for artificial reservoirs that are cracked and can't hold water.
3. We have given up the old-fashioned way, the way of common sense and reason, and sought the council of the ungodly.
4. We do not appreciate our cultural artifacts.
5. There is no urgency to pray.
6. We are a people with an attitude problem.
7. We have abandoned who we are and who God is.
8. We are not thirsty now. We have chosen to go to an artificial source that can't hold water.

The language for God and people was inclusive throughout the presenta-tion. This psychologist carefully articulated words. Her voice was affirm-ing and urgent. She knew her listeners and engaged them in a culturally specific manner.

Veronice Miles preached a narrative, expository sermon in "God Is Doing a New Thing" (Numbers 26:1-2 and 27:1-10). She preached at her home church for a "Sister to Sister" Weekend. Preaching with persons who knew you before the call to preach and who have watched growth and development is a daunting task. There is a subconscious desire to be better than the last time they heard you and still please God. Reverend Miles acknowledged the support she had received from the listeners. She immediately went to the background of the text about the Daughters of Zelophehad, giving their names and the cultural context of the times. She mentions the absence of the other women in the story. She spoke of the cultural parallels in the contemporary context: "No promise in the land." "We are these daughters." "Hoping they will show us how to move on. We have been told no for too long." She describes the sisters going before Moses to petition for their inheritance.

> I can see them making their way to the front of the congregation. Walking past the women's section. Proceeding to the front. Men wondering if they are bringing something in the court for food. (Yeah, yeah, laughter) Women who walk with great confidence and delibera- tion. Confidence growing with each step. Hearts beginning to leap inside of them. As they whispered, "Girl, you can do it," to themselves and possibly to each other. "Just keep walking, everything is gonna be all right."

She celebrates throughout the sermon. Her voice is used for transition between points. There is a refrain of "Sister you can lean on me! We are reaching forth," punctuated with "Um" and "Hallelujah!" as the sermon resolves into an invitation of discipleship.

Thirty-eight ministers used a format similar to James Harris's adapta- tion of the Hegelian thesis-antithesis-synthesis model.[9] Harris posits a "dialectical topicality" paradigm—ideal (this is what is), real (this is what's wrong), and the blend (this is what will be done). The women using this form stated their purpose, asked the relevant questions of the text, critiqued the church or society, and sought to present not solid answers, but a thought, goal, action, or something on which the people could focus. Two of the sermons were a string of stories or biblical texts connected to the title with minimal exegesis.

Illustrations, Imagery, and Content

Illustrations are like titles. An illustration is supposed to throw light, illuminate, reinforce, or explain. Illustrations are supportive material that fleshes out content. Stories, images, songs, sounds, body movements, poetry, jokes, headlines, testimonies, or whatever is placed within the proclamation used should elucidate rather than obscure the intent of the biblical text.[10] The well-prepared preacher knows the most important illustration is the biblical text. This means not randomly reciting texts *ad nauseam*, but making exegetically sound choices in supportive material. The following excerpts reveal the variety of illustrations, images, and content used by black women.

Preaching at a Seven Last Words service, Bridget Piggue presents a twelve-minute textual/topical sermon on Jesus' cry from the cross (Mark 15:34).

> A cry of dereliction, a cry of destitution, and a cry of desperation. A cry filled with the deepest pain imaginable. Pain that comes when one is trying to make some sense of feeling abandoned, alone, and forsaken. Jesus is no stranger to feeling forsaken. Peter denied him three times, and Judas, in communion with a kiss and thirty pieces of silver, abdicated Jesus to his enemies. Yes, feeling forsaken was not new to Jesus. But the depth of this cry, an emotional state, as he hung there on the cross, was different this time. It was reminiscent of the anguish he felt in the Garden, when he had picked three disciples to go with him [and] pray with him just for an hour.

Her delivery is slow, not distractingly slow, but deliberate. Every syllable is clear. She uses her voice to paint the picture through emphasis and inflection.

Stephanie Thompson's sermon, "Lighten Up!" from Ephesians 5:8-14, describes the myriad forms of lightbulbs and their function. "A person separated from Christ cannot shine." The purpose of life is illustrative of the mandate for Christians to live as "children of light." Using a manuscript, a decidedly masculine image of God, and knowledge of the congregation, she uses humor, varied pacing, and inflection to transition through the sermon. She employs, "Turn to your neighbor and say, 'Neighbor, you need to lighten up.'" This verbal exchange instituted a pattern of her saying, "If this is you then, . . . " (call), followed spontaneously by the congregation saying, "You need to lighten up" (response).

She developed six points, including "aspects" of light as the way something looks to the eye or mind and the "flame" of light equated to knowledge of God. She ends with an invitation, "But you have to be willing to let God be your Savior. He is waiting. Follow his light."

In her initial sermon, Debra Matthews describes the 1970s television program "Mission Impossible" as the controlling image for Christian living in "Mission Unstoppable" (Matthew 28:6.) She illustrates the opening scene of each program concerning a mysterious message given to "Mr. Phelps," supposedly giving him an option to accept a dangerous mission or turn it down. He is cautioned that should he accept the mission, he and his team (she describes each team member and his or her strengths in depth) will be on their own. She equates the IMF work on the show to the text. She, too, uses humor, familiarity with the congregation, movement back and forth across the pulpit, hand gestures, clapping, and powerful pregnant pauses. She testifies about her call to ministry and emphatically says. "Can't stop me. Lord told me I have a mission."

Raquel St. Clair preaches "Things That Money Can't Buy" (Isaiah 55:1-4), beginning with a prayer. She speaks with high energy, a rapid but emphatic rate, and pausing and punctuates by hard consonants. In an Advent oration, she supplies a critique of consumerism. The mantra "Money can buy . . . , but . . . " was the centerpiece of sermon purpose elaboration.

> Money can buy some books, but not an education.
> Money can buy a bed, but not sleep.
> Money can buy a Bible, but not good religion.
> Money can buy a computer, but not common sense.
> Money can buy clothes, but not character.
> Money can buy cosmetics, but not self-confidence.
> Money can buy a following, but not friends.
> Money can buy food, but not an appetite.
> Money can buy lingerie, but not love.
> Money can buy medicine, but not health.
> Money can buy Prozac, but not peace.
> Money can buy sex, but not a soul mate.

She ends the run by looping back to the text: "If we are not careful, we will be like the people in the scripture text." She ends the sermon with a call for acceptance of the "one-stop shopping" available with God, reiterates the text, and issues an invitation.

Sandra Blair preaches the sermon "Cracked Cisterns and Watertight Wells," taken from Jeremiah 2:13, referencing a manuscript, a steady rate, effective pauses, hand gestures, slight rocking from side to side, wrinkling of her forehead for harder points, and a calming smile for reassurance. She removed her glasses after reading the text and remained at the podium microphone throughout the thirty-five-minute discourse. She began her delivery with recognizing ecclesial protocol, prayer, and centering. Exegesis was evident with extensive background on Jeremiah and the social climate of the text. She wove contemporary examples with ancient wells, drought, and cisterns. She depicted "Cracked Cistern Syndrome" and "churchaholics." In this expository, thematic sermon, she spoke of the "imperceptible cracks and gaping holes in our lives." She ended the sermon with the story of a cracked watering jug.

One must choose battles wisely, or the information related in the sermon will be overwhelming to the listener. An apology for preaching about a particular subject diminishes the authenticity and power of the message. Preachers who say one thing and then do another are an anathema. Cognitive dissonance is when a preacher evokes equality while using derogatory or oppressive language and imagery. The status of a black preacher in a black congregation at times prevents the listener from disagreeing with the premise of the sermon. If the preacher said it, it is right. The awesome responsibility of preaching means that it is the duty of the preacher to filter and re-filter the sermon.

For the black preacher, there is a confidence that the biblical text holds the key to how we are to live. It is not God's intention for persons to suffer continually. Sin is said to be the root cause for humanity's barriers, oppression of others, and lack of love for one another. Preachers proclaim the possibility of change. They assist the listener in identification, examination, and resolution of alienation, conflict, and oppression located within the biblical text and society. Preaching in an African American context is predicated on the cultural imperative that it is not a crime to be black, no one has the right to oppress another person, and God is a God of justice and equality. God is a God of love. Everyone has equal value and dignity. The present situation does not define one's total existence. This means that in spite of the encounter with societal ills such as racism, sexism, ageism, classism, materialism, or even academic elitism, there will ultimately be an equitable resolution, a healing, a change, a sense of empowerment for the better. Hope for transformation or change permeates the healing, saving, preaching, and teaching Christ of the New Testament. Hope is alive in the preaching that raises critical questions about the lives and lifestyles of all persons. When one proclaims transformation and newness in Christ, one is resting but remaining in tune. The succeeding chapters will analyze the communicative proficiency of black women and the distinctiveness of their presence in ministry.

"Hold On to Your Hope"

The following sermon was originally preached in a chapel service for the 2001 "Year of Reconciliation" at the Candler School of Theology at

Emory University in Atlanta. It was then modified to fit the idea of hope in an African American congregation

Old Testament Reading: Ezekiel 37:13-14

> 13 "And you shall know that I am the LORD, when I open your graves, and bring you up from your graves, O my people.
> 14 I will put my spirit within you, and you shall live, and I will place you on your own soil; then you shall know that I, the LORD, have spoken and will act," says the LORD.

Dire predictions of the end of life as we know it fill the media, crowd around coffee machines, echo down academic corridors, float through church parking lots, and reverberate in the halls of political power with regularity.
Faith quakes abound
    Too many dreams are deferred by drama.
    Too many ministry moments are missed by madness
    Too many Hallelujahs are halted by hatred
    Too many beliefs are battered by bluntness
    Too many realities are wrecked by wrath
    Too many excuses are echoed by enmity
Where is the hope the faithful speak of on Sunday morning?
    Does faith take a vacation on Monday?
    Is God active in our lives only when everything seems to be going our way?
Walk back with me for a short time through the sacred text to the book of Ezekiel
A parable of how the church, the ecclesia, the called-out can experience restoration of relationship with God and the resuscitation of hope in the midst of despair.
As you know, in chapters 36 and 37, we are told of God's restoration promise to God's people. Through the prophet Ezekiel, we observe a vision of unity after the receipt of the blessing of the Holy Spirit
    Ezekiel [God strengthens] was a visionary, prophet, and watchman.
    He was given a mission by God to minister to a rebellious, faithless, spiritless, and defeated people.
    He had been proclaiming the word of God for twenty-two years
Still the people refused to listen

Temples were torn down
This preacher lived during the exile, Diaspora, scattering of Israel and
Judah.
    People scattered, killed, and imprisoned
On the tenth anniversary of their deportation, a once-proud, mighty
    people stood separated from their land, their temple, their families,
    and they had separated themselves from God.
    They had not listened to the instruction about obedience.
    They tried to run their own show.
    They became stiff-necked, stagnant, stupefied, shameless people
    Perhaps they thought they could get by treating people anyway they
        wanted
    Perhaps they thought God was not paying attention to their actions
    Perhaps they began to think they were God.
God was not pleased and began to teach the Israelites about suffering,
    hope, and restoration.
        Forty-six hundred enslaved persons were forced to walk nine hun-
            dred miles to the Tel-a-Bib in the valley of the Tigris-Euphrates
            (once the cradle of civilization)
        [Pishon, Gihon, Tigris and Euphrates Rivers flowed].
    They had lost their hope. [Hebrew *towcheleth*—expectation]
        Hope: expectation of attainment, trust, anticipation, belief, faith
    They became dry, parched, and lifeless.
        No vision, no wisdom, no ingenuity, imprisoned in societal graves
            of despair.
    They slipped into a form of spiritual and physical death right there
        in the valley
    No hope, no anticipation, no aspirations, no belief, no desire, no
        endurance, no goal, no expectation of any change.
Walking back through the text, you know the story
    In a vision, God takes Ezekiel to the valley and instructs him to walk
around, observing the decimation of the people, now dead, dry, dull, lifeless, fragments of the promise of yesterday
    These leftovers appear to be beyond repair
God asked, "Can these bones live?"
    Is it possible to restore life when broken dreams,
        Broken relationships
        Broken promises
        Broken aspirations

Broken ministries
Broken spirits
Broken people have been pronounced dead?
Could God restore Hope?
Hope had died with a little help from her friends
In my sanctified imagination, I can see Hope's obituary in the *Jerusalem News* or *USA Today* or *New York Times*
Hope's Obituary
Here lies Hope
Hope had been so popular, now Hope felt abandoned, overlooked, discarded
People came from everywhere just to see Hope
Someone was always looking for Hope, now they looked for something else
One could feel a change in the room whenever Hope entered
Darkness gave way to light when Hope returned
Faces lit up when Hope made contact
Hope was on life support for a while, but then just seemed to give up
Hope made a slow transition from life to death
Hope was once a song in a weary throat
Hope was the evidence not seen but believed
Hope was the validation that every mountain would be made low and every valley would be raised up
Hope was the shelter in the time of storm
Hope was the unmerited favor of God
Hope was the steadfast love *(hesed)*
Nicknamed joy, peace, and faith, depending on the need of the friend
Once synonymous with vibrancy, life, action
Hope was filled with such promise, but her life was cut short
Symptoms of Hope's Demise
How could so much promise be replaced, lost, stolen, strayed?
Why didn't someone see it coming?
Intelligence, personhood, belief systems, family structure, sexuality questioned
Two steps forward, thirteen backward
Watched enemy prosper
Brick ceiling replaced the stained glass ceilings
Congregational rebellion—sedentary erosion of faith

Immobilization of press toward mark by separation from family
Lack of support for ministry
Overworked, underpaid
Ecclesiastical apartheid
No time to work out her own grief in disappointment, distrust
Financial difficulty
Name-calling
Jokes to keep her in her place
Construction of barriers of race, age, gender, class, ability were used
    to strangle her articulation of possibility
Some say that Hope was healthy until she began to accept the standards
  of others who sought only her demise
    No matter how hard she tried to fit in
Those whom Hope thought were her friends could not be found
    Even some of Hope's family members started to disown her
Hope tried to play the games, but the pressure slowly ate away at her
  heart, soul, and mind
    Hope even forgot the mantra that God has given us a Spirit not of
      fear, but of love, power, and self-control
In latter days, Hope's shoulders seemed to slump under the weight of
  responsibility
    The smile that usually greeted the people at the down had become
      a sour frown
    The energetic body movement had become perfunctory gestures
    The sharp mind had been numbed by disappointment and doubt
      Just going along to get along, faking the funk
    Playing political games, being pawns of so-called power brokers
    No prayer, no praise, no song, no sermon for fear of criticism of her
      joy.
Hope was sitting in the midst of brokenness
    She needed to be restored to her former relationship with her power
      source
Some of the responsibility for her slow painful death was the answer to
  life and was in front of her, but she refused to, or could not, see it
    Like Israel, down in the valley with Ezekiel
Hope was part of the chosen ones of God, yet could not see God in the
  midst of the storm
Hope forgot the essence of her being
    She began to look at the problem and not to the solution

Have you ever met Hope?

    Perhaps you visited with Hope?

    Maybe she was in one of your classes?

    Maybe she reminds you of someone?

    Perhaps you forgot Hope's address.

Hope found it overwhelming to try to exist in a seething caldron of death, dissension, distrust, and depression

    No light, no tunnel, no dreams, no vision

    Unable to find the joy she once knew when she first found the Lord

    Hope seemed to be gone

God begs the question of Ezekiel

"Can these bones live?"

    Do you believe, Ezekiel, that life can come from death?

God asks each of us the same question today

    Do you believe that hope can be resurrected in these fragments of faith?

Ezekiel answered, "Lord, you know."

    How do you answer?

God said preach to the bones and they will live.

These leftovers appear to be beyond repair

    Ezekiel responded, "Bones, hear the Word of the Lord."

You biblical scholars know the rest

    The bones began to change form

    They became reconciled with parts that had long been separated

    And all the fragments in the valley began to take shape

    Bones became skeletons that became carcasses that became bodies, with all the parts in divine order, covered with flesh, skin, and hair.

What was dead was reconciled, restored by the power of God doing a miraculous work in the valley of seeming death

    The potter put it back together again

God reconciled what was, by appearances, lost, dead, without a future.

    Reconciliation (Greek *Katallage*) is a change in relationship, restoration

    Reconciliation presupposes that something was together or whole at one point

    The relationship was breached, and it seeks to be brought back into right relationship

Identify that something or someone is out of order

Stages of Reconciliation
>Forgiveness—requested and granted
>Repentance has taken place—new ways of doing and thinking
>A period of pruning and correction has been scheduled
>Rebuilding relationship, and restoring faith, hope, and love
>Healing is beginning
>Hope for actualization of God's promise is restored

Reconciliation is not a committee process—it is work
>It must be maintained
>It must be nurtured with all the energy of the reconnection

God reconciled the bones, the fragments, and the remnants.
>But that is not the end of the matter

After God put them back together
>God energized them for service.

Once a body is reconciled, it is not time to set and congratulate each other on how well we look; it is time to be about God's business
>Each was then imbued with the breath of life by the indwelling of the Holy Spirit
>Life returned
>>Hope began to grow again.

Ezekiel's vision was a message of hope for the nation of Israel that even after they ignored God's directives
>After they were pronounced dead by their enemies
>After all hope seemed gone
>>God's promise to restore them would take place.
>Beloved of God
>The truth is that nothing is too hard for God
>>It is not over until God says it is over

Hopelessness became hope in Ezekiel's vision
>Death became life
>God's promise was affirmed
>Reconciliation was actualized

God understands that sometimes the mountains seem too high and the valleys seem too low
>Some of us shout on Sunday, but face Monday burdened with cares
>Sometimes, no matter how hard we try, all hell regularly breaks lose in our lives

God wants us to know today there is a plan to preempt the death of hope
Verses 11 to 14: the crux of the matter

Look at God's promise in the valley
    By the power of the Holy Spirit
    Not by power, nor by might, but by God's Spirit
Spirit, which condemns us
    Convinces us
    Convicts us
    Converts us
    Counsels us
    Covers us
    Commissions us
By my Spirit
    I will open up your graves
    Put the obituary aside
    Cancel the funeral arrangements
I will send my Spirit to unearth those things that are of no value in your
    lives
    Don't you know God made the dirt they try to throw on you?
    God can command that dirt and dust to move
I will uncover stuff you've been hiding, and you will breathe in fresh hope
    I will open up your graves
        I will move those persons, places, things that seem to keep trying to
        steal your joy.
I have to leave some enemies around you so they can see my victory in
    you, but I will open up those graves that you keep digging to defeat my
    program
I have no place for "Mr. I'm in charge." I can use people like disposable
    tissues
    Mrs. Judge, jury, prosecutor, and executioner
God tells us in the Word that we need to maintain our character and
    believe in God, not the committee report
    We are to seek the face of God even when others tell us that God is
        dead, that hope is gone
God says when we trust God more than we trust humanity
    God will restore us to the hope of our salvation
    God will reconnect us to the correct source of our being
    God will unearth the gifts that have been placed within us
God says, remember this is my world
    I created it
    I run it

I decide when it will end
I dispense my favor on my sons and daughters
I bless and curse
I am in control
I open doors that no one can shut and shut doors that no one can
    open
Didn't I tell you that no weapon formed against you would prosper?
    Didn't I say that no water would drown you?
    No fire would burn you
I would make your enemies your footstool
    I called you
    I anointed you
    I appointed you
    I set you before the nations
    I will put my word in your mouth
You don't have to answer to anyone but me
    I am with you always even until the end

The prophet continues
I will open up your
    Crypts of "I can't"
    Shrines of "I'm not smart enough"
    Mausoleums of "It's not my fault"
    Sepulchers of "They won't believe me"
    Resting places of "I'm too old, too short, too poor, too dumb"
    Tombs of "But I'm a woman. But I'm black"
    Coffins of shoulda, coulda, woulda
    Caskets of "My family doesn't want me to be a minister"
    Sarcophagi of "The congregation won't support me"
    Graves of "The professor doesn't like me"

I am that Hope that springs eternal
    When the church, home, seminary, clique
This is the blessed hope
    Take your head out of the
Look to Jesus the author and finisher of life
    Paul from prison reaffirms the need to hold onto hope even when it
        looks like the end is near
        It is never over until God says it's over

He says when you are facing any disappointment
> Hope appears gone

Think (use your own minds, stop checking your brains at the door, rest in your faith in God)
> Your attitude should be that of Christ Jesus
> Hold on to God's standards
> Think about God's goodness

Believe whatever is
> True (*alethe*)—not lies, rumors or embellishments, deceit, but what is loyal, faithful, proper, reliable, and genuine
> Noble (*semnos*), worthy of respect, dignified, exalted, excellent
> Right (*dikaios*) by God's standards
> Pure (*hagnos*), free from contamination, morally correct
> Lovely (*prosphiles*), pleasing to God
> Commendable (*euphemos*), admirable, positive, constructive
> Virtuous

Lift up your drooping hands and strengthen your weak knees
> Make a straight path for your feet, so what is lame may not be put out of joint, but rather healed

Get up, do something
> Pray
> Sing
> Moan if you have to
> Don't sit around on your hands.
>> No more dragging your feet

Empty your venom bags
> Trash you messianic complexes
> Vacuum out the inability to say no
> Discard self-destructive behaviors
> Check snobbish spirituality
> Obliterate snobbish superiority

God has the last word.
> Only by the grace of God is hope kept alive and well

When we reconnect to our understanding that God will do exceedingly abundantly above anything we ask, God will save us even from ourselves
God will not leave us without a comforter even when it seems that we are "way down yonder by ourselves and can't hear nobody pray."
> Just like in the valley that day, Jesus is saying get up from your graves
> Shake the dirt of this world off your minds

> Look to the hills for your help
>> All is not lost
> Turn off the old tapes
>> Stop giving the devil a place in our lives
> I know you are tired, but you still live
> For those of us who seek our own destruction
>> Cover ourselves up
>> Relinquish our hope willingly
>> Seek comfort in complaining
> God says
>> I will open up those
>>> Dark
>>> Dank
>>> Dim
>>> Dirty
>>> Disgusting
>>> Depressed
>>> Demented
>>> Disturbing
>>> Debilitating
>>> Disrespected
>>> Distressed
>>> Destructive
>>> Dying
>> Places in your life
> I will place you on your own soil
> Stop begging for a place at the table
>> In the pulpit
>> In the group
>> In the school
>> In the church
>> In the neighborhood
> Don't sell your inheritance for a cup of instant gratification.
>> I have joy that no one can match
> All you have to do is hold on, hold up, hold out
>> Joy will come after a while
> You are sons and daughters of the Most High God, so act like it
> I will give you your own little spot to stand
>> No need for competition

No need to compare
No need for jealousy
No need to try to run over anyone
No need to constantly critique someone else's life when yours needs
    work
Hope is alive
    We just need to look under all the dirt around it and recover it
Our God lives and moves and has being
    Stop those fleeting, frivolous, fashionable flights of fancy.
Live in unity
    Prayerful dependence on God
God's promise to Ezekiel is also God's promise to all of us who have wan-
dered in deep places, looking for hope, only to be told that hope is
deferred
    Hope is not for us,
    Hope is a dream
    Hope is dead
This day
God says Hope is not dead,
    You read the wrong report
    Stop preempting hope with hype
Hope is not on CNN, C-SPAN, HBO, CINEMAX, ABC, CBS, PBS,
ESPN
    Hope is not coming to a theatre near you
    Hope is not an appointment, power or position
    Hope is not a spouse or a child
    Hope is not a credit card or bank balance
All this will pass away
    God has swallowed up the death of hope in victory with the sacri-
        fice and resurrection of Christ on the cross of salvation
God has promised by amazing grace that if we just stand on the promises
of God, we, too, will actualize our hope of eternal life
    If we hold onto our hope
        We'll receive more blessing than we know what to do with
            Blessed in the city
            Blessed in the field
            Blessed when we go out
            Blessed when we come in
    Enemies will be scattered

Come at us one way, God will make them leave seven other
ways
Lend and never borrow
God will make us the head and not the tail
Blessed
Hold on to your hope
How do you know preacher?
Psalmist writes,
My hope is built on nothing less
Than Jesus' blood and righteousness
I dare not trust the sweetest frame
But wholly lean on Jesus' name
On Christ the solid rock I stand
All other ground is sinking sand
All other ground is sinking sand
Hold on to your hope.

CHAPTER FIVE

SINGING THE SONG IN A STRANGE LAND

On the willows there we hung up our harps. For there our captors asked us for songs, and our tormentors asked for mirth, saying, "Sing us one of the songs of Zion!" How could we sing the LORD's song in a foreign land? (Psalm 137:2-4)

This Psalm is one of the passages used in black churches to denote the quest for freedom. It is one of remembrance. It is about remembering whom God is and how God protects us regardless of what transpires on the surface. There are women proclaimers who have never faced repression. There are some who are still bound and will not enjoy freedom of speech in their lifetimes. Still others have endured, and God has set them free to sing their song in strange lands and in relative free spaces. How do black women sing the Lord's song wherever they are?

As women press their way in ministry it is imperative that they take their harps off the tree. They're not abandoned. In the face of those who do not want to hear women as they answer the call of God, God provides new songs. In spite of ecclesiastical oppression or some denial of our own gifts, women praise and proclaim God in the distinctive sound of women's voices—mezzo soprano to bass. Some have loud, deafening voices. Others have soft, soothing voices. Some have irritating sandpaper-sounding voices. Others have voices that sound as smooth as warm chocolate.

Regardless of the sound, women are singing the Lord's song. They have learned the process of preaching the same way men have—"sitting at the feet" of other preachers. Some take on patterns of their role models. Some emulate the senior pastor. Some imitate the up-and-coming "powerhouse evangelist." Some have to watch every televangelist they can Monday through Sunday so they can "sound" like them, "really deliver the word" like them, and gain opportunities to preach. After all, one has to do what is popular so lives can be changed. The difficulty is that some never find their own voice. Some develop a comfortable self-identity and sound feminine yet powerful. There's a new group that move in and out of a principally "masculine" or "feminine" voice depending on the occasion. Some even believe that the louder you are, the more powerful you are as a preacher.

When I worked as a speech pathologist I taught the anatomy, physiology, neurology, and endocrinology of the parts of the body associated with speech production. I learned that the vocal structures of men and women are generally different sizes with the same function. The muscles known as vocal folds are approximately the size of a dime. The folds of men are, however, somewhat thicker than women. This is not that archaic argument about the so-called Adam's apple. It is just a physiological fact. As a speech and language pathologist, I assessed voice production with children and adults in schools, hospitals, clinics, and in private settings for seventeen years. I listen intently to preachers and can usually pinpoint the source and quality of their vocal production. So much depends on the voice of the preacher. The emotion, tempo, articulation, texture, intensity, and even the meaning of the words sound *of* the preacher rather than sounding *like* a preacher.

There is a section in the sermon analysis form I developed for classes that looks at how the text is embodied. Areas of assessment are authenticity, language, facial expression, use of space, voice, nonverbal cues, listener engagement, presence, and emotion. This chapter addresses the orality (voice and diction) and aurality (sound and audibility) of the proclaimer. It will also assess call and response and celebration as heard on a variety of tapes submitted for review.

Historian Albert Raboteau describes the tradition of black preaching as a person addressing the day-to-day concerns of the congregation in a stylized chanted form.

The preacher first and foremost understands that the sermon is from God. Sacred speech is not a human possession or invention. It is God-breathed. It is not about the manuscript or the preacher. Credit goes to the inspiration of the Holy Spirit. Raboteau continues, the preacher should be familiar with the biblical text and know that one cannot talk about God unless one knows who God is from personal experience. Information contained in chanted or folk sermons is based on Bible stories, mother wit (common sense), and life experience. Humor, wordplay, emotional pitch, gestures, using the body, and the vocal energy are essential to the experience. The preacher's voice is calm initially, gradually increasing in volume and rate until there is a regular chanting exchange with the speaker and the congregation. Words are elongated and sounds are collapsed. The respected preaching time, Raboteau says, was 20 to 40 minutes. At an emotional peak, there may be tonal changes, and there may be gasping for air at the end of sentences. It may result in singing, clapping, or sounding and shouting of the congregation.[1] Recognition that the preaching moment does not go forth without God is evident in some of the prayers or statements that began the sistah preaching moments.

Sermon Introductions

In establishing protocol prior to the sermon, the preacher thanks God and then names the ecclesial leadership, the host pastor, officers of the church, and the membership. One may also extend greetings from his or her home church and senior pastor, if applicable. This shows that the preacher has manners. She understands that the invitation did not have to be extended. He is visiting in someone else's home and is expected to follow the rules of hospitality. It is a means of affording respect while building rapport. The length of the protocol depends on the denominational setting.

Zina Jacque intones a traditional introduction to the preaching moment. She moves through praise of God to a prayer for anointing to preach.

> God is a good God. God is an awesome God. Now I'm Baptist, so I have to do the Baptist thing. Giving honor to God who is the head of my life, and to my Pastor ____.

Greetings for the one who created us, the one who knew before the dawn of time we would be in this room. For the one who ordained your ministry and mine. The one who knows about the mess in your life that you tried to hide from the people in this room. And who chose you and is using you anyway. Cracked vessels that we are. Got a plan for our life. Hallelujah, Hallelujah, O God, Oh, is there a word from the Lord?

Speak, Lord, that we, your people, might hear from you. Hide your daughter behind the sacred redemptive power of your cross. None of me and all of you. And let the words of my mouth and meditation of my heart be acceptable in your sight for you, and you alone are our strength and our redeemer. And God's people together said, "Amen."

Prayers specifically recognize the special day and the preacher's need for endowment and empowerment of the Holy Spirit. Betty Hanna-Witherspoon passionately prays for guidance during a Good Friday service:

Our Father and our God, our mother and our father.
A father to the fatherless, a mother to the motherless.
We come now on this Good Friday, leaning and depending on you.
Holy Ghost, we ask you to come. Move Betty out of the way.
Take over the pulpit and speak to the hearts and minds of your people.
Holy Ghost, you're in charge now.
Get Betty out of the way.
In the name of Jesus we pray, Amen.

The acknowledgment of the attributes of God establishes the preacher's relationship with God and makes intercession for the people's reception and understanding of the sermon. Evoking numerous images of God, Zelia Brown-Harvey speaks for the congregation and herself:

Most Holy, Most Merciful, All-knowing, Almighty God. This morning we come before you, asking you to step through our inadequacies to ensure that your people hear a word. Lord God, we pray that the words of our mouths be acceptable in your sight. You are my Rock, my Strength, my Redeemer, and we further pray that something said here will touch hearts, souls, minds of the hearers that they may use this word in the days to come. It is in Jesus' name we pray, Amen.

The song before the sermon affects the entrance into the preaching moment. A song that is well received, up-tempo, and leads to ecstatic praise may be excellent for setting the tone for the sermon. It may also pitch the preacher so high or leave her so wound up that she is unable to begin the sermon. The song that is less than stellar, sluggish, or off-key, may result in a heavy, breathless service. In both situations, the preacher may have to "talk it down or talk it up" in order to reach the tune that fits the content of the sermon.

In the following excerpt, the Reverend Marie Davis uses the words of the song "I Just Want to Be Right" as a transition into her opening remarks:

> Just want to be right. Do you want to be right today? Just want to be right, want to be right when Jesus comes. Just want to be right. O Hallelujah, thank you, Jesus. You sing and you shout like you want to be right. The choir singing today like they're already right. O thank you, Jesus. For if it had not been for the Lord on our side, where would we be? Just want to be right. Thank you, Jesus, Hallelujah. Be all right, right now. The Holy Ghost is already here. We can just say the bene-diction and go home. 'Cause the Holy Ghost has already shown up. Showed out. Just want to be right. Hallelujah. Just want to be right. Oh, thank you, Jesus. To the great pastor of this church, Reverend Hall. I want to thank you for allowing me this opportunity. Thank you for allowing me to come this way. In the name of Jesus. For my sister, my partner, Reverend Smith. To my mother, my teacher, my mentor, Reverend Fry Brown. And he could be my son, you know, but to my brother in the ministry, Reverend Brown. To each of you that makes up this fine congregation and those of you who came from far and near. And all the class leaders today. It is a pleasure and an honor for me to stand before you this day to proclaim the word of God. We thank God for Jesus. And here we say all the time, "We won't worry you long," but we don't know (I'm not gonna say it). But the Holy Ghost we don't know. Whatever the Lord says we're gonna do today.

African American preaching is experiential. Black preaching is based in establishing black identity as God's people by the assurance of grace or good news. Through concrete, logical, ethical, emotive, and reflective thought, the black preacher illuminates the possibility of reconciliation, restoration, and healing.[2] Preachers are also in need of assurance. What if the preacher is having a Zechariah moment? While preaching about a loving, caring, forgiving, grace-filled God, her or his voice may feel as if there is cotton clogging the throat. Other times, vocal fatigue sets in when one is straining to be heard or so invested in the sermon that one is exhausted. This emotional overlay may be due to hearing loss, fear, excitement, fatigue, imitation, abuse, medication, illness, or just mismanaged expectations of what a preacher should sound like. The result is harsh, strident, muffled, strained, and weak voices, all of which affect delivery and reception of the message. There is loss of voice due to some emotional factors that, at times, are unidentifiable. How can one sing the Lord's song when the strangeness of the land chokes off our voices?

There are individual factors that may affect one's emotions and subsequently one's voice during the preaching moment. One's health and emotional maturity are at the top of the list. Preachers, particularly women who tend to care for others and put themselves last, need to take time to rejuvenate and care for their bodies. Excessive weight, illnesses, and medications can all affect breathing and vocal production. Issues of authority and call may produce hesitant, weak, or inaudible "I'm not really here" or "I'm sorry to bother you" or "I'm just a woman" voices. At the other end of the continuum are the "Listen to me," "I'm going to stand here until you get it," "I know I'm gifted" loud, abrasive voices. When one is comfortable and assured that God has given both the call and authority, he or she can speak in his or her voice and stop masquerading. The vocal structure may not be able to sustain a style or voice spoken in imitation of someone else.

In terms of ministry, there is the consideration of the congregational sensitivity to the preacher. Persons insist on talking with the preacher before, during, and after the service. Time must be built into the day so that the preacher's voice can rest. The preacher sometimes talks nonstop on Sunday. One should, if at all possible, be on voice rest on Monday. Sound systems should be set to one audible level for the preacher and the listener without leading to shouting. The level of physical and emotional energy for preaching is affected by the number of persons on the ministerial staff. If the preacher is the sole minister, she has to talk through much of the service, and fatigue can easily arise. The activism of the church may mean preaching in the morning and again in the afternoon or evening. The preacher's status, church polity, and congregational expectations may demand more preaching than in other churches. The importance of voice care for preachers will be discussed in a later publication. Preachers need reassurance that God is in the midst of the experience. Then they can continue to sing the correct song with holy boldness.

Pastor Anne Lightner-Fuller of Mt. Calvary AME Church in Towson, Maryland, exemplifies the effect of situations on the emotional content and intent of the sermon.

She preaches "Making It Through Your Night Season" at a September 11 community memorial service. Her focus text is Psalm 77:10-12. In the ten-minute time slot, she immediately exegetes, describing Asaph's life experience as a night season. In this expository, topical sermon, she reread the Psalm saying, "The suffering Israel is not suffering out of hatred. Our God is about love and compassion, he's not indicted of hatred." Connecting with those who had experienced personal loss, she intones Jeremiah 3:23.

It is because of mercy we're not consume, because of God's mercies we are renewed every morning. Great is thy faithfulness. As ironic as it seems at a time like this, suffering grows faithful men and women, grows faithful and determined disciples. United we stand. What terrorists met for evil, God met for good. God will use for good what terrorists threatened to do to us. But look at how blessed America is. I have not ever, I've never seen us more united. I have never seen us more united until now. I have never in all of my life, men hugging at the opening of the American stock market. People who ordinarily don't have time to speak to each other are now looking at other human beings in another way.

She remains at the podium microphone and looks over the crowd as discernible emotional shifts infuse her voice. She returns to the text after about two minutes of supportive comments.

The psalmist gives us one of the ways to make it through our night season. To say this is in my mind firmly. This is the Lord in my flesh right now. This is something we have to live through; it is not something we can deny. I came to help you to understand tonight, to accept something does not necessarily mean that you allow it to control your life.

She then moves to the celebration evening in the midst of one of the strangest lands most have ever experienced. Pitch breaks, hoarseness, volume increase, movement of the right hand, furrowed brow, a glistening forehead, and, at times, reassuring smiles accompany her closing remarks.

Whatever the situation is, do not let it keep you down, because God is still on the throne. God is the same yesterday, today, and forever, forevermore. Don't ever forget, don't ever forget, that God can be trusted. And we will make it through this tragedy. God has never failed me yet. And I have no reason to turn back on him now. Hallelujah, somebody. I will bless the Lord in all times. God's praise will continually be in my mouth. . . . But when I think of the goodness of Jesus and all he's done for me, not only for me, [but also] for you, my soul cries out Hallelujah! God has blessed America and God is continuing to bless America and the God we love and we serve will continue to bless America.

Although she is preaching in a racially diverse, ecumenical gathering, all the elements of black preaching, including testimony, scriptural quotation, and celebration, are present. There are times that black preachers drop cultural elements when preaching in contexts different from their own. Other times, as Dr. Lightner-Fuller demonstrates, the effectiveness of one sermon remains true to who the preacher is regardless of the listener.

Delivery

About fifteen years ago, Dr. Charles G. Adams, Senior Pastor of the Hartford Memorial Baptist Church in Detroit, Michigan, and extraordinary homiletician, taught a two-week summer school class called "Preaching, Black and White." In one lecture, he gave a list of "do's and don'ts for the preacher." Over the years, I have used them for preparation and delivery of sermons. I also coupled them with my technical background in speech pathology to assist preachers in enhancing their delivery effectiveness.[3]

1. Avoid being dull, tedious, or laborious. Vocal energy paired with sound theology and knowledge of language give life to a sermon.
2. Never apologize for the sermon. "I know you don't want to hear this but . . . " or "I'm sorry, but . . . " Apologies defuse the authority of the preacher.
3. Audibility is essential—reach the furthest person from the pulpit. In an age of sound bites, there is an overreliance on microphones. I have students practice projection without microphones and do exercises to increase their speaking endurance. Abuse of the vocal mechanism is rampant among preachers, with the trend of "yelling" instead of learning to use the voice wisely.
4. Don't be monotonous. Inflection, melody, and tempo changes are essential. If used correctly, the voice can paint a picture with minimal language.

5. We preach with people not at, over, or under them.

6. Don't steal another person's sermons no matter how good the sermon sounds. In black preaching, we borrow from other preachers. There may be an introduction, some captivating point, alliteration, closure, or unique take on a passage one admires. Linguistically it sticks with us, and we model the pattern and language. We should at least credit the person we are imitating. One lacks homiletical integrity, authority, creativity, character, calm, and spirituality if one's entire preaching life is stolen.

7. Don't repeat a sermon unless it is filtered. In every opportunity to preach, the communicants are different. New experience, new information, new communication. If we believe that God does new things, then we can read over the sermon and make modifications as led.

8. Don't imitate others. Be yourself. I believe that God calls each of us as a particular instrument. Our vocalics, carriage, beliefs, and sound are distinctive. I realize that some sistahs operate under the death-dealing attitude that to be a good preacher one must sound, think, move, and look like a man. If God had wanted everyone to be men, I think God could have pulled that off and saved everyone the trouble.

9. Don't preach too long. The shortest sermon presented for evaluation was eleven minutes. The longest was forty-nine minutes. The average length was thirty-three minutes.

Two other aspects of sermon delivery are use of microphones and extemporaneous versus written sermons. Currently there is a subtle assessment of one's ability to preach based on walking with a microphone. This is tied to the belief that those who use manuscripts are not "anointed." Of the thirty-eight videos submitted or commercially purchased, one preacher used a headset microphone, six used lapel microphones, nine made use of a cordless handheld microphone, eight used the podium microphone but picked up a handheld microphone toward the end of the sermon, and fourteen used the podium microphone exclusively. Mobility of the preacher, for some, means that the "Spirit is moving." Analogous to the microphone seems to be the mistaken belief that a manuscript preacher is not "led by the Spirit."

There are some preachers who appear tethered to the podium. Their written material—manuscript, notes, or outlines—is on note cards, handwritten, on plain paper and in elaborate leather binders, folded in Bibles, on yellow legal pads, on lap-top computers, and on something resembling a teleprompter. Some read rather than reference their manuscripts. Some are more comfortable at the podium and do not move around in normal conversation. Some are able to use written material and still move around in the pulpit. Some who move around a lot are not able to give organized sermons and may resort to a diatribe or listing of scriptural texts or song titles. Answers to the question regarding whether one is a manuscript, outline, note, or extemporaneous preacher indicated that it changed according to the situation, the occasion, and the time. Fifty respondents said that they use a full manuscript. Twenty-seven use an outline. Notes were given as the answer for sixteen persons. Fifteen said they were strictly extemporaneous preachers. Six people use both manuscript and notes. Two use webpages exclusively. The transition and eye contact with the listeners are vital in using a manuscript. The effectiveness of what is preached is not dependent on the use of manuscript or extemporaneous delivery or handheld or podium microphones.

Call and Response

Call and response is dialogical. The preaching moment is not a solitary, performative act, with the herald on a great stage as if she were Juliet or even Hamlet presenting a soliloquy and waiting for the end of the act and a rousing applause. In a communicative cycle, one speaks and another listens and responds. The original speaker then counters the original listener's rejoinder, and the pattern is established. The timing, rate, and volume of the exchange depends on both the speaker and the listener. In black preaching, this cyclical pattern may be momentary, permeate the entire sermon, evolve as celebration increases, accompany the end of a sermon, or be verbally absent. It is important to remember that call and response in the black church setting may be verbal, nonverbal, or both. Persons may wave a hand, clap, stand up, run, cry, shake their heads, rock back and forth, moan, hum, kneel, or even throw items at the preacher, in an affirming sort of way.

Musicologist Jon Michael Spencer, in *The Concise Dictionary of Preaching*, details the folk mannerisms of black preaching. He says that the preacher begins in a normal speaking voice then modulates as momentum grows. He calls black preaching a "danced religion."[4] Call and response is not a planned activity (although there are some preachers who practice it and write sayings into their manuscripts). Call and response is like hearing a song; memories begin to flood your soul, and before you know it, you are either humming the tune or attempting a dance you haven't done in ages. You may even turn the music source up as the melody overtakes you, and, much to your children's chagrin, you move all over the family room. In another instant, you may hear a word or phrase, and tears begin to cascade down your face before you recognize the pain, the joy, the depth of the memory you thought you were past.

"It's Time to Believe" was preached the Wednesday after Resurrection Sunday by the Reverend Bernadette Glover-Williams. She uses four points to encourage the congregation to maintain faith even in the face of difficulty. Using an outline and handheld microphone, she peppers the sermon with "You won't hear me," "I won't be long," "Ya'll don't hear me," "Oh, don't you hear me?" "Ya'll won't help me tonight," "Honey," and "Look at your neighbor." She demonstrates that call and response is evident in complex sermons as well as in more simplistic presentations. The four points of the sermon reinforce her premise that "seeing is not necessarily believing."

1. Grief can do a number on you. She uses the character Forrest Gump at the White House as an illustration.
2. Jesus' signs and miracles for the people were motivated by compassion. He acted in obedience rather than compassion for himself.
3. If God had planned for the innocent to be overtaken by the corrupt, jealous, and envious, why would God ever perform a miracle for what could have been a way of escape unfolding?
4. Just because God restrains his power does not mean he has lost his ability.

The celebration centers around knowledge of God's work in the world. She reminds the listeners, "We are viewing things after the fact. The disciples weren't so sure." She walks away from the podium at the end of the sermon during the celebration.

Idiosyncratic statements, community sayings, or preaching clichés generally occur in the sistah preaching with regularity. They are a cultural element of black verbal exchange. This is a listing of some of the comments used in the sermons evaluated. They are representative rather than exhaustive. The function is to prompt listener feedback. They become part of the oral tradition, particularly in preaching circles. Some catch you off guard. Some are planned. Some are identified with particular preachers, denominations, or worship styles. Like steps to a dance, the movement flows naturally. The manner in which they are spoken and their placement within the sermon depend on the individual and the listeners. Like harmonizing on a song with a group of friends, the give and take is natural.

Do you hear me?
Stay with me!
I know you don't know what I'm talking about!
You don't know like I know!
Do you feel me?
I know you want to know where I'm going.
Don't make me tell my story.
Am I talking good?
Amen!
Praise you, Jesus!
Are you following me?
Praise God.
Bless the name of Jesus!
God is good.
I don't know if you know.
Hallelujah!
You catch that?
Hear me now!
I promise I won't keep you long.
Can I get a witness?
Anybody know what I'm talking about?
Pray for me now.
Are you praying?
Now, now, now.
Amen lights!
Y'all get that.
Turn to your neighbor.

I won't be before you long.
It's preaching time.
You pray with me.
I'm glad you ask.
Stay with me now.
Glory to his name.
Bless God.
Hallelujah to his name!
Hear me good.
Hallelujah to God.
I wish I had a praying church.
You got to help me now.
Can I get some help up in here?
Am I helping somebody?
Glory to God.
It's the truth anyhow.
Come on now.
Nobody but the Lord.
Hey, God.
Hey! Hey! Hey?
Listen, listen, listen.
The Lord gave me this word.
First giving honor to God.
The devil is a liar.
Oh, glory?
Clap your hands and say, Amen.

Am I close?
Ah, God.
Help me, Lord.
Praise 'em.
Give God some praise.
Praise the Name of Jesus.
You don't hear me.
Somebody say, Amen.
Somebody say something.
Well.
Look here!
See! see! see!
Time to give God praise.

I need some help up in here.
I feel my help coming.
Help me, Holy Ghost.
I wish I had someone to pray.
I'm going to preach anyhow.
You don't hear me.
You're not following me.
Go with me now. (Come with me now.)
Walk with me now.
This word is deep.
I want you to get this.
Stand up and give your neighbor a high five.
Now, now, now.

Evans Crawford details the "homiletical musicality," or audible responses, from the congregation during the preaching moment. Crawford lists five possible responses: "Help 'em, Lord!" " Well?" "That's all right!" "Amen!" and "Glory Hallelujah!" Crawford says that timing, pauses, inflection, pace, and the musical qualities of speech engage the listener during proclamation.[5] Other responses I have heard over the years include, "Make it plain," "Stay right there," "Paint it," "You preaching now," "Yes, sir," "Preach, Preacher!" "That's good, that's good," "I know you're right," "Teach," and "You're on target." The response "yes, sir" may be used when a sistah is preaching. Sometimes the response is perfunctory and the individual doesn't make the gender switch. Call and response drives the sermonic celebration.

Henry Mitchell depicts celebration as integral to call and response. It is a meaningful identification with God's truth. Sound theological preparation is a prerequisite of celebration. Celebration should relate both to text and to the purpose of the people and not pushed or manipulated. It is not an occasion for emotional manipulation. Celebration takes place throughout the sermon rather than as a cliché at the end of the oration. Celebration, he says, is rejoicing and praise at a spiritual feast.[6]

The excerpt of a sermon given by the Reverend T. Renée Crutcher begins with thanksgiving and acknowledgment. She was apologetic and compared her skill level to that of the senior pastor. She immediately moves to the text, defining the term *midwife* in the text and in contemporary society. She gives thorough background on the cultural setting of the text, including genocide, isolation, and the fear of God. Her voice is expressive, dramatic, visual, intense, and articulate. Language is inclusive. She uses a cordless podium microphone and manuscript.

> Will we be midwives? We will have to aid in the birth of life. We need to assist in deliverance of the child from hopelessness, from degradation, from despair, from the pools of underachievement, from an educational system that has little intent of educating, from children having children, from the deference, from an underprivileged existence, in the midst of self-hate, abuse, and being disenfranchised, and because of race, sex, or denomination. And God counts on us to help build lives.

She celebrates throughout the sermon and gives a testimony at the end of the sermon: "Having been raised [from] the abyss of suicidal depression, I needed a midwife. Is there anyone here who needs a midwife? Let me tell you about the midwife who delivered me." Further utilizing the theme of the midwives in the focus text, she goes on to give nine features of the midwife who brought her through. Music is underscoring what she's doing. Her hands move throughout the sermon in coordination with her words. She picks up the handheld microphone and prepares to move away from the podium. Her contralto voice melodiously flows, setting the tempo as the call and response drives the ending. In the black preaching tradition, she creatively "ends at the cross."

> He (Jesus) left the glory of heaven.
> He entered as a back door, barnyard divinity.
> He laid his little head on a pillow of straw in an animal trough.
> His little body was kept warm by the breath of an ox.
> They named him Jesus.
> On Calvary's Hill, He aided in the process of my birth.
> On Resurrection morning, he pushed me through the birth canal to everlasting life.
> And I've been sucking on the breast of the Holy Spirit for my nourishment and growth ever since.
> He delivered me.

He gave me life.
Do you need him to see you to serve as your midwife?
Has he ever been your midwife?

She ends by singing, "He Delivered Me."

The Hoop

"To hoop or not to hoop?" is a lecture topic in my class on black preaching history, content, and delivery. Once associated with uneducated, rural, Baptist, Pentecostal, or charismatic blacks only, this form of sermon presentation is used with regularity by white televangelists who understand the historical link and effectiveness between call and response.[7] It is a form of singing the songs of Zion in a strange land. The use of "hoop," "tune," "holler," "rap," "call," "shout," "dance," or "celebration" depends on the preachers' experience, linguistic proficiency, spirituality, and cultural location. There is an expectation in some geographical areas and denominations that the preacher does not proclaim God's word unless she or he "hoops." It is evidence of spiritual endowment and Christian experience. In other denominations, "hooping" is viewed as an outdated mode of listener manipulation or a cover for the preacher who has not adequately handled the text. This is especially true in contexts where the person "teaches" the word. In my minority report, I contend that all preaching should teach something. The form of the lesson is what changes.

"Calling the roll," or listing the names of the heroes of the faith—Moses to John on Patmos—having a "Stephen" moment and reviewing the entire history of God's action in the world; talking about a Christian grandmother or mother; taking Jesus to the cross, Resurrection, and Second Coming; singing a song; telling a story, particularly one that has been a fixture in the oral tradition; or sharing one's testimony are common elements of the hoop. The hoop is an intensified, poetic, alliterative, verbal or nonverbal, spirit-endowed (although there is a school of thought that says one can practice a hoop and be just as effective) rhetorical device. The hoop is usually at the end of a sermon. There may be vocal gymnastics that require gasping for air, panting, long pauses, or rapid speech; or in some cases, the voice quality becomes so harsh that the natural voice is just a memory. The voice runs the entire tonic scale. Articulation is marked by elongation of vowels, repetition of phrases or initial consonants, or omission of word endings. Action verbs and adjectives and nouns are the order of the day. Emphasis is placed on pronunciation of "Jesus," which may become "Geesuz"; and "God" many become "Gahd." Hooping is physical, and the preacher, at times, is drenched in perspiration. There is a curious ritual of immediately wrapping one's neck with a large handkerchief or towel or putting on a coat "to keep the heat in." Actually, perspiration is a natural cooling and toxin release system, and one loses the voice not because of heat or drafts, but because of vocal exertion. Affect is influenced by listener familiarity with the preacher, understanding of what is taking place, predictability of the hoop, and the context. I caution my students to make sure they have fed the people a good sermonic meal before rushing to the hoop. The danger of manipulation and emotional overload is like a sugar high if one has not had protein before dessert. There is a growing expectation that a "good" woman preacher be able to hoop. The reality is that some women hoop and some men do not hoop. The choice is up to the Spirit and the preacher. To hoop or not to hoop remains the question.

Telley Lynnette Gadson is an under-thirty, seminary-educated "hooper." She is a product of the black preaching tradition and the South Carolina Island culture. Her energy is at the same level throughout the seventeen-minute and fifty-nine-second presentation. In a sermon entitled "Who Do You Think You Are?" she spends seventeen minutes and nineteen seconds exegeting the text and celebrating God's presence and power. She pastors two churches, and, at the time of this afternoon message, she had already preached twice that day. This excerpt is the close of the message. The people are standing, and the call and response pattern is sustained with organ riffs. She encourages the young people at the Youth Day service.

> Who do you think you are?
> I'm so glad you asked.
> Some, some call Him Mary's baby
> Some call Him the Lily of the Valley
> Some say He's a Bright and Morning Star
> Some say He's a Rose of Sharon
> Some say He's the Fountain of Life [Leans back and hits the handheld
>   microphone on the corner of her mouth.]
> Some say He's the Light of the World
> Some call Him the Alpha and the Omega
> He's the Beginning and He's the End.

He's the first and last
He's my very best friend
There were times I didn't have a dime, He was my provider
I can call on Jesus in the morning
Jesus in the noonday
I say "Father, I stretch my hands to thee, no other help"

"I know if you withdraw yourself from me, where can I go?"
I came by to let you know He will provide for you
[Reaches for a handkerchief, leaves the pulpit, moves toward the first
    bench; eye contact is limited, looking up to the ceiling; turns around,
    sits down, and ending]
If thou withdraw yourself from me, whither shall I go?
Who do you think you are? (Reiteration of topic)
[Still seated]
You are a child of the king, act like it
I came by to tell you that He is God
Early one Friday afternoon
the sun stopped shining
the wind stopped blowing
the moon dripped with blood
But early one Sunday morning after three days in the grave
after three days in the grave (jumps up off the bench and walks back to
pulpit)
He got up with all power in his hands
Who you think you are?
[The audience responds with applause and standing; she is wiping her
face]
Who you think you are?
Who you think you are?
Who do you think you are?
Every now and then we need to take some time for your personal reflec-
    tion
Even the preacher needs a preacher every now and then
Take some time to do some self-image
I have been busy lately
Haven't taken time for my inventory
If you don't mind I need to spend some time with Telley
If you don't mind,
[Picked up mirror and repeatedly asked self]
"Who do you think you are?"

Martha Simmons cautions that there are pitfalls in black preaching, particularly when one has not adequately prepared.[8] Proof texting, or rattling off a series of texts without proper exegesis or connection to the sermon purpose, is evident in many contemporary sermons. Some believe the more texts they quote, the more connected they are with the "word." The difficulty is that they may leave the listener with a list of texts and little understanding of their meaning. Simmons writes that celebration is decidedly people glad about the behavior they have been asked to continue. Care should be taken so that the celebration is not premature and the text is sufficiently worked. The preacher must also filter the stories, illustrations, and images so that they do not leave the listener emotionally drained. The temptation to rely on clichéd endings neutralizes the effect of the text.

"Lord, Please Show Me Your Glory" (Exodus 33:18-22) was preached at a denominational planning meeting in Texas. This preacher, the Reverend Ida Kenner, used a podium microphone and did not leave the podium. She evidently had a manuscript or notes due to the occasions of looking down and reading. The sermon content focused on ways in the Old Testament that God reveals God's glory to believers. She first defines glory and then lists biblical examples of God's glory. In the progression of the sermon, she talks about how one misses an opportunity to receive God's glory and ends in celebration of what not to do. She went immediately to the text and interjected, "Lord, God" throughout the sermon. She holds a white handkerchief, which she later uses to wipe perspiration. Her body language included turning from side to side, leaning back or to the right side, shaking her right hand for emphasis, and looking primarily to her right in the pulpit. Musicality through repetition combined with a hoop interspersed with focus text is her style. She ends each sentence with "Huh" or an increasingly abrupt vowel pronunciation.

> You can't see God's glory unless you're thankful before the Almighty God.
> You can't enter into the gates unless you're thankful before the Almighty God.
> He will not take you in with your high and lofty self.
> You got to bow down before God.
> You got to thank God.
> At the end, if you're so pious and cute, you can't praise God.
> You got to get to God's glory, the past to the brazen altar.
> That's where the prosperity is, at Jesus' feet.

Do you want his glory?
Let me tell you about God.
You got to be cleaned.
You can't hold dirt and think you're going to get God's glory.
You can't lie on your neighbor and think you're going to get God's glory.
You can backbite and think you're going to get God's glory.
You got to walk upright.
You can't take your tithe and spend it at Dillard's now.
You can't take your offering and give it to Saks Fifth Avenue.
You got to obey God if you want God's glory.
God, please show me your glory.

This chapter has, through the voices of sistah preachers and pro-claimers, discussed voice and diction, sermon introductions, delivery, call and response, and the hoop and celebration. The next chapter will look at nonverbal factors in the proclamation of black women. Singing a song in a strange land is not an easy proposition, but with God, all things are possible. The writer of Psalm 137 says that if there is no remembrance of Jerusalem, no thought of the source of our call and memory and of the one who leads, guides, and protects our lives, we will be voiceless. This is why sistahs keep singing.

"Just Preach!"

This sermon was first preached in 1999 for a preaching conference. It was published in the *African American Pulpit*.[9] It stemmed from my discomfort with sermons that were theologically illogical, were joke- or story-centered rather than Bible-centered, were performance-based, or were overwhelmingly manipulative.

Old Testament Reading: Isaiah 52:7-9

> 7 How beautiful upon the mountains are the feet of the messenger who announces peace, who brings good news, who announces salvation, who says to Zion, "Your God reigns."
> 8 Listen! Your sentinels lift up their voices, together they sing for joy; for in plain sight they see the return of the LORD to Zion.
> 9 Break forth together into singing, you ruins of Jerusalem; for the LORD has comforted his people, he has redeemed Jerusalem.

New Testament Reading: Romans 10:8-15

> 8 But what does it say? "The word is near you, on your lips and in your heart" (that is, the word of faith that we proclaim);
> 9 because if you confess with your lips that Jesus is Lord and believe in your heart that God raised him from the dead, you will be saved.
> 10 For one believes with the heart and so is justified, and one confesses with the mouth and so is saved.
> 11 The scripture says, "No one who believes in him will be put to shame."
> 12 For there is no distinction between Jew and Greek; the same Lord is Lord of all and is generous to all who call on him.
> 13 For, "Everyone who calls on the name of the Lord shall be saved."
> 14 But how are they to call on one in whom they have not believed? And how are they to believe in one of whom they have never heard? And how are they to hear without someone to proclaim him?
> 15 And how are they to proclaim him unless they are sent? As it is written, "How beautiful are the feet of those who bring good news!"

Do you remember the last time you were able to read a newspaper, channel-surf, log onto the Internet, send E-mail or snail mail, receive a page, or even hold an "old-fashioned" face-to-face conversation without encountering bad news?

Our lives are permeated with talk of social injustice, infectious diseases, familial decimation, racial profiling, political machinations, global poverty, ethnic cleansing, terrorism, unmanageable addictions, interpersonal alienation, and spiritual bankruptcy.

The Bible says there is nothing new under the sun. My brothers and sisters, we are a people of hope. God has an answer for any situation careening down the information superhighway. God knows, in times like these,

Too many dreams are dying at dawn

Too many aspirations are asphyxiated in apathy

Too many visions are eviscerated in valleys

Too many blessings are buried in boredom

Too many joys are jilted by jealousy

Just as in the days of the prophets, God is still the author and finisher of the "good news," the "saving word," the "empowered message," and the "naked truth" that frees us from debilitating rumors and unsubstantiated predictions of the demise of God's world.

We do not need meandering wordsmiths, pretentious provocateurs, or supercilious shockmeisters. The world is in need of persons who will just preach.

God sends persons to proclaim liberty, even when some wish to remain in Egypt. [Have you ever stayed too long in Egypt?]

God anoints peculiar instruments to dispense that "balm in Gilead to make the wounded whole."

God still hears the cries of people and commissions new prophets to preach the word with passion and clarity.

God assigns heralds, preachers, ministers, teachers, leaders, and proclaimers to just preach.

In our focus text, the apostle Paul writes of conditions similar to what we face today.

Paul—born a Jew in Tarsus

Educated in Gamaliel's seminary

Persecuted the People of the Way

Knocked off his elitist horse in Damascus

Convicted to ministry by the Spirit of God

Devoted to establishing his citizenship in heaven

Paul knew the price, the cost, the hardships and hallelujahs, the majesty and misery of ministry; look at his record

Five times flogged by Jews [forty lashes minus one]

Three times beaten with rods

One time stoned

Three times shipwrecked

Danger at sea

Danger on rivers

Danger on banks

Danger in the wilderness

Danger from bandits

Danger in the cities

Danger in the county

Danger from own people

Danger from false sisters and brothers

Daily pressure because of concern for the churches (2 Corinthians 11)

Paul was given the task of taking the good news into the whole world regardless of the cost.

Paul usually wrote to the people, the believers, Jews and Gentiles in the known world of the only one who is able to save them in spite of their current circumstances.

On his third missionary trip to Corinth, Paul addresses his letter to all who are in Rome, the beloved of God, and those called saints.

The Christians in Rome were a depressed, disturbed, disrespected, and disillusioned group.

At one time, they held different values than the Romans.

There were united in love.

There were no class distinctions.

They helped one another.

They were a big extended family.

The church began as a Jewish cult but after twenty-seven years had added Gentile converts.

There was diversity in culture and nationality, but they still lived in love and charity with their neighbors.

As we look at the tenth chapter of Paul's letter to the church at Rome, Paul explains that his soul is troubled because of disturbing trends of unbelief growing unchecked in the church.

Some, Paul writes, are existing in darkness.

They were beginning to pick up habits from those around them. They were in Rome, so they started acting like Romans.

They were turning from the law of God because of political pressure and a desire to be socially accepted.

Where communal sharing once existed, competition raged.

The idea of being equal before God (no distinction between Greek and Jew; the same Lord is Lord of all and is generous to all who call on him) was becoming a distant memory or fairy tale for many of the believers.

Sound familiar?

The ecclesiastical landscape has changed little.

Children are still dying.

Adults are still abusing one another.

Diseases are still killing thousands of our brothers and sisters daily.

Nations are still fighting over land.

Political opinions are still overshadowing spiritual discussions.

Check out many of our churches, communities, families, and pastors.

Folk running around looking for salvation in all the wrong places.
  Church-hopping and Holy Ghost-shopping.
  Denominational damnation.
Advertisements of "We preach and teach the whole word," as if the
  gospel can be segmented.
Throwing away one's religious heritage for a cup of instant popularity.
Perpetrating the prosperity of a few, while millions exist in poverty.
Competitions for same market share while millions remain unchurched.
Big churches with little spirituality.
Loud music with no theology.
Hand-clapping with no mention of Christ.
Choreographed praise, as if humans command the Spirit.
Sermons about serving the pastor, but no realization that God is still on
  the throne.
Preachers, leaders hiding behind artificial barriers of
  Powder-filled vials
  Weak theology
  Cloned delivery styles
  Unlimited credit lines
  Competitive market shares
  Private jets
  Faddish clichés
  Designer labels
  Back-scratching officers
  Made-up titles
  Colorful, oversized, flowing robes
  Calvary-sized crosses
  Multiple rings
  Ill-fitting collars
  "Big chair syndrome"
  Perspiration, anticipation, handkerchiefs
  Cowering committees
  And powerless positions.
Is it a wonder that the people are in darkness? Look at their models of
  Christian love.
Paul sends warnings and correctives for strengthening the church and its
  leadership.
Paul says stop looking around for the word. It is already here. It is in your
  hearts and minds. The word is Incarnate.

If you confess the word of God with your mouth—outward confession—and believe it with your heart—inward confession—you shall be saved.

In a four-point sermon [for Jews and Gentiles, churched and unchurched, clergy and laity]

Paul outlines what is needed for the church to recover the "joy it once knew." Paul instructs us about this ministry called preaching.

    a. Preachers are sent by God

    b. Preachers are sent to proclaim the message of God

    c. People have to hear the message of God

    d. Once they have heard, then they can believe

    e. Once they believe, they can live the message

This is the task of the preacher: to proclaim the unadulterated word of God, to spread the gospel full and free, to preach the good news, to preach not a cheap gospel, but a transforming word.

How are they—God's sons and daughters—to call, plead, entreat, request, ask, and seek the one—the answer, hope, savior, supplier, help, and liberator—in whom they have not believed?

How can they believe when the one they were to believe in was rarely the focus of the service?

How can they hear above the maddening noise of "sound and fury signifying nothing"?

How can they call on the name of Jesus when the subject rarely comes up?

Three stories and a joke save nothing but the preacher's popularity and often his or her appointment.

Superficial, diabetic, all-fluff and no-stuff sermons to please the people rather than to challenge their walk with God.

Paul writes across the ages—*just preach.*

Paul's questions continue

How are they to proclaim unless they are sent?

So many of us start this journey of carrying God's word with joy, vitality, awe, fear, trembling, and unstoppable energy.

We answer the call of God with boldness, declaring, "Here I am, send me. I'll go."

When the rubber of reality hits the road of revelation, some drop out of the race

Some can't stand the pressure

Some think it was all praise and no work

Some looked for a power trip and forgot all power comes from God.

Some become *functional atheists*—they think they are God, that nothing happens until they arrive, and that no one can take their place.

My brothers and sisters, think of all the time we waste in fruitless discussions about who is called to preach.

Some refuse to allow others to say or to herald God's Word because of gender, denomination, sexual proclivity, race, wealth, poverty, education, hoping, or imprecise pronunciation.

Wasting precious time arguing about who is worthy to be ordained.

None of us are Levites, but some act as if they own the pulpit and are worthy enough to sit in judgment about someone else's call.

[1 Corinthians 1:26]

Consider your own call. Think of how mind-boggling it is that God called you to preach. [Lord, I hear of showers of blessing; thou are scattering full and free. Showers the thirsty soul refreshing. Let some drops now fall on me, even me]

The promise of God is that anyone who believes will never be put to shame. We don't have to be ashamed of this gospel of Jesus Christ.

1. Not many were wise. God is the source of wisdom. Why waste time arguing about human intelligence. We do not know enough to try to run God's employment program.

2. Not many were powerful. All power comes from God. This ministry is about God, not about us.

3. Not many were of noble birth. Through the blood of Jesus, we all become heirs to God's kingdom. Most of us do not have a window or a pot, except for God's blessings

God chooses what is foolish in this world, the message of the cross to shame the wise. Not everyone will believe; not everyone wants to be saved.

God chooses what is weak in the world to shame the strong.

Paul says if we boast, we are to boast about what God has worked in, through, and in spite of us.

God chooses the despised, disregarded, disrespected, dejected, disenfranchised to do God's will.

God takes the most unlikely persons—sinners saved by grace, the last one picked to be on the team, the one everyone else overlooks—and uses them to build up the earthly path to a heavenly destination.

God takes the fragile, fractured, fragments of vessels and fixes, purges, prunes, cleans, trains, and raises them up to bear the word of life.

All we are to do is *just preach!*

My brothers and my sisters, when we are doing the will and work of God, all hell is going to break loose.

Those closest to us will not always understand why we have to do what we have to do.

Our friends will criticism how we do our job.

Sometimes the people will not follow.

Sometime we will be "way down yonder by ourselves and can't hear nobody pray."

Sometime we will not be able to see the tunnel or the light.

Sometime we will want to give up and go back.

Sometime we will find ourselves in the Garden at Gethsemane during "let this cup pass" moments.

Examine yourself:

Who called me to preach?

Who validated my mission and ministry?

Whose command urges me to say a word for the Lord?

This call to proclaim did not emanate in the mind of a bishop, a senior pastor, a board, or a committee.

It did not begin with family members at the Thanksgiving table, talking about how you sounded like, looked like, or acted like a preacher.

I have a friend who says, "The real ones never do."

There would not be automatic assumptions that, because a parent was a preacher, you must automatically follow in that path.

No, God is the only one who can give the assignment.

This call (when taken seriously) did not even begin as a figment of our own imaginations.

Paul says God's preachers are sent.

Who in his or her right mind would boldly step forward to be castigated as an impostor or pimp?

Who would willingly give up jobs, family, friends, prestige, and security to go to school at age 30, 40, or 50?

Who would go from one assignment to another, with no guarantee of staying long enough to find the church, except one who is called and sent by somebody greater than you or me?

What bit of insanity courses through us that we would offer ourselves as vessels to stand on holy ground and proclaim God's word to a world that stands in darkness?

All we know is that God has sent us out to *just preach!*

The Bible says that tomorrow is not promised.

Now is the time to stop waiting for someone else to say when to preach, what to preach, when to shout, when to praise, when to witness, who to preach with, how long to preach, or where to preach.

We are to be obedient to the will and direction of God, not to some Pavlovian behavior modification program.

How do we expect folk to be saved if they don't believe?

How do we think people will be relieved of the pressures of this life if they do not believe there is a possibility for change?

How can they hear unless someone opens her mouth and preaches the word of God?

God has made arrangements for sending out preachers. Remember, God sends preachers.

God calls preachers.

God anoints preachers.

God appoints preachers.

God elects preachers.

God ordains preachers.

God protects preachers.

This preaching thing is not easy.

It is not for cowards.

It is not for the faint of heart.

The word instructs us that some will abandon their faith.

Some will follow diverse spirits.

Some will be hypocritical liars.

Some will have no conscience and numb the listener with his or her words.

Some will give stringent rules for the people and follow none themselves.

If the preacher responds to the illumination, guidance, and direction of the Holy Spirit during both preparation and presentation, the word will be powerful.

In order to preach, we must undergo spiritual kenosis—empty ourselves for the sake of others. We must be prepared to be worthy to
carry the word anytime, any place, anywhere God says.

We must seek God's affection, forgiveness, love, and mercy

We are earthen vessels, not carbon copies, not clones, not perfect,
but peculiar, particular, proven instruments with an assignment
from God to *just preach!*

Preachers are human beings, sons of soil and salvation, daughters of dust
and divinity, called according to God's purpose.

Preachers are not gods. The expectation is that we try to become
Christlike.

Preachers are God's children, called to a different standard of
service.

Preachers do not save; Jesus saves, and we just point the way to Jesus.

Some forget that all have sinned and come short of God's glory.
They damn the people to hell as if the truth that all have
sinned and come short of the glory of God does not include
them.

Some choose to manipulate the people into some ill-conceived
power trip rather than persuade them to convert to God's plan.

It is not about us. It is about God.

We are able to preach only when we realize that the Word of God is
preached through us, not by us.

We are merely conduits of God's treasure hidden in our earthly
vessels.

If God called you to preach, no ordination board, good ol' boys club, or
good ol' girls clique will be able to stop the move of God. This fool-
ishness called preaching will be birthed even if we try to abort it.

God will perform a spiritual C-section on us to birth the sermon that
is growing in our souls.

Just preach!

Quoting Isaiah, Paul concludes the matter as he writes of the results of
carrying, birthing, relating, or bringing forth a message of hope in times
of darkness.

"How beautiful are the feet of those who bring good news!"

How wonderful are the feet of those who are eager to take the word
to the people of God anytime, any place, anywhere, anyhow! How
beautiful are the feet of those whose speaking of the word is like
pouring water onto parched ground!

How refreshing are the feet of those who enable others to hear words of comfort, compassion, and chastisement!

How beautiful—hot, dusty, aching, tired, bruised, blistered, broken, battered, smelly—are the feet of the brothers and sisters, of men and of women who bring good news.

How beautiful, blessed, and bought are the lives of the ones who know there is no choice but to go into all the nations and *just preach*. Didn't Isaiah preach, "How beautiful upon the mountains are the feet of the messenger who announces peace, who brings good news, who announces salvation, who says to Zion, 'Your God reigns'? Listen! Your sentinels lift up their voices together, they sing for joy, for in plain sight, they see the return of the Lord to Zion."

Nothing is new under the sun. Yesterday, today, and forever, we are to tell the salvation story.

We, the priesthood of all believers, are to *just preach*.

Preach, not clown, preach

Preach, not beg, preach

Preach, not control, preach

Preach, not manipulate, preach

Preach, not lie, preach

Preach, not perform, preach

Preach, this is our calling, this is our purpose, this is our story, this is our responsibility.

Just preach—until sinners ask what they must do to be saved.

Just preach—always faithful to the text.

Just preach—live out the word in actions and words.

Just preach—believing that the Lord will make the way.

Just preach—speaking the truth in love.

Just preach—with all you heart, all your soul, all your strength, and all your mind.

Just preach—with the courage of your convictions.

Just preach—letting nothing and nobody turn you around.

Just preach—without apology or manipulation.

Just preach—until everyone knows that Satan is a liar.

Just preach—until the wicked cease from troubling and the weary are at rest.

Just preach—until all the graves open up and all our dead places are revived.

Just preach—until Pentecost is everyday.

Just preach—until the blind see, the lame walk, the deaf hear, and the dumb talk.

Just preach—until the lonely feel love, the houseless have home, and the naked get clothes.

Just preach—until everyone, everywhere knows that Jesus is real and God is alive.

Just preach—Christ as people who hear, believe, and are sent by God to say the word.

Just preach—with a weary throat until all the world knows about the blessed hope.

Just preach—until every knee bows and every tongue confesses that Jesus Christ is Lord.

Just preach!

CHOIR ROBES AND CHOREOGRAPHY

When I directed or sang in choirs after all the work of preparation for a Sunday service or a concert, there was always the dreaded business meeting about what attire the choir should wear. The long hours of learning the music and even the purpose of the musical presentation were often overshadowed by vehement arguments about what was appropriate for the occasion. "Dresses or suits?" "Long skirts or short skirts?" "White pumps or black pumps?" "It's too soon to wear white." "What color should we wear?" "No, we wore that last year." "I think all the women should wear white shoes." "Drop earrings or stud earrings?" "You know we are all supposed to look alike." "Perhaps we should wear our regular robes with special stoles." "Let's do Afrocentric this year." "No, I don't like to wear that stuff." "Maybe we should just let everyone wear whatever they want." The discussion would lag on for what seemed like days. Some would decide not to sing because they do not have money for the proper dress. Some would eventually show up in whatever they wanted or something close to the assigned attire. Others insisted on uniformity regardless of how the choir sounded. There was no difficulty deciding what men would wear—identical ties, vests, shirts, or jackets. For some reason, enormous stress was associated with selection of appropriate choir robes. The same tie or a vest and shirt seemed to fill the bill in men's attire considerations.

The choir robe business meeting format seems to be gaining momentum among sistah proclaimers. The fashion police are raiding pulpits and convention centers across the nation. The focus of the proclamation is sometimes pushed aside for virulent appraisal and oppressive standard-setting of women's attire. "What should we wear?" "What color should we wear?" "How long should our skirts be?" "Are pants in order?" "What about that hair?" "No makeup, of course. Holy women do not wear makeup." "You need to wear a robe to cover up your body. You don't want to make people (men) forget the word do you?" "You're standing out too much. Put on some black and pull your hair back so you'll look like a preacher." I always thought the argument about toning down women's appearance, as if women were birds or animals, was such a joke. Unless God comes and performs spiritual body reconstruction, there is little women can do to hide themselves. They are black women. They have physical features that naturally stand out. Black women stand out in most places. Black women who happen to preach really stand out. Still the debate rages on about what is "appropriate liturgical attire" for women preachers, evangelists, speakers, and teachers. I have a friend who once said, "If they say you don't look like a preacher, tell them the real ones never do!" What does appearance have to do with the proclamation of the word? Does one's dress impinge on one's communicative ability? Who sets the standard? Being raised in the black church, I was taught that one always wears her best when working for the Lord. Spotlighting choir robes rather than content is complicated.

Joseph Webb, author of *Preaching and the Challenge of Pluralism*, discusses "symbolicity"—the signs and symbols of communication. Signs, he says, are sensory input that prompt our senses to respond. Symbols represent something that is absent. Signs and symbols form the basis for human response to cultural, conscious, and visual stimuli. Each symbol stands for ethical, moral, religious, or cultural meaning.[1] Response to symbols is either positive or negative and cognitive or emotive. In the preaching moment, "symbolicity" affects language production and nonverbal presentation—clothing and movement. In the preaching moment, certain stimuli represent present reality, and other, the past memory. Clothing evokes meaning and feeling in the speaker and listener. This creates a nonverbal call and response.

Geography alone, or geography coupled with denomination, produces conflicting attire standards. I remember a meeting of AME women where one of the topics was appropriate dress for women in ministry. One of the sistahs began to harangue about what women need to do to be "accepted" as equals in ministry. As she waxed authoritatively on the need for women to look more like real preachers (men), or at least not to call attention to themselves, she said quite emphatically, "Don't dress like those whorish women in the ___ district. They wear all sorts of loud colors, nail polish, and hair all over the place. They would not be allowed in the pulpit at my home church in all that red." Three of the women sitting at the table were from that assailed district. They just made eye contact and knowingly smiled. Sistah was dressed in a the drab beige jacket, short hair, no jewelry, no makeup, and flat shoes and was convinced that everyone had to look alike to be granted a place at the "big people's table." The women in the room wearing makeup, nail polish, colorful outfits, and an array of footwear were being castigated yet listened patiently. They had already moved to a place of self-identity and moved, at least in a supportive system, to other battlegrounds. The ecclesial leadership, ordination board, or senior pastor is frequently the determinant of what one is to wear, the color, and accessories. One's own comfort level, rapport with the leadership, and understanding of the purpose for clothing influence compliance. Age, experience, occasion, ecclesial status, and personal preference are also determinants. Often sistah proclaimers risk rejection due to their individuality. In other instances, their style is refreshing, praised, and imitated by other women. If there has not been a model of how women proclaimers dress then the status quo choir robe rules. When there is a feminine model for clerical wear, acceptance is more likely. The effect of the attire of women proclaimers and emulation of dress by both laity and clergy are worthy of research.

Other than the statement that most women do not sound like preachers or dress like preachers is the claim that women's pulpit presence is too soft, lacking energy, or not representative of the prophets of the Bible, Paul, or Jesus. I wonder at times who has access to an audiotape or videotape of their preaching? What peer group assessed their homiletical effectiveness? How do we know if Paul's preaching was charismatic? He fussed so much in his letters. The physicality aspect of preaching includes eye contact, physical engagement with the congregation, embodiment of the text, use of hands, handling of distractions, physical energy, stance, posture, and carriage. Once the choir robe is selected, the choreography is charted.

Choir choreography is an interesting phenomenon. The trick is to get everyone, regardless of size, shape, or ability, to move in concert. Inevitably, Sister Joyce rocks a different way. Sister Veronica claps on the wrong beat or is unable to sing and clap at the same time. Brother Frank just stands still as others crash into his shoulder. Some choreography is carefully rehearsed for a professional appearance. Others vow that the Holy Spirit directs their moves. Yet another group testifies to familiarity with the rhythm and a natural connect takes place. They can't help moving in a certain way. The choir director becomes the chief choreographer. In the black church, choreography is prized particularly for mass choirs that have the opportunity to preach at a conference or "mega church." Some preachers are the same way, as seeking a large venue means more prestige. The soloist is left to move as directed. In the preaching moment, choreography is said to depend on the move of the Holy Spirit. At times, however, proclaimers just as the choir soloist practice where to place their hands, when to move their arms, when to stomp their feet, when to dance, or when to walk away from the podium and toward the congregation. Others say that they do not realize their movement in the pulpit. Some comply with pulpit decorum set by the pastor. There are sistahs who stand still during the entire presentation, using one hand and facial expressions to connect with the listeners. Reverend Jeanette rhythmically rocks back and forth. Sister Elsie flails her arms like she's bringing in airplanes. Mother Naomi braces on the podium. Other sisters pound on the podium for emphasis. Dr. Wanda dances back and forth around the pulpit or preaching area. Actions such as running around the church, jumping up and down, taking off a watch, adjusting glasses, unzipping robes, mopping sweat, gulping water, kicking, stomping, or spinning around are genderless physical manifestations in black preaching. These steps are choreographed according to worship style, experience, denomination, congregational acceptance or expectation, sermon content, and the endowment of the Spirit.

A sampling of research replies is presented according to denominational regulations, ecclesial status, physical attributes, particular ministries, and church attire. Appraisal of videotapes, commercial presentations, and televangelists provide information regarding both attire and physicality of sistah preachers and proclaimers. Five sermons will be evaluated for delivery, congregational engagement, celebration, language, content, attire, and nonverbal language.

Vestments define a clerical office—different robes, stoles, colors, and attendant regalia—and set proclaimers apart from the laity. Vestments provide a "covering" from being in the secular to operating as representatives in the sacred. Vestments are used as marks of authority and validation of the call to ministry. In the early stages of my ministry, everything was made for men. Rarely was a robe designed in a woman's size. There was no accounting for breasts or behinds. The length of the robe was also problematic. Many times I felt like I was playing dress up; so overwhelmed by the amount of fabric and velvet that smothered me, I had difficulty breathing. In the 90s it seemed as though someone realized that women were also preachers and we were here to stay.

The choice of vestment depends on the faith system. Some wear robes because of denominational requirements and personal preferences. In this research pool, rationale for what sistah preachers wear was dependent on theology, type of ministry, geography, church event, culture, and physical comfort or movement. Fifty listed wearing a robe. Thirty-seven indicated that they wear suits. Twenty chose dresses. Afrocentric robes or dresses accounted for twenty replies. Business casual or casual dress was listed on seventeen survey forms. Several women listed other options.

The first group speaks of denominational requirements for vestments. Cynthia Vaughn says, "I wear a robe most often because I usually preach only in churches; it helps to establish official status: one less decision to make about appropriate attire." Cynthia Vaughn is on the staff of one of the larger United Methodist Churches in Georgia.

Rosetta DuBois Gadson of the AME Church in New York says:

> My attire . . . is primarily a black or white robe when preaching the pulpit because it is the tradition of our denomination. I also wear suits of various colors, as in the colors for a particular worship service, and in African dresses and robes which the occasion dictates.

Sister Darlene Smith, also of the AME Church, says:

> Oftentimes, I wear a robe when proclaiming. I guess I wear the robe especially when preaching outside the AME Church to send a message that even though women are proclaimers, the robe helps convey that symbolic meeting of authentication. Although, I know demons can and will use robes. However, there are occasions when I will wear a dress or

a suit and even African attire when I think it is appropriate, because the attire does not validate who you are in Christ and the call to proclaim his word.

Nondenominational proclaimer Raedorah Stewart-Dodd of California says,

[It] depends on denominational expectations. Conservative black robe with no ornamentation, black robe with kente accents, "regular" clothes that are, for me, African dresses (as opposed to tailored or sequined suits). I design and sew most of my vestments and prefer very ornate textiles in simple designs. Seldom wear black or collar, but do when culturally appropriate.

Stephanie Crowder is a Disciple of Christ proclaimer in Tennessee and says,

Most (70 percent) of the time I wear a black robe because I preach during morning worship. If not, I wear a dress or suit. At my home church in Nashville, I preach in a dressy pantsuit since I feel more comfortable wearing such there.

Sermon Analysis

LaTrelle Miller Easterling, AME Elder, preached at a Women's Day service at a Baptist church in Colorado. The pastor of the church did not wear a robe. Reverend Miller Easterling wore a white alb, a purple stole pinned with a flower, stud earrings, medium length hair, a wedding ring, a watch, and two-inch black heels. She sat in the front row on the right side of the altar next to her husband. Directly in front of her was a lectern used to greet visitors and make announcements. She preached from the floor at that lectern. The pastor sat in the pulpit. During the sermon, she remained at the lectern. She is a manuscript preacher and variably maintained eye contact with the congregation. The women in the choir stand were nonresponsive for the first seven minutes. Her language was balanced in imagery, names for God, and textual information. She slowed down for particular words such as "aggrandizement." Body language included stretching out of hands and waving of fingers on each hand for emphasis of the text. She looked mostly to her right, braced at times on the lectern, held her head to the right, dropped her right shoulder for emphasis, and occasionally pointed at the congregation during a difficult section of the sermon. She utilized repetition and alliteration toward the end of the sermon. The sermon was driven by call and response. Her voice ranged from soft and affirming in the beginning to guttural toward the end or in times of dramatic presentation. Transitions were made through celebration or brisk tempo changes. This narrative, expository sermon was about Deborah (Judges 4). She began with background on Deborah as prophetess, judge, leader, and extraordinary woman. The behavioral purpose of the sermon was to keep your mind on the mission regardless of what human beings say about you. Do what God has called you to do.

> Deborah was a wise woman, so that means that she had to have a relationship with God. Because the word says that the fear of the Lord is the beginning of wisdom. Do you fear today? Do you have a relationship with him today? Do you talk to him in the morning and in the noonday and in the evening? Do you know how to call him way [actually, waaaay—elongation of vowels were evident through most of the sermon], way down in the valley when you couldn't hear nobody pray?

She referenced multiple biblical texts to support celebration. She preached a four-point sermon associating Deborah's life with the lives of black women:

1. Deborah knew that God has saving power.
2. Deborah kept her mind on her mission.
3. When called into service, she did not try to give an excuse.
4. Deborah did not major in the minors

"Deborah did what God told her to do," and that is the challenge issued to the women in the congregation. She ends with a classic run of phrases to resolve the purpose and engage the listener.

> If your mission is teaching, then teach.
> If your mission is preaching, then preach.
> If your mission is evangelizing, then evangelize.
> If your mission is serving, then serve.
> If your mission is mentoring, be a mentor.
> If your mission is to clean, then clean.
> If your mission is healing, then heal.

> If your mission is standing in when all else has been done, then stand.
> No matter what others say
> When God says so, it is so
> No matter whether others agree, God agrees
> Nobody else can tell your story
> If you keep your mind on your mission and know your position, God will
> provide.

Keeping her mind on her mission, this sistah preached from the floor with as much vigor as when she preaches from an "official" pulpit. Some sister proclaimers accept the invitation regardless of the location, while others refuse to preach anywhere except the designated pulpit. This is a decision that women must make for themselves. The other item for contemplation is the black church Women's Day pinning of flowers on preachers. Some women accept them and place them on their garments. Others ask to take them later. When sistah proclaimers are able to see their mission about the madness, they can move past the choir robe discussion. The minutia catches some women off guard. Some miss the call on their lives and mission. It seems trite, but pressuring oneself to be someone else is in fact playing dress up until Mom or Dad asks for their clothes back.

Vestments, for some sistahs, represent their ecclesial status. Bishop Nellie Yarborough, of Mt. Calvary Holy Church in Maine, wears special clergy robes with overlays. Apostolic pastor Sherada Allen (Apostolic church in Connecticut) reports, "As a minister, I wear clergy robes to honor the position as one that carries the word and to avoid any distractions while I preach. And also I perspire, so I need to change attire after I'm done ministering." Pastor Shermella G. Egson, of the AME Church in California, says, "[I wear a] robe because it gives me a sense of authenticity. Dark suit because it stands for reverence. No clothing that would bring attention to me. Finally, Bishop Jenniefer Hightower, a nondenominational proclaimer in Maine, explains, "Apostolic vestments because they are the reminder of [the] holiness and excellence of God."

Robes come in many forms—handmade to tailored, Wesleyan to cassock, fitted to flowing—and cost from one hundred to one thousand dollars. Regardless of the pastor's attire, if the word is overshadowed, the preacher is totally naked. Pastor Toni Alvarado wears cassocks, suits, and dresses depending on the occasion.

Sermon Analysis

Pastor Toni Alvarado reports that she wears robes, dresses, and suits when preaching. On this occasion she wore a black cassock with red trim and diamond earrings. She preached a forty-seven-minute topical, narrative, expository sermon entitled "The Power of Prayer and Praise" taken from Acts 13:11-27. She used thorough exegesis on Luke and Acts, the Holy Ghost, power, and praise. She exemplifies the marriage of the academic and the spirit-filled. She shifted through four texts and used a behavioral purpose of the necessity of having both a prayer and a praise life.

> That's interesting because people that do not know how to persevere in prayer don't like going back to the valley. They like to stay on the mountain. But this Christian walk is a series of mountaintops and valleys. There's a theology out there that teaches us that when we get saved, we come to Christ, that we're not going to go through anything. Somebody say the Devil is a lie. The truth is, baby, you are not going to skip from mountaintop to mountaintop. For every mountaintop experience, you got to go in the valley. The mountaintop experiences are wonderful but you can't live on the top of the mountain. Because no one would die if the only thing you have is the mountaintop experience. We have got to go down to the valley where the life is. Oh, come on, somebody. I wish I had two or three people that will thank God for the valley experience. We just want to shout about the mountaintop experience. But we would die if we [stayed] on the mountain, baby. You got to go down to the valley. Does anyone know I'm talking about valley experiences this morning? There's no vegetation on top of the mountain. There is no life on top of the mountain. You see, mountaintop Christians are shallow.

This manuscript preacher uses a handheld microphone that she constantly transferred from side to side. Mannerisms include using the full pulpit space and engaging the other ministers, the choir, and the congregation when talking, pacing back and forth across the pulpit, particularly to her right, articulating the refrain of "Come on, somebody" and wiping the side of her mouth with her fingers. After a reiteration of her purpose and her sermon points, she leads the congregation in a celebrative moment. She then transitions to a quiet invitation to discipleship. Wiping the mouth, fiddling with hair, loosening a collar, shaking shoulders, stretching neck, popping knuckles, and rapid blinking are just a few of the mannerisms exhibited by preachers. Most are unconscious movements to release tension or to quell excitement. I have been told that I roll my shoulders or smile when I approach a transition or hard sermon point. I did not believe it until I watched a tape. For some reason I have been preaching barefoot for the past six or so years. I feel more connection to the Holy Spirit and feel "grounded" in God's presence after I take them off. The urge to remove them happens about three to five minutes before the preaching moment. Explicable and inexplicable idiosyncrasies are present in both men and women who proclaim. They are as varied as the chosen attire.

Sermon Analysis

Michelle Loyd Paige describes her attire in this matter: "Oh, I like to wear the Sunday suits you see in the Essence catalog or JCPenney Fashion Influences. I don't wear the hats (they would fly off), but the big glitter earrings, high heels, usually have my nails done, and usually have the sistah hairdo—French twist or bun with height and tons of gel!" She proclaims at a women's conference. Using Isaiah 61:1 and Romans 8:5-9, she talks about depression ("sleeping with sorrow"). She wears a black suit with a gold braid down the sleeve, white shell, heavy gold necklace, high French roll, rhinestone buttons, and diamond earrings. She began the discourse with shoes on and then removed them after ten minutes. She had a lapel microphone to which she was tethered. This became obvious when she tried to leave her notes on the podium and move toward the women. She walked back and forth behind the podium as she worked from a manuscript. She kept moving her hands up to her face in a contemplative manner. She summarized the behavioral purpose of overcoming depression in an acronym for RENEW.

R—recognize your unbeliefs and doubts
E—empty your trash
N—neutralize the opposition
E—earnestly desire the presence of God
W—walk as an act of belief

She spoke with dramatic flair and effective modulation and embodied phrases such as "How can I lift my hands when the burdens of life are calling my name? They've gotten so close that they even call you by your nickname." She knew her audience. This sociologist read the text inclusively, saying, "Because there are women in here, we're going to change the gender, but it's all the same." She resolved the moment by referencing Hebrews 11 and asking the listeners to be self-reflective.

Choice of clothing is like the choice of language. Some of the sistahs unapologetically use exclusively masculine images of God and humanity, some use a blend of images, and others use inclusive language. Language is personal. Further research on theological language usage in sermons is required but is outside the scope of this particular project.

Physical attributes often dictate the choice of dress. Some preachers use the lap cloth as a means of modest covering. This eighteen-by-eighteen usually lace-trimmed, color-coordinated cloth is sold in Christian bookstores, homemade, or is sold in specialty boutiques. The point is to cover the preacher's knees if her skirt is short and she is sitting on a pulpit or even in the first row of the sanctuary. There are men who sit with their legs sprawled out, exposing their genital areas, but do not use lap cloths. I have also seen women wearing almost ankle-length skirts use the cloth. The lap cloth must be repositioned when the women stand up or move abruptly. I suppose it serves a purpose, but it seems to imply that women do not know how to sit modestly.

Regina Groff of the AME Church in Colorado says of dressing for proclaiming,

> At my home church I wear a robe because it is protocol. When I preach outside my home church, it depends on the setting. Sometimes, I wear a suit or dress because it's more appropriate. It seems to be a little pretentious to wear a robe in a setting like a hotel or even the fellowship hall. If I am at another church, I carry my robe and seek the direction of the pastor or ministers of the church. If they wear robes, I will. If they do not, and my skirt is long enough to cover my knees, I won't. If my skirt is not long enough, I may go ahead and wear my robe. But typically I wear a long skirt.

And Bridget Piggue, of the Presbyterian church in Georgia, says,

> My attire when proclaiming is primarily a robe. When I do not wear robe, I wear a suit that is not too "form-fitting." Why? I basically do not want to draw attention to my "curves." I'm fairly shapely and want to be sensitive not to draw attention to myself in any manner. I do not feel stifled by it but do want to be conscious of what my goals are when

197

preaching, not one of which is to have people focus on my attire. I still, however, want to look nice in whatever I choose to wear.

Body shape, height, muscular physique, hair length and style, weight, and general health contribute to one's dress as well as one's mobility. Assistant pastor Zelia Brown-Harvey, from the AME in Georgia, says: "I prefer a robe when I preach. If my hair is long, I wear it up. The robe symbolizes the covering of me so that it takes the focus off me and keeps it on God." Thelma Chambers, president of the Progressive Baptist Women's Department in Oklahoma, relates, "Usually clergy robe/attire. It releases me from self-consciousness about my appearance." Physicality determines Zina Jacque's dress: "Unless it is an informal setting, I wear robe. As a large woman, I feel that it is important to cover up those body parts that might have extra movement and distract those who are listening." Mobility and congregational concerns drive Pastor Betty Hanna-Witherspoon's (of the AME in California) clothing selection, "Preaching in a robe because it gives me freedom of movement that street clothes don't give, and the robe keeps the congregation's mind off the pastor's attire and on the message."

Keeping the congregation's mind off the pastor's attire is a difficult proposition at times. As I watch my sistah proclaimer, even I—a clothes lover from way back—have to shake my head. I see tassels, spangles, fringe, feathers, rhinestones, 1980s Patti Labelle hair, four-inch earrings, five-inch talons, and some of the worst shoes on the planet (another one of my vices). I also see all kinds of head coverings ranging from lace doilies to kufis. The "church lady" suit with or without the "church lady" hat is a contemporary ensemble. Hair styles run the gamut—locks, braids, Caesar cuts, Afros, twists, shoulder lengths, lacquered French rolls, natural, relaxed, platinum blond, and salt-and-pepper gray. Heavy makeup or no hint of cosmetics is the order of the day. Earrings are hoops, studs, drop, button, costume, and diamond. Fabrics are wool, cotton, silk, fur, leather, linen, and polyester. Sistah preachers dress in black, dark blues, and browns. Some wear three-inch heels with matching hosiery, while others opt for flats and basic brown or white hosiery. There is a struggle between ultra-feminine and masculine dress. Which is appropriate? Is there some middle ground? The choir robe debate continues. The preacher should have a well-prepared and delivered sermon for the listener to see past her attire, regardless of the choices.

Considering how the presence of a woman in the pulpit affects the current and next generation of women in the church, attire may serve a sociopolitical interest. Melinda Contreras-Byrd, of the AME Church in New Jersey, says,

> I usually wear a robe in churches—no worries about how I dressed. I think it's important for little girls and women to see women in clerical vestments . . . for the sake of the occasion. In other settings, I usually wear African or other ethnic garb—long and loose-fitting for movement and comfort and cultural pride.

Lisa Rhodes, Dean of the Chapel at Spelman College in Atlanta, preaches in an expository, narrative style with a few rhetorical elements. Using the title "A Test of Faith," she works the Matthew text on Jesus walking on the water. Wearing a black robe with Afrocentric stole, goddess braids that ended in a French roll, gold-framed glasses, tasteful makeup, stud earrings, two rings, and a watch, she begins by asking the congregation to repeat the sermon title after her. This is a rhetorical motif she repeatedly employs during the sermon. Her vocalics range from strong emphasis on content to almost whisper for effect. Nonverbal communication (use of hands and body) was in line with vocal gymnastics. From time to time, she smiled at an ironic point she stated. Facial expression was engaging as she smiled at times, looking at the audience over glasses. She read from a manuscript; however, eye contact was evident the entire time. Idiosyncrasies included clinching her fist, splaying her hands, and other bodily gestures, including moving her papers. Toward the end of the sermon, the body language followed the verbs in the sermon such as howling, walking, tossing, or being quick. She demonstrated an effective use of pausing and deliberate articulation for clarity. Alliteration as well as pictorial language was evident during the sermon. At the section about walking on the waves, her hands emulate the rolling of the waves. Exegesis was evident with background given immediately on the focus text. Rhetorical questions pepper throughout in order to call the listener to the refrain, "A Test of Faith."

> How many of you have experienced the waves embedded in the storms of life?
> How many of you have had a moment, or perhaps a season, in which you have been battered and bruised by the conditions of life, by the swelling waves of financial hardship or by an abusive relationship?
> How many of you have been beaten down by the cold hands of discrimination, racism, racial profiling, sexism, ageism, or classism?

If only you were a better man or woman, if only you had more money, if only you had more education, if only you worked harder. Yet if only, if only, if only, if only.

She ended the discourse with a litany of names for Jesus associated with black preaching: Lily of the Valley, Bright and Morning Star, bridge over troubled water, and the same Jesus. Vocal fatigue was evident during stronger emphasis in celebration and repetition near the end of the sermon. Transition was effective as she ended by singing "My Hope Is Built on Nothing Less."

Two sistahs reported wearing clerical collars. In terms of dress, one sistah from the American Baptist Church in New Jersey, Bernadette Glover-Williams, said, "It varies; most consistently, a collar whether a robe is worn or not. The collar reminds me of the authority and weight of responsibility that accompanies ordination." Lenora Nicholas Welch (Progressive Baptist in California) prefers the predetermined attire of ministry. "I usually wear a robe and ethnic stole. Sometimes I wear a suit and clerical collar. It is professional. I see it as "uniform," which identifies the work I am doing. Twenty years ago, when I entered ministry, collars for women were the order of the day. It was "suggested" by female seminary colleagues that I purchase a collar for hospital calls. Because of my physical attributes and the fact that, at that time, shirts were tailored for men only, I wore the shirt once. I discovered that sick people just want someone to pray; rarely do they critique the fashion of the minister. Like robes, collars are individual choices.

The dress of laywomen who proclaim varies also. What is your attire? Bible teacher Kim Martin of the Pentecostal church in Colorado says, "Long skirt, long sleeve blouse, or jacket (suit). I do not want people to focus on what I am wearing, but I want them to hear what God is saying through me." Richelle Fry Skinner, a woman with a passion for youth ministry and from the AME Church in Colorado, reports, "Usually casual dress. I work with young people and I try to support them in their own environment." And Carrie Dunson, a Baptist adult class teacher in Missouri, relates, "Business casual because my location is the Midwest, which is on the casual side of dressing for most events. Less distracting." A Missionary Baptist woman from Georgia, Dorcas Ford Doward works in youth and women's ministries stipulates, "My attire when proclaiming is usually what I have on at the time. But in the classroom, it is usually a suit (skirt) not pants. The reason for this is my upbringing and teaching that when you proclaim God's word in front of a class, you present yourself accordingly." Finally, Marcia Williams of the AME Church in Colorado, a woman who writes plays, coordinates music presentations, and serves routinely as mistress of ceremonies at church events, writes, "From be-jeaned to bejeweled. My attire is a function of the venue, audience, and personal inclination."

Regardless of ordination status, some women opt for suits or dresses. Yet another group opts for Afrocentric dress. Each is a distinctive vessel with the same purpose. In answer to the question, the location of the preaching event and its designation determine the attire also. Black churches are notorious for color coordination for Women's Days. I imagine I have either a stole, dress, or suit in every conceivable color. My collection of Afrocentric garb began long before my call into ministry. It represents part of my heritage and is comfortable. As I mature, I find that comfort is essential. Robes seem to be the "ensemble" for most Methodist services. The sistahs share their fashion sense.

Concerning her proclaiming attire, Carolyn DuBose of the Baptist church in Michigan says,

> My attire is usually an all-white suit because of the Women's Day speaking that I do. Otherwise, I proclaim in regular business attire especially when in the workshop, conference, prison ministry, or classroom setting.

JoAnne Robertson, a Baptist woman proclaimer in Tennessee, reports,

> If I'm not wearing my robe (which usually means I'm not preaching at Metropolitan), I have on one of four outfits depending on season and occasion: white solid, red, black, or royal blue dress. I like my attire to be relatively simple; if you're wearing flamboyant clothes, then you need to preach that much harder otherwise folk will be looking at your outfit, not listening to the word. I think it is especially true for women proclaimers. I love clothes and fashion. I also don't always want to fall into "working my outfit" instead of preaching the text.

Cultural identity is another attire aspect. The culture in which one grows, lives, or identifies with also affects the dress. Afrocentric dress has to do with identity with one's heritage. Although growing liturgical acceptance is on the horizon, many still avoid or dismiss Afrocentric dress. T. Renée Crutcher, a Baptist proclaimer in Georgia, says,

> My dress varies. It can be African attire, suits, dresses, dressy pantsuits. It depends on what I feel and where I am. I'm not terribly conservative

or necessarily a conformist. I wear jewelry that I feel will not be too distracting, but don't limit my jewelry to small conservative pieces. Because of my height, I wear heels so I can see above the pulpit. If I'm inclined to remove my shoes, I do or do not wear hosiery. When wearing long African attire, I will not [wear hosiery].

Pleshette Harris is a nondenominational proclaimer in Georgia and had this to say about her attire:

I will dress according to the setting and occasion. At my monthly women's prayer and discipleship meetings, I will wear a nice dress outfit or nice pants and shirt, or I may wear some jeans and a jacket. I dress this way because this is who Pleshette Harris is, and I have to be who God has made me to be, and not according to what others expect of me.

Another proclaimer, Roslyn Satchel of the AME Church in Georgia, says,

The person of the preacher sends a message that ought not contradict or send a mixed message. I am an Afrocentric woman and preacher whose ministry is both Afrocentric and Christian—informed by an African Jesus Christ and African ancestors and our "mighty cloud of witnesses."

Self-disclosure by black women goes beyond what they wear. The vulnerability and transparency in sharing one's past before salvation, health crises, family difficulties, childlessness, poverty, oppression, or addictions is common in the proclamation of black women. Through tears and shouts for joy at the victory, black women proclaimers share the stories of their deliverance.

Sermon Analysis

In "Hungry Hearts with a Passion for His Presence," based on Luke 7:36-50, all of which is read before preaching, Pastor Diana Branch reveals her deliverance eighteen years prior to the service. She gives a general background to the text and then launches into a narration about hunger and passion for Christ. After a celebration associated with the song, she settles into a slow and deliberate rhythm. Language and imagery is decidedly masculine based on her preference for the King James

Version of the text. She is dressed in a black robe and dress. Her hair is in a French roll, with tendrils on each side. Holding a cordless microphone in one hand and a white towel in the other, she walks back and forth in a short pace. Her conversational tone is infused with elongated vowels, pitch breaks, pauses with deep inhalations (Whew!), and stresses on initial syllables. Mannerisms include wiping the corner of her mouth and placing her hands on her hips. "Oh, don't make me tell my story," "You don't know like I know what he's done for me," and "Honey, you don't know the half of the testimony" proceed her personal testimony about eighteen years of deliverance. She provides a major critique of church folk, "Religious folks always either evaluating or speculating but not participating," because "they are trying to figure out if my praise is real." She ends the forty-two-minute topical sermon on a decrescendo, inviting the people to unlock the passion for Christ.

Passion for Christ is sometimes demonstrated in the inflection of the voice and the movement of the body. The minister's body language, her approach to the pulpit, the walk between the chair and the podium, the rigidity or looseness of the body, the facial expressions, her willingness to "get ugly for Jesus," and her use of the space at the podium—wherever it is located—speaks loudly about the confidence level and investment in the text. Claudette Copeland proved this point in a sermon before a national women's conference in Atlanta. "Seek Thy Face," based on Psalm 27:1-7, challenged women to establish an obedient relationship with God rather than with a person. She cautioned them against becoming "conference junkies." In a dark blue two-piece dress, with jewels on the button placer and cuff, short, feathered hair, and black pumps, she strode to the Plexiglas podium with self-assurance. Vocalics produced were emphasis on elongated words, effective pause, elongation of vowels (aaa as in anguish), and variable volume. She is a manuscript preacher and used a handheld microphone. Vernacular phrases incorporated throughout the forty-plus-minute presentation were:

God said don't preach about women today
Come on and go with me
Y'all got to help me stay up in here
I can hear you all
Somebody say . . .
That's all right, baby
You better call somebody

I know I wasn't gonna get no help right there
Touch your pretty self and say . . .
Put your feet in the stirrups, baby.
Such a pretty self and talk about your own self
You want circus religion
I'm fixing to get out of your way
I'm closing
You ain't gonna help me in here, I see

Mannerisms observed were walking back and forth in the pulpit area, leaning forward toward the listener, a hop interspaced with running backward from the podium, bending at the knee when acting out the narrative, patting the back of her head as if to smooth her hair, and consistent eye contact with the congregation. Her controlling image was that of an exterminator removing squirrels from the attic of her home. She paralleled the process to her behavioral purpose of seeking God's face.

1. Begin to see self rather than what is going on around you
2. Call for self-examination.
3. It's going to make the demands on you
4. Look around and get rid of your stuff
5. Need God to pull out your stuff and help you throw it away
6. Seal off the places where stuff keeps getting in
7. Set some traps to get rid of the stuff

Call and response was sustained by repetition of "Clean it out." Her testimony of recovery from a life-threatening illness and how she learned to seek God's face in the depths of that experience places ended with a prayer and invitation.

Chapter Summary

The symbols are everywhere. They stand for what once was and will be. Through the years, women have been symbols of sin in the eyes of some "God-fearing folk" who think all women should be shrouded and invisible. There are those who believe that women are created in partnership with men and have voices, minds, and gifts just like men. They move to open the way for individuals to confess and profess their faith in their own way. Women can dress up in ways someone else dictates or make their own choices; in their nakedness, they are still women. Sistah proclaimers can stand sedately and whisper a word or vigorously and yell; after the sermon, they are still women. The choir robe committee refuses to adjourn. The choreographer is still in the studio. The word of God is still alive.

"Spiritual Makeovers for Cosmetic Christians"

This sermon was preached at a combination Pentecost Sunday and Women's Day service at Bethel AMEC in Harlem in 2002. It is a challenge to be true to who we are.

Pentecost Sunday:

- The age of fulfillment or the coming of the kingdom of God is at hand
- Ministry, death, and resurrection of Jesus has prepared the way
- Jesus sits at the right hand of God
- The Holy Spirit in the church is a sign of Christ's present power and glory
- The second coming of Christ is promised
- Repentance, the metanoia, the turning from sin and turning to God leads to forgiveness and salvation
- In order to grow in faith and love, we must accept the cleaning power of the Holy Spirit and learn to love in the manner God has prescribed.

Two passages of attention address this need to seek perfection.

Old Testament Reading: Psalm 51:10

Create in me a clean heart, O God, and put a new and right spirit within me.

New Testament Reading: 1 Corinthians 6:19-20

19 Or do you not know that your body is a temple of the Holy Spirit within you, which you have from God, and that you are not your own?

20 For you were bought with a price; therefore glorify God in your body.

Lord, prepare me [get me ready]
To be a sanctuary *[Sanctus]*, set me aside, Lord, move whatever is not right out of me
Pure and holy [*qadash*, separateness, withdrawal]
Tried and true [tested, refined, as in the process of making steel]
With thanksgiving [gratitude]
I'll be a living
Sanctuary
Lord, for you

How many times have we heard these lyrics, sung with passion and believability?

Sanctification is the state to proper functioning.
　　To sanctify someone or something is to set that person, place, or thing apart for use as the designer intended.
　　Eyeglasses are sanctified to improve sight.
In a theological sense [The Greek word sanctification], *hagiamos* means holiness.
　　Persons are set apart to be used for God's purpose in God's kingdom—endowed with God's Spirit.
　　When we say we'll be sanctuaries,
　　In essence, we pledge to present our bodies to God for cleansing, renovation, overhaul, molding, and making after God's will.
The words sound beautiful on Sunday in the congregation of the saints or when things are going well in our lives, but what about after church
　　After the people have gone home
　　When we hit that first bump on Monday morning
　　Grace can change us from who or what we are
　　To whom and what God wants us to become
When we look at ourselves in the spiritual mirror and see what's beneath the surface
　　Our inner beings
　　Our true intentions
　　Our character/reputation

Who are we?

    Are we worthy of God's love?

        Are we able to show loving-kindness, goodwill, and compassion wherever we go and with whomever we meet?

I invite us this morning to take a good look into our spiritual reflections, our sanctified mirrors

        To take a look at the women, persons, we are before we begin to cover up our scars and stars

        The persons we are when we first wake up, before the makeup.

        The deep down, really us before the cover-up.

The persons we are on Sunday afternoon

    Monday morning

    or Saturday night

    Rather than our Sunday-morning cleaned-up-nicely, looking good selves.

Take a little time personally to assess needs and ask for a little help from God's cleansing power.

If we are honest with ourselves, most of us are from time to time cosmetic individuals

We have parts of our lives we do not want anyone to see

    know

    glimpse

    because we think they will not like us or accept us if they know who we really are.

We have been conditioned by the world to present false faces to hide our vulnerable selves.

We even are taught by the world that there are standards of beauty we should attain, or else we are of less value.

We are even tempted to cover up the temple God has given us just so we can fit in.

Some feature, blemish, that we don't like

This leads to dermabrasion, liposuction, plastic surgery, miracle diets, body shapers, artificial nails, extra hair, false eyelashes, hair color, and so on

It is a wonder we remember what we really look like

    When was the last time we saw ourselves as we really are, cellulite and all?

Black women spend over $7.4 billion a year on cosmetics, hair care, manicures, pedicures, and massages.

I remember reciting
Paul Lawrence Dunbar, 1896, "We Wear the Mask"

> *We wear the mask that grins and lies,*
> *It hides our cheeks and shades our eyes,*
> *This debt we pay to human guile;*
> *With torn and bleeding hearts we smile,*
> *And mouth with myriad subtleties*
>
> . . . .
> *We wear the mask*

Black women have the panache to make an outfit work whether we have
$1 or $1 million.
  We will pay $35 a month on a layaway because we saw another sis-
    ter in an outfit and thought we would look better in it.
  We try to lose fifty pounds in one month to go to a party where the
    people will not remember us the next day.
  Some even purchase an outfit, leave the tags in, and return it the day
    after the special day so others will complement their fashion
    sense.
  Some of us are wearing borrowed clothing today because we put the
    outfit on a charge card we will not pay off for another fifty years.
After all, we have a social image to uphold.
  No one needs to know we can't afford to keep up the front.
For many, our service depends on how good we look.
  Not on how much God has given us
Historically, black women have presented their best self to the world.
  Not letting too many people know them for fear they would take
    advantage.
We shield our inner selves
  Our secrets
  Our pain
  Our abilities
  Our beliefs
  Our needs
  Sometimes our faith
With loud voices or no voices
  Rolling hips or shuffling feet
  Expressive hand movements

Head snaps
Downcast eyes
Winning smiles
Disgruntled frowns
Extravagant dress or understated shrouds.
Forgetting that God sees and knows all about us.
Our actions, mannerisms, deportment, and vocal gymnastics are often cosmetic, cover-ups, facades, masks to protect us from "others"
Cosmetic Christians
    1. cosmetic: skilled in adornment
    2. done or made for the sake of appearance
    3. not substantive: superficial
Many of us wear the mask every Sunday.
    We check our brains at the door and do whatever is asked of us, forgetting we are to do what God says do.
    We say we are part of the praise and worship team that affirms the goodness of God in our lives
    But shy away from individual confessions and professions of faith.
    Following whatever seems popular
    Saving up hundreds of dollars each year to be loosed as if God did not already set us free when we confessed Jesus as Lord
Christian women religiously watching Oprah and Dr. Phil for tips on how to be in relationships, while ignoring the model of living in a long-term relationship without intention of marriage
Afraid to ask God for a blessing because we feel so unworthy.
Sometimes we get caught up in the collective effervescence of worship and do not examine our personal relationship with God.
    Hoping that no one will ask what we really believe because we will have to make up an answer or parrot what we heard on television.
    Some of us just like to get lost in the crowd so we will not have to use our gifts and talents for the building of the kingdom of God.
    We say we are bringing it all to the altar of sacrifice to lay, to take our burdens to the Lord and leave them there, but we pick them up on the way back to our seats because we have become comfortable with grief.
We can all easily become cosmetic Christians, forgetting God's favor.
    We start out brimming with trust and utter dependence on God but begin to hit peaks and valleys, slowly sinking into automatic pilot.

No investment, no duty, just doing what everyone else is doing.
Going along to get along
Saying one thing and doing another
So busy trying to look like Christians we forget how to be a Christian
Trying to please the world and neglecting to shine for Jesus
We forget that humans look on the outside but that God looks at our hearts
God knows who we are beneath all our cosmetics
God is not pleased with cosmetic Christians
Cosmetic Christians—In the word, but the word is not in us.
Bible carriers, but not Bible readers
Choir members deaf to the tones of God's mercy
Clean robes, but soiled souls
Believers on Sunday in church, but doubters on Monday at work
Cosmetic Christians
Hypocritical lifestyles
Impersonating Christians
Counterfeit charity based in applause
Masquerading as missionaries as long as we do not have to touch a diseased person
Simulating support as long as we get to be chair
Cosmetic Christians
Pretending to be who we say we are, falsifying information
Check your driver's license
Age, weight, height, hair color
Purporting abilities
Look at your resume, what have we finessed to get something?
Have we prayed for someone lately, or do we prey on everyone?
Cosmetic Christians
We cover up life's bumps and bruises, we mask the physical distress, and we drape our financial difficulties with new wardrobes
We hide our eyes from the light of truth
We pretend that we have not sinned and come short of God's glory
That all we need to do is apply a little cover-up and everything will be all right.
Cosmetics, carriage, conversation, costumes, coiffures—clean on the outside but what about our inner temple.
More concerned about our reputation than our soul's salvation.

Reputation—that's who others think we are.

Character—that's who we really are

We have allowed so much junk to clutter our temples that God's Spirit is often blocked from dwelling within us.

> Weighed down with junk and unable to run the race due to sheer physical and spiritual exhaustion

Beloved, God's spirit, cannot abide or reside in superficial, cosmetic temples.

Paul cautions us about our responsibility for these vessels God has gifted us with:

> *Or didn't you realize that your body is a sacred place, the place of the Holy Spirit? (The Message)*

Before we can proclaim that we are women united in prayer, faith, and love, we each must undergo spiritual makeovers, refurbishing the wonder and marvelous temples God has given us

We must give up the lifestyles of cosmetic Christians

> Pretending to be in love and charity with our sisters and brothers, pretending to love the pastor, pretending to do the work for God, all the time waiting for our names to be called

> Pretending to be better than everyone else, forgetting that all have sinned and come short

> Professing being saved, sanctified, filled with the Holy Ghost, until after the service in the parking lot or on the sidewalk, sometimes even in the fellowship hall or back of the sanctuary, the cursing and drama begins

Time for a spiritual makeover

If we want to be fit for God's kingdom, we must stand under God's spiritual microscope,

> If we wish to be sanctuaries of God's Spirit, undergo spiritual MRIs

> Head to toe, front to back, top to bottom, inside and outside

> If we desire to reach the goal, we must lay it all on the altar of sacrifice

> Submit our bodies—our hearts, souls, minds, and strength—to spiritual power washing

We need to take off the societal makeup and become clean vessels for Christ, worthy to receive the gift of life.

> Every crack, crease, and crevice of our beings must be cleaned.

Clean [Hebrew, *tawher*]

To be pure, bright, uncontaminated
To remove all foreign matter
To prepare
To free from flaws
To heal
To alleviate temptation
To make whole
David, who knew about being a servant of God but slipping back into lives that are not pleasing to God, gave us a model request for spiritual makeovers
Create in me a clean heart, and renew a right sprit within me.
Soak me in your laundry and I'll come clean, scrub me and I'll have a snow-white life. [The Message]
If we want to be made over, we must let God remove all that is not of God.
God chooses the cleaning products.
For some of us, God has to use special chemicals to thoroughly cleanse us
Cleaning agents
Not Noxzema, Oil of Olay, Mary Kay, Avon, Prescriptives, Iman, Clearasil, Dove, Safeguard, Fashion Fair, Flori Roberts, Clarians, Givenchy, Cheer, Tide, or Clorox—these are topical agents.
God uses deep-cleaning, grace-filled methods on our spiritual houses.
Kindness, leniency, generosity, pardon, reprieve, benevolence, love, goodness
Enables us to receive the promise of God's unmerited blessings, God's grace.
We have to take off our old selves and put on new clothes that fit us individually
Spiritual makeovers involve
Pruning
Cutting
Tearing
Changing
Reforming
Touching us with a penetrating cleansing power
We all need an appointment at God's spa
Don't even consult your day planner or checkbook, and make an appointment now.
No waiting

This spa is always open

Take the full treatment

Submit our hearts, minds, souls, bodies, spirit so God can

Power vacuum the hatred and malice from our hearts that sour our souls. Allow us to look within and stop criticizing others.

It's me, it's me, it's me, O Lord, standing in the need of prayer.

Reupholster the spiritual furniture; broken, wounded spirits; feeble minds; lying lips; tattling tongues; envious eyes; itching ears; cold hearts

Remove the decaying coverings of hearts and minds; apply tapestries of love, joy, peace, patience, gentleness, meekness, goodness, and self-control

Sweep away the cobwebs of self-deception, when we critique the faults of friends, while problems are perched precariously on the precipice of our own lives

Dust the little places we store the grudges we refuse to let go. You know, that thing that happened five, ten, twenty, forty years ago.

Flush out the prayers against others while be beg God to forgive us our sins

Liquefy the greasy buildup on the windows of our souls that block the light of our blessings and our view of the cross

Demolish the false walls that partition people based on pathetic power games and politically based oppression growing out of sexism, racism, classism, heterosexism, handicappism, ageism.

Scrub away, excoriate the idea that we created ourselves or have the right to abuse, misuse, beat, cure, demean, or kill another child of God. We did not create a thing and do not own it. God gave us dominion and care of the world, not ownership

Patch up leaks caused by wear and tear of anger and stupid controversies

Haul away the garbage that emanates from our mouths, defiles our bodies—cursing, grumbling, complaints, gossip, and criticism—acting like hell Monday through Saturday and pretending to be pure and holy on Sunday—saved, sanctified, and filled with the Holy Ghost.

Today is the day beloved daughters of dust and divinity, sons of soul and salvation

Clean up our cosmetic exteriors and renovate our decaying insides so we can be the sanctuary, the temples of the Holy Spirit

Take off the mask
Empty venom bags
Cancel reservations at the "oh, poor me hotel"
Trash messianic complexes
Shake off the inability to say no
Lay down self-destructive behaviors
Soak away the snobbish spirituality
Lay aside anything that slows or distracts or confuses or blurs or impedes our view and pursuit of the goal God has placed before us.

Time for a Spiritual Makeover
We can accept the pardon of our sins—that's positional perfection
God will make a change, if we are willing to be made over

The blood of Jesus shed for us will enable us to discard, remove
The foundation of old relationships
The eyeliner of old anger
The mascara of old rage
The lipliner of old malice
The lipstick of old slander
The blush of old filthy language
The powder of old impurity
The wig of old immorality
The perfume of old lust
The deodorant of old greed
The lotion of old jealousy
The mouthwash of old lies
The gel of old thoughts

We can benefit from working in faithful ministry—that's relative *perfection*

Love never gives up
Cares more for others than for self
Doesn't want what it can't have
Doesn't strut
Doesn't have a swelled head
Doesn't force herself on others
Isn't always "me first"
Doesn't fly off the handle
Doesn't keep score of the sins of others
Doesn't revel when others grovel
Takes pleasure in the flowering of truth

Puts up with anything
Trusts God always
Always looks for the best
Never looks back
Keeps going to the end
Love never dies
We can prepare to receive the gift of eternal life—*that's ultimate perfection—New Jerusalem, already but not yet*
Looking toward Jesus, the author and finisher of our faith
 Then we can stand in the congregation of the saints
  Anchored in the faith of our mothers
  No longer cosmetic Christians
  Clean vessels pressing toward the mark of God's calling
  Looking at models of all the women who have gone before us
  seeking love, faith, and unity through prayer
God will bless us with
 Second Chance of Eve
 Willingness of Sarah
 Belief of Hagar
 Nurture of Jocabed
 Devotion of Zipporah
 Healing of Miriam
 Ingenuity of Shiprah and Puah
 Fearlessness of Rahab
 Beauty of Sheba
 Decency of Vashti
 Courage of Esther
 Obedience of the Widow of Zarapheth
 Selflessness of Ruth
 Justice of Deborah
 Fortitude of Naomi
 Vision of Anna
 Patience of the Woman with the Issue
 Hospitality of Martha
 Gratitude of Magdalene
 Sermon of the Woman at the Well
 Teaching of Priscilla
 Diplomacy of the Candace
 Inquisitiveness of Mary

Charity of Dorcas
Faith of Lydia
Thankfulness of the Widow of Nain
Wisdom of Elizabeth
Resourcefulness of Joanna
Song of Mary, the Mother of Jesus
Passion of Big Sis
Boldness of Baby Sis
Grace of Auntie
Dignity of Big Mamma
Anointing of Grandmother
Foresight of Ma Dear
Mercy of Mother
Love of Jesus
It's time (5X) for a Spiritual Makeover

CHAPTER SEVEN

NEW SONGS

W hen I hear the promise of deliverance and change in Psalm 98:1, I cannot help complying with the director. We are entreated to sing a new song. God has done great, wonderful, marvelous things in our lives. No matter what we have encountered in this life, God is in control. Our foremothers sang with weary throats, but they kept on singing. They sang of hope, liberation, spiritual endowment, new life, and the ultimate removal of all obstacles to their personhood. They understood that God and God alone called them and made room for them. God kept them safe as they traveled around the country, leaving families, churches, and societal standards in order to do the will of God. They modeled the necessity of singing in the key of G-O-D, for only the name of God saves. Yes, some dressed in heavy, dark frocks and looked and sounded like men, but they were willing to do whatever was necessary to "say a word." The foremothers never said their lives were easy—some died all alone—but the promised reward for obedience was in sight.

Like their foremothers, many contemporary black women have creatively moved beyond the "Big Chair Syndrome." Many know that all ground is holy. God is everywhere. The tremendous power of the pulpit in the black church tradition can be liberating or oppressive. It is, in fact, the freedom of the black pulpit that enabled cries for justice and civil rights to ring throughout this country and around the world. Why not for black women proclaimers everywhere? Thankfully, there are denominations that welcome women and recognize their call to be singers, speakers, evangelists, teachers, and preachers. Contemporary daughters of Zelophehad sing whole notes and half notes, but they are singing. These sistahs seek their inheritance boldly and quietly. They sing the Lord's song in strange and familiar lands. They take rests to deepen their relationship with God, realizing who they are and who has called them "for such a time as this." These sistahs come to the table prepared and fully engaged in the preaching moment. Not everyone is a stellar preacher, but they come with a passion for the word of God. They come in choir robes or no robes. The come fully choreographed or prone to stillness. They come with raw throats filled with passion and fleshy healthy throats filled with love. Sistah proclaimers come as women of God ready, willing, and able to do the work. They are no better or worse than any other preacher, male, female, black, White, Asian, Hispanic, or multiracial. The are distinctive vessels because they are black, female, Christian, and live in a society that is still maturing in gender, racial, social, economic, and political equality. Their passions and thematic thrust are influenced by their social location just like anyone else. They do not fit a mold. They are as diverse as they are in number. Laboring under the unction of the Spirit, sistahs are sight-reading, listening to, and singing new songs, for God has and is doing marvelous things.

This research project has been, for me, a sistah proclaimer, a cleansing event. It has been a burden in that I desired to honor black women who trusted me to handle their words and ideas with care. It has been a privilege because I have been afforded the opportunity to illuminate the gifts and graces of black women in the preaching moment. It has been deeply moving as I read over survey answers and reviewed taped information. It has been a spiritual event as I read the joy and pain between each line and behind each expression. I desired to include all the responses that each sistah so painstakingly contributed but realized that is would take me into retirement. Selecting a representative sampling for each chapter was emotionally and intellectually taxing. Once again, I had to rely on prayer and direction of the Spirit of God. I realize that this is neither a sociological nor an academic method, but I am a black woman and that is what most of us do first.

The initial proposal was a book on how different black women preachers are from black men preachers. As the information arrived, I decided that I wanted this to be neither a contentious gender politics work nor an apologetic for black women. I knew I wanted to write more than a sermon collection without explaining preaching elements. After much prayer, that behavioral purpose began to take shape. This book is a survey about how and why black women prepare and present God's word.

The evolution of this homiletical task took me to places I did not anticipate. The difficulty mailing surveys following the events of last fall were aggravating. Mail did not reach some sistahs. Mail was returned as "no longer at this address" from women I speak with at least once a month. In the next project, I will resort to E-mail or personal contact only. The number of surveys distributed was due to anticipated slow return. I also desired to reach as many women from different denominations as possible. Their reasons vary from too busy, forgot to mail the information, lost it, or there was no response. Only one person wrote me and said that she did not want to participate due to her belief system.

This is one of the first homiletical research projects using a large number of "live" cohorts. Black women, as a rule, do not tape themselves unless they have an opportunity to preach at churches with tape ministries. Some of the women called to say they did not have anything worth showing but sent manuscripts. As mentioned in chapter 3, I was amazed at the preferred translations and exclusive language and imagery for God. Perhaps I have been teaching too long. Maybe my passion for justice and equality has clouded my vision.

In each chapter, the women speak for themselves as I critique a homiletical task based on the forms in the Appendix, Charts 6 and 7. Black women's voices have been muted in ecclesial settings and even in some academic circles, but I decided to let them say what they wished to contribute to the discussion without the editorializing present in numerous historical texts. I understand that this process may make the work appear cumbersome, but it is necessary to lend integrity to the process. I did not want to be viewed as the voice, but as one voice on black women's homiletical process.

In my final analysis, I discovered that black women's process, sound, and movement are dependent on the duration of their ministry, presence, or absence of female role models, what is accepted as preaching in their places of worship ministry, personal preference, education, age, exposure to congregations, and self-affirmation. I have observed similarities between black women and black men in the areas of call and response, celebration, length of sermon, sermon type, idiosyncratic phrases, and in some mannerisms such as carrying handkerchiefs or towels and using handheld microphones. Based on the information in this study, black women have distinctive preaching passions, body movements, voice quality, and pressures to be perfect or someone other than who they are. Many of the women in this study exhibited a willingness to share intensely emotional testimonies in celebration of deliverance. The content of the sermon was driven by thematic choice. In the end, no one can speak for black women's issues the way a black woman can. Apologies for preaching were repeatedly observed. Attire is an obvious difference particularly for the women who choose not to wear robes.

The study resulted in renewed interest in further study in this area. Future research will include a five-year follow-up on this group of sistah proclaimers, finding any changes in their preaching preparation, passion, and presentation. There is a need for a book on contemporary black women who have founded denominations or are pastors. The Reverend Dr. Cynthia Hale pastors a 6000-plus-member Disciples of Christ Church in Atlanta. She began the church ten years ago with eight people. She is well-read, intensely prepared, exegetically sound, and well-organized. Her delivery is graceful, feminine, celebrative, and confident. She lives into her call and unapologetically proclaims God's word. Her story should be put in conversation with other black women. I also see an opportunity for an analysis of women televangelists. Along that same line is an opportunity to study preachers in cross-racial or multiracial appointments or preaching opportunities to discern similarities or differences in homiletical tasks, language, text, style, and delivery. The Reverend Bridgette Young, Associate University Chaplain in Atlanta, helped unearth this research area by submitting one tape of a sermon in a predominately white church and one in a black church. The difference in her delivery, energy, textual handling, and sermon length caught my attention. My next magnum opus will be a book on sexuality and preaching. I am interested in how physical attributes, dress, voice, and mannerisms affect the preaching moment from the perspective of the preacher (male and female) and the congregation.

This piece of music is over, but the refrain continues. It's time to sing new songs. The old school melody of exclusivity can be weary and worn. The contemporary tune of inclusivity can be vivacious and compelling. Sistah proclaimers are singing new songs. Can you hear them?

"Wake Up! It's Time to Make a Change"

The sermon was preached at a Watch Night service in 1999. Watch Night, in the black church tradition the last day of the year. Black worshipers gather to testify about how they survived the outgoing year, sing God's praises, preach some thematic word about resolve in the new year, and enter the new year (at the stoke of midnight) in prayer.

Old Testament Reading: Proverbs 6:9-11

> 9 How long will you lie there, O lazybones? When will you rise from your sleep?
> 10 A little sleep, a little slumber, a little folding of the hands to rest,
> 11 and poverty will come upon you like a robber, and want, like an armed warrior.

New Testament Reading: Revelation 3:1-6

> 1 "And to the angel of the church in Sardis write: These are the words of him who has the seven spirits of God and the seven stars: I know your works; you have a name of being alive, but you are dead.
> 2 Wake up, and strengthen what remains and is on the point of death, for I have not found your works perfect in the sight of my God.
> 3 Remember then what you received and heard; obey it, and repent. If you do not wake up, I will come like a thief, and you will not know at what hour I will come to you.
> 4 Yet you have still a few persons in Sardis who have not soiled their clothes; they will walk with me, dressed in white, for they are worthy.
> 5 If you conquer, you will be clothed like them in white robes, and I will not blot your name out of the book of life; I will confess your name before my Father and before his angels.
> 6 Let anyone who has an ear listen to what the Spirit is saying to the churches."

Now I lay me down to sleep
I pray the Lord, my soul to keep
If I should die
Before I wake
I pray the Lord my soul to take

Remember when you learned to repeat this prayer?
    Some of us still say it each night.
Remember all the hope tied up in going to bed at night, anticipating what
    we would do tomorrow?
    Okay, I'm going to take a little nap. Hope my toys are still there
        tomorrow.
    Daddy says that if I pray, the monsters will not bother me tonight.
    Maybe I can do better tomorrow.
    I just need some sleep.

Sleep—Hebrew, [shenah s-h-e-n-a-h], yashen [y-a-s-h-e-n],
Greek, hypnos [h-y-p-n-o-s]

    Physical rest, gift from God, period of replenishing, rejuvenation

Sleep—a natural, healthy, but temporary and periodic, suspension of the
    functions of the organs of the senses and voluntary and rational soul.
Science tells us that we need 5 to 6 hours of sleep a night depending on
    our age. Four hours is the minimum needed for maximum effectiveness
    in waking hours.
    But we can overdo a good thing when we become so set in the
        reclining position—no vision, no plans, just the same old routine
    Some of us put more effort into sleep than we do waking up
    Mattress selected for firmness and good sleep
    Pillows fluffed and stacked
    Perhaps one in front and one in the back for good support
    Maybe even a body pillow between our knees for spinal support
    That spot in our own bed that fits our particular bodies just right
    Covers on or off
    Right pajamas or lack thereof
    Temperature setting appropriate to the season and our internal
        thermostats
    Answering machine with caller I.D. visible

Television on or perhaps favorite music
Snack by the bedside
Water or milk
Remote control
Alarm clock within easy reach
Reading materials
If we could figure out how to cook, clean, or care for ourselves from bed, we would be set for life
  Comfort supreme, all is in order
    Creature comforts are satisfied, our interests are being served, we are ready to get some good sleep
Some even believe they can catch up on so-called lost sleep. Some of us stay in bed so long we awaken with muscle aches, headaches, and after tossing and turning all night.
The problem is that instead of becoming strengthened by God's gift, we oversleep, stay in bed too long. We become bedridden Christians, making pillow promises to God that we know we will not keep in the morning.
The writer of Proverbs, however, tells us that too much sleep is not good for us:

Lazybones, go to the ant
Study its ways and learn
Without leaders, officers, or rulers
It lays up its stores during the summer
Gathers its food at harvest
How long will you lie there, lazybones
When will you wake from your sleep?
A bit more sleep, a bit more slumber
A bit more hugging yourself in bed
And poverty will come calling upon you
And want, like a man with a shield (Proverbs 6:6 The Message)

When we sleep too long, we become sluggard
  Lazier than a pig on vacation
  Only exercise we get is turning over.
You know, too much sleep is like putting things off
  Making excuses
  Avoiding responsibility

Blaming others for our lack of motivation

Running away from a problem

Is your spiritual bed so comfortable that you refuse to get up? Do not move to fluff up the pillows of imagination, head sunk down, just lying there without hope and action, no incentive, just spiritually sleepy sluggards.

Beloved, God has a word for us today about the beginning stages of a change, transformation, revolution

Walk back with me for a brief time through the sacred text to the book of Revelation

In a familiar story,

John, the beloved Disciple,

> Stayed with the women at the cross with Jesus after the other disciples left
>
> Now an old man
>
> Exiled and imprisoned on the Isle of Patmos located in the Aegean Sea (a small rocky prison colony for enemies of the state) by Emperor Domitian
>
> because he preached the good news of the kingdom of God.

On the Lord's Day, John received a vision

> In part of the vision, God sends letters through the resurrected Jesus Christ by the power of the Holy Spirit to John the Apostle in a seven-part vision with seven parts each.

In this revelation or vision, John hears and sees the letter delivered to seven angels who represent seven churches in Asia Minor and may represent various conditions of contemporary churches.

Revelation 2 to 3 pertains to "things as they are"

God wants each representative church to know about the eschaton

the end of time

the hard things each believer should know and do

the second coming of Christ, the Parousia

the reward of faithfulness to God's word

the consequences of oversleeping

The text setting is the end of the first century, facing a new millennium, and the Empire is in trouble

Churches—lower classes

No long history

No glorious institutions

Meetings in private homes

Leadership unpatriotic—concerned only with inreach, no outreach

Scapegoats for any and all disasters

Under constant harassment

Called outsiders and Jesus fanatics

Conflicts between church and state

In Revelation 2 and 3, Ephesus, Smyrna, Pergamum, Thyatira, Sardis, Philadelphia, and Laodicea are each given a specific command; commendation or condemnation, correction and challenge, based on their individual spiritual characteristics and needs.

Sardis, fifth of seven churches

Arts, crafts, and textile producer

First center to mint gold and silver coins

Capital of Lydia under Croseus, located on the north spur of Mount Timolus

Metropolis—located on the mountain (older section, which became overpopulated)

And in the valley [1500 ft below]

Sardis, state of apathy, no movement, no progress

Trapped in *traditionalism*—dead faith of living people rather than modifying *tradition*—living faith of dead people

Filled mainly with sleeping, stagnant, stinking, supercilious, sanctimonious, stiff-necked people

Chapter 3, verse 1

And to the angel of the church in Sardis write: These are the words of him who has the seven sprits of God and the seven stars: "I know your works; you have a name of being alive, but you are dead."

Look at *Sardis*

No information shared, except with select leadership

Cringing at entrance of disabled

Castigation of the poor, diseased, ignorant, unchurched

Just sitting around congratulating one another on how big the church building was and how many people joined on Sunday

Marquee boasting open 7:30–2:30 each Sunday, with three services; but no one could get a prayer in at the throne of grace after 5:00 P.M. the same night

Sardis Wonderful *reputation* (what others think about us), little knowledge of its character (what we really are)

> Nice buildings often erected to the glory of the pastor and not to God
>
> Comfortable pews reserved for the big tithers

Sardis Great choir singing "I Won't Complain," yet refusing to sing if he or she is not the lead, as if God inspired them to write it in the first place.

> Bulletins listing forty ministries, with ten actually in operation, thriving, and sustained
>
> Advertisements stating, "We are in the word," but nothing about whether the word is in them

Sardis Preachers passionately proclaiming God's desire that we turn away from sin five minutes after gossiping about the people, about what someone is wearing, which woman looks good, what man we would like to date, or how much the offering should be by the size of the crowd.

> Congregants proudly carrying Bibles on Sunday morning, throwing them in the trunk or back window until the next Sunday or Bible study—spoon-fed, diabetic Christians
>
> Barriers set up to keep others out—out of pulpits, out of worship, out of fellowship, out of power

Sardis Populated mainly by unredeemed, unregulated people

> Was infested with sin, gradually decaying like a house with silent working termites in its foundation
>
> Not our usual list of sins—sex, drugs, and alcohol

Sardis was full of itself, bragging about how much it did for the community, competition with other churches, denomination for who is the most holy, proselytizing

Sardis had a reputation for being alive (animated, energetic, vigorous, united in body and soul), but the word says:

> It was spiritually dead—cessation of all vital functions, termination of any form of existence

Sardis was on life support and didn't even know it.

Sardis was sound asleep, had suspended its consciousness, was floating through life on automatic pilot, was a community of the living dead, had spiritual mediocrity, was in desperate need of revitalization

Sardis needed a revolution, a change; it needed to be transformed from what it was to what God wanted it to be in order to be fit for the kingdom.

> Sardis needed to stop sleeping and get itself together.

Have you ever worshiped in Sardis?
Have you ever lived in Sardis?
Have you ever been to Sardis?
Check your own papers.
Sardis was asleep.

> Sleep—the state where there is a lessened acuteness of sensory perception, a confusion of ideas, and loss of mental control followed by a more unconscious state.
> It is the loss of power.

Consider the state of the world. Are we asleep?

> It seems the hope and hype of December 1999 has slid into the hesitancy and hollowness of December 2000. The year is almost over, and some of us are just reading our resolutions.
> Persons who proclaimed the new century as a time for social change, religious prosperity, and personal growth have become
> tepid
> apathetic
> languid
> inert
> lethargic
> somnolent
> dormant and comatose leaders.
> Some have decided that the cost of change is too high.
> Some have opted for token promotions, while others remain locked out of leadership.
> Some have encountered disappointment that human promises became counterfeit checks that no denominational bank could cash.
> Some get so caught up in the "But I Can't" or "They Won't Let Me" theology, they do not focus on God's possibilities and promise.
> Some have slid into a zombielike trance, allowing cankerous leadership to grow like unchecked spiritual cancer.
> Some have been lied to and been complicitus with self-deception so long the truth is a vague memory.
> Some have continued to voice opinion in private telephone conversations, E-mail messages, chat rooms, conferencing messages, and sidewalks or parking lots after the meeting they were afraid to speak up in because of fear of demotion or ostracism by a group of people who do not like you anyway.

"But we have always done it this way" became the mantra of those who are afraid of change or are too lazy to try anything new.

My sisters and my brothers, brothers and sisters, God is not pleased. It is time to make a change. It's time to wake up. Wipe the sleep away.

There are five stages of sleep

Stage One—Twilight Sleep

Wakefulness

Irregular waves

Muscles relax

Breathing smooth

Try to follow the commandments of God; at times we slip up but don't have sense enough to ask for forgiveness and recover

Stage Two—Quiet Sleep

Slower brain waves

Sudden burst of activity

Commemorative day tripling of attendees, Mass choir singing, church filled. High service one Sunday, but on the fifth Sunday or during football season, summer, or holidays, numbers go down, or we act as if God took off work

Stages Three and Four—Delta, Slow wave, Deep sleep

No control of large muscles

No knowledge of surroundings

Most susceptible to attack

Totally vulnerable

No praise, no fellowship, no offering, no love, no commitment

Verse 2a: *Wake up! And strengthen what remains and is on the point of death*

Sleep is the rehearsal for spiritual and physical death. Too many of us are at the point of sleeping into death. God says "wake up!"

God is trying to do a new thing, and many of us are sound asleep.

Blessings we prayed for have been given, but we missed them.

We talked to God, fell asleep, and snored so loud we couldn't hear the answer.

1. Wake up, be watchful, regain your attitude of life, wait for Christ's promised return

2. Strengthen what remains and is on the point of death—protect yourself

Flex your spiritual muscles

Study the Word of God to show yourself approved by God

Read and read Christ's teachings

Pray without ceasing, not just when trouble arises

Rejoice always in the Lord, even when you can't find the tunnel or the light

Stay in love and charity with all persons regardless of age, race, ethnicity, gender, bank balance, or belief system

Change attitudes—same mind in us that is in Christ Jesus

Verse 2b: *for I have not found your works perfect in the sight of my God.*

Sardis was replete with those whose work was not pleasing in God's sight

Mind manipulators

People pleasers

Money hoarders

Comfort seekers

Smooth talkers

Pulpit dominators

Verbal abusers

Poor mouthers

Sex chasers

Offering beggars

Perpetrating believers

Cowardly grumblers

Walking, talking, sleepy, spiritually dead people

Perhaps you have visited Sardis, stayed too long, and gradually became a part of the community.

Perhaps you purchased a summer, vacation, or time share residence in Sardis.

Just a place to relax and forget responsibilities.

God is calling us to wake up, time to change our ways.

Verse 3: *Remember then what you received and heard; obey it and repent.*

God's counsel to the church, every believer

1. Receive

Receive—What has God given to you?

How do you handle holy things?

Have you used your talent—gifts and graces—as stipulated by God, or are you exerting energy only when it pleases you or you get to stand in the spotlight?

Too many times we pray—worrying God—for something that God gave us years or months ago and we were too sleepy to comprehend the gift.

2. Heard—Listening involves passive perception of sounds; hearing is the integration of sensory information into intelligible resources for action

3. Obey God, hold on, hold up, and obey all of the commandments, not just the ones that seem easiest.

Reward for waking up, obeying God, and going back another way

Blessed in the city

Blessed in the fields

Blessed when we go out

Blessed when we come in

Lord will cause our enemies to be defeated before us

They will come at us one way and flee seven ways

Established as a holy people—if we keep God's commandments

Lend and never borrow

Lord will make us the head and not the tail (Deuteronomy 28)

We know the rules, taught by mothers and grandmothers

Greatest Commandment—*Love the Lord with all our hearts, souls, and minds, and neighbors as self.*

Forgive everything and everyone that is within your power to forgive; forgive yourself

Anna Julia Cooper—*Learn to love yourself, discipline yourself, determine for yourself who you are.*[1]

Let the same mind be in you that is in Christ Jesus.

We are to be imitators of Christ's compassion and forgiving attitude.

We are not ordained to be Christ.

Too many demigods running around proclaiming they are the next Messiah; God only assigned one.

Obedience means we affirm our trust in God's presence

Stop the madness.

Align us with the goals of God's purpose

Accept the reliability of God's promise.

4. Repent—*metanoia*, turning back toward God; *teshuvah*—turning back time

Feeling of regret. Changing of the mind, turning from sin, returning to covenant relationship with God. Covenant relationship means we are sons and daughters, daughters and sons, of God our father.

Tomorrow is not promised, change must be rapid, now is the time God says that we do not have to remain the same.

Martin Luther King, Jr. once preached, "*And one of the great liabilities of life is that all too many people find themselves living amid a great period of social change and yet they fail to develop the new attitudes, the new mental responses that the new situation demands. They end up sleeping through the* revolution."[2]

Revolutions are conceived in our minds, like John's revelation.

How?

a. Acknowledge our need for change.
b. Assess the need. What is the purpose?
c. Plan a course of action
d. Select person or persons to change a situation
e. Secure proper resources
f. Set time lines
g. Begin the work
h. Re-evaluate the purpose
i. Complete the task
j. Maintenance

The entire cycle must be followed for a successful revolution

Failure to complete all the steps means the cause is lost.

Some of us missed the call, the change, because we were waiting for someone else to do the work.

Didn't believe that God would ask us to do the "impossible."

Saw the vision and closed our eyes.

Hit the alarm clock [*chronos*] and snoozed past the moment [*kairos*].

Wanted a large committee before engaging the problem.

No clue about our purpose or our plan.

Didn't pray first.

Stayed out too late last night, couldn't keep eyes open long enough to see the salvation of the Lord the next morning.

Wanted to wait for budgetary approval instead of stepping out on faith.

Standing like lifeless bones in the valley

Praying the same old prayers,

Singing the same old songs,

Preaching the same old sermons,

Giving the same old amount

Griping about the same old things

because we were so relaxed the newness wore off before we opened the package.

God does a new thing each and every day,

Stop looking back at what was, and focus on what is and will be.

Remember, just because we are not part of the revolution because we opt to sleep through it does not mean that it has not taken place. Seven last words of a failed revolution: "We haven't done it that way before."

Thirty-five years ago, Gil Scott Heron wrote, "The revolution will not be televised."

Too many Christians are looking for change in the wrong places.

It will not be on CNN, CBS, ABC, HBO, Showtime, ESPN, PBS, FOX, UPN, BET, the Playboy Channel, Nick at Night, Jerry, Rickie, Maury, or Oprah.

We can channel-surf all we want, but the revolution will not be the next story line on *As the World Turns*, *Guiding Light*, *The Young and the Restless*, *Days of Our Lives*, or *Passions*.

It will not be discussed on *Judge Judy*, *Judge Mathis*, *The Parkers*, *Steve Harvey*, *Monday Night Football*, *Monday Night Nitro*, or WWF.

God's transformation, change, and revolution begins in the believer's heart and mind.

A major stumbling block to individual and collective revolution and transformation is fear.

Too many believers are paralyzed by fear

Fear of the unknown, of failure, of success, of own abilities

Fearful

Trauma of transformation

Cost of change

Pain of possibility

Fear of freedom

Liability of liberation

Risk of recuperation

Burden of birthing

Wake up, time to move from deep, powerless sleep to a new life, a new day.

God has not given us a spirit of fear, but of love, power, and a sound mind.

Successful revolutions are accomplished when we struggle until daylight and walk away with a limp.

Sometimes, wounded in battle, but savoring the victory. Knowing God is in the midst of it all.

Mothers and fathers used to sing, *"God don't want and he don't need no coward soldiers in his band."*

Courage is the willingness to sacrifice for the good of the order.
God gives us instructions and life support and provides the means for change.
>God wants us to move past the first four stages of sleep and look to the fifth stage.
>Real change is birthed in the fifth stage of sleep.

Stage Five—Rapid Eye Movement
>Brain activity begins to increase, waking
>R.E.M. sleep—in midst of nightmare
>A troubling in the soul
>Struggling to come back from the brink
>Receiving dreams and visions
>Trying to take hold
>Crying out for God's help
>Realization of environment
>Reflection—*anamnesis*—remembering
>Resurrection
>Rapid change from one form to another—revolution

Remember, too many are sleepwalking with selective amnesia.
Wake up!
>The day of revolution is passing us by
>>Wipe the film off your eyes so you can see God's creation
>>Rinse the filth out of our mouths so we can sing God's praises.
>>Wash the odor off of the temple so God's Spirit can dwell within us.
>>Stretch the muscles before they atrophy and movement in the Sprit becomes impossible.
>>Listen to what God wants you to accomplish this day
>>Reflect on those who did not make it through the night
>>Thank God you have a new chance to get it right.

Remember that without God, there is no change, no conversion, no revolution, no new thing, no vision, no hope, and no rescue
>Remember, God has liberated our souls from hell and opens us up to freedom in mind, soul, body, and spirit.
>God gives us a second chance, new opportunities to get right, a new way to walk, a new way to talk, and a new self.

Verse 3b: *If you pull the covers back over your heads and sleep on, oblivious to God, I'll return when you least expect it, break into your life like a thief in the night* (The Message).

Get up on your feet!

Take a deep breath!

> Maybe there's life in you yet. I wouldn't know by the busy work.
> Nothing is complete.

Beloved with all its faults, with all of the noise of complacent sleepers.

> God had a message to send through Sardis.

Sardis was the church of hope.

> With God, there is always the possibility for change

Verse 4: *You still have a few who haven't ruined themselves (faithful remnant) who are wallowing in the muck of the world* (The Message).

There are a few in Sardis

> Faithful few of 300 left with Gideon
>> Two out of twelve with the good report from the promised land
>> One out of ten lepers who said, "Thank you."
>> One out of twelve disciples who stayed at the cross until the end
>> One out of four who remained awake in the Garden at Gethsemane

There are a few who have not soiled their clothes.

There are a few who have proved their worth.

> Passed character
> Remained true to Christ
> Dedicated to cause of Christ
> Keep the faith regardless of the current fad or fashion.

Wear clothing designed to fit individual lives instead of everyone else's

> It is difficult to be revolutionary if we are wearing the wrong garments.
> God may send us to do battle in armor, and we're wearing cotton because we got too hot engaging evil.

REWARD FOR CHANGE

Verse 5: *If you conquer, [Faithful are more than conquerors thorough Christ Jesus] you will be clothed like them [the faithful] in white robes.*

> Like the number that no one could number in the latter part of the Revelation, coming from every nation

Sardis was known for its rich textiles. God's promise is that the faithful will be clothed in garments of righteousness—clothing that will protect us from anything the adversary has to offer.

> No weapon formed against us will prosper.
> No fire will burn us

No water can drown us
Hope is in the Lord.

I got a robe, you got a robe, all of God's children got a robe
When I get to heaven, gonna put on my robe and walk all over God's heaven
    Everybody singing 'bout heaven ain't going there
And I will not blot your name out of the Book of Life.
I will confess your name before my father and before his angels.
    Name will be listed on the permanent record of the saints.
    No hackers, computer glitches, power outages can destroy our per-
    manent record.
    God's promise is the backup system for our inclusion in the Book
    of Life
    Jesus' blood is the right protection so nothing and no one can
    overshadow, record over our file
    No one can take it out but God.
God can erase our names if we sin against God, do not put our trust in
    God, are not born again, or take nothing away from God's prophecy.
God places a name on our foreheads that only he knows to verify our
    right to the tree of life.
Verse 6: *Let anyone who has an ear listen to what the Sprit is saying to the*
    churches.
    Get out of the bed of complacency
    Start those spiritual strengthening exercises
    Obey God's word
    Go back another way.
    We do not have to live at Sardis.
God told me to tell you that if we accept the challenge to wake up, he
    will transform our dying, sleepy reputation into a living, redeeming
    character
The end of the call to revolution, to change for Sardis, is the same call for
    us would-be, slumbering revolutionaries in 2000.
    Listen, open your ears
        Hear what Christ our Savior says
        Pay attention!
        Open your eyes!
Wake up! Time to make a change
    It's not about us, it's about God
Wake up! It's time to make a change

Take your head out from the under the covers of deception, denial, and
   degradation.
Wake up! Prepare to engage evil in all its forms
Wake up! No time for a meeting to plan another meeting—today is the
   day of salvation
Wake up! Let nothing and nobody separate you from the love of God
Wake up! Worship is not theater; it is honoring God's goodness in our
   lives
Wake up! It's time to make a change
   Stop letting others
      Define our family structure
      Determine our intellectual capacity
      Delineate our economic strength
      Regulate our advancement
      Restrict our communication
      Restrain our belief
      Define who are
We are children of the most high God
Wake up! It's time to make a change
   We serve a God of action, not reaction
Wake up! It's time to make a change
   We are not imprisoned by who we were yesterday
      Morning by morning, we are blessed with a second chance.
Wake up! It's Time to make a change
   Stop living below your birthright; honor God's gifts and grace within
      you
Wake up! It's time to make a change
   Nothing is too hard for God
      If God has given you a vision, write it down, work the plan, and
         plan the work and then run with it.
   My brothers and my sisters,
   When we are fully awake, God will begin the process of changing us
      from who we are to whom God wants us to become
God, our Creator, through Jesus Christ our Savior, by the power of the
   Holy Spirit, is writing us a letter today, saying wake up!
   Wake up, wake up, wake up
   It's time to make a change!

Appendix

Chart 1. Brochure Questions

1. Name, title, address, contact numbers
2. Denominational affiliation, status
3. Name of church or ministry affiliation
4. Age range
5. Highest education level
6. Postsecondary degree, area(s), e.g., Seminary, Bible College
7. Why do you proclaim God's Word?
8. How long have you been proclaiming God's Word?
9. How often do you proclaim?
10. Primary location of your proclamation.
11. What steps do you follow in preparation to preach/proclaim, e.g., text selection, supportive materials, topic selection, form or style, manuscript, outline, notes, or extemporaneous
12. What Bible translation(s) do you use? Why?
13. Who is (are) your proclamation mentor(s)/role model(s)?
14. What is your attire when proclaiming? Why?
15. Who was the first woman you heard proclaim? When? Where? Your reaction?

Follow-up Questions (randomly selected E-mails)
1. Do you use the Old Testament and the New Testament equally or one more than the other? Why?

2. Are there topics, themes, or texts you find yourself using often or avoiding?
3. What is your passion ministry? What do you know in your heart people need to hear more than anything else?

Chart 2. Top Four Translations by Time in Ministry

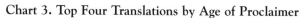
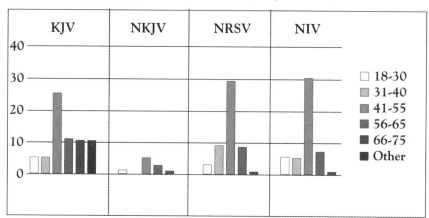

Chart 3. Top Four Translations by Age of Proclaimer

Chart 4. Top Four Translations by Education

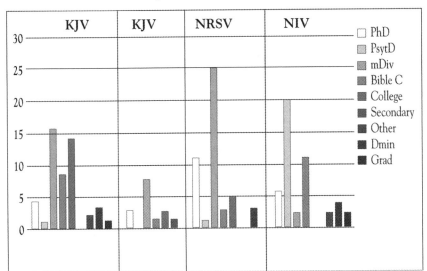

Chart 5. Sermon Critique and Feedback

A. Sermon Content

1. **Text selection**—appropriate, obscure, liturgical, special occasion, manageable, assigned, how selected
2. **Exegesis or isogesis**—research evident, background given, language consideration, definitions, cultural perspective, time and date consideration, related texts
3. **Translation**—how many are considered, consulted, or used in body of sermon
4. **Use of stated scriptural text**—number of texts used in sermon, place of text[s] in sermon
5. **Purpose of sermon**—accomplished, clear, hidden
6. **Illustrations and images**—appropriate, culturally specific, connected to sermon focus, variety, type, balanced, woven, add-ons
7. **Topic**—[if applicable] appropriate, length, clearly stated, pertinent to sermon content and text
8. **Cultural specificity**—gender, race, class, education, denomination, age
9. **Sermon focus**—to whom does the sermon speak? How?

B. Organization

1. **Sermon type**—narrative, topical, textual, dipolar, expository, first persons, dialogue, rhetorical, monologue, etc.
2. **Introduction**—relevance, length, connection with sermon body
3. **Body of sermon**—Is selected text integral to sermon? Works the text? Connection between ancient text and contemporary context? Were images and illustrations integrated into body?
4. **Movement**—stagnant or dynamic, transitions, identifiable central point, number of points [balance of point explication]
5. **Conclusion**—predictable, pronounced, celebration, opened, connected, tagged on, closed, absent

C. Person of the Preacher

1. **Authenticity**—original work, cliché, rote memory, regurgitation, plagiarism, citations, credit
2. **Presence**—fearful, energetic, commanding, engaging, tyrannical, domineering, self-righteous
3. **Believability**—invested in sermon, committed to content
4. **Preaching with listener**—pastoral, prophetic
5. **Appearance**—dress, carriage, hair, shoes, colors, vestments, jewelry

D. Communicability

1. **Audibility**—too loud, too soft, appropriate, good use of varied volume
2. **Articulation**—clarity, cluttering, stuttering, pronunciation
3. **Dialect**—regional, ethnic, national, cultural
4. **Breathing**—breath control, panting, gasping, labored, etc.
5. **Pacing and pauses**—too fast, too slow, variable, too long, pregnant
6. **Language usage**—gender, culture, race, geography, denomination, age
7. **Nonverbal communication**—body engagement, language, eye contact, gestures, use of hands, spatial relationships
8. **Emotive**—inviting, affirming, demeaning, open to feedback
9. **Distractions**—handling, ignored, impact, integration

Chart 6. Assessment Elements for Women Preachers

1. age
2. education
3. geographical
4. personal experience
5. denomination
6. example/models
7. congregation composition
8. family support/obligations-role balance
9. occupation
10. sense of call
11. authority issues
12. context
13. recurrent themes

NOTES

Introduction

1. Judith Weisenfeld and Richard Newman, eds., *This Far by Faith: Readings in African American Women's Religious Biography* (New York: Routledge, 1996).

2. Richard J. Douglass-Chin, *Preacher Woman Sings the Blues: The Autobiographies of Nineteenth-Century African American Evangelists* (Columbia: University of Missouri Press, 2001), 1-19.

3. Catherine Wessinger, ed., *Religious Institutions and Women's Leadership: New Roles Inside the Mainstream* (Columbia: University of South Carolina Press, 1996); Bert James Loewenberg and Ruth Bogin, eds., *Black Women in Nineteenth-Century American Life: Their Words, Their Thoughts, Their Feelings* (University Park: The Pennsylvania State University Press, 1976); Susan Hill Lindley, *"You Have Stept Out of Your Place": A History of Women and Religion in America* (Louisville: Westminster John Knox Press, 1996); Lee McGee, *Wrestling with the Patriarchs: Retrieving Women's Voices in Preaching* (Nashville: Abingdon Press, 1996). Teresa L. Fry Brown, *God Don't Like Ugly: African American Women Handing On Spiritual Values* (Nashville: Abingdon Press, 2000).

4. Barbara Brown Zikmund, Adair T. Lumis, and Patricia Mui Yin Chang, *Clergy Women: An Uphill Calling* (Louisville: Westminster John Knox Press, 1998); Frederick W. Schmidt Jr., *A Still Small Voice: Women, Ordination, and the Church* (Syracuse: Syracuse University Press, 1996); Vashti M. McKenzie, *Not Without a Struggle: Leadership Development for African American Women in Ministry* (Cleveland: United Church Press, 1996); Delores C. Carpenter, *A Time for Honor: A Portrait of African American Clergywomen* (St. Louis, Mo.: Chalice Press, 2001).

5. Christine M. Smith, *Preaching as Weeping, Confession and Resistance: Radical Response to Radical Evil* (Louisville: Westminster John Knox Press, 1992); Carol M. Norén, *The Woman in the Pulpit* (Nashville: Abingdon Press, 1991).

6. Cheryl Sanders, "The Woman as Preacher" in *African American Religious Studies: An Interdisciplinary Anthology,* ed. Gayraud Wilmore (Durham, N.C.: Duke University Press,

1989). Ella Pearson Mitchell, ed., *Those Preaching Women: African American Preachers Tackle Tough Questions*, vol. 3 (Valley Forge, Pa.: Judson Press, 1996). Bettye Collier-Thomas, *Daughters of Thunder: Black Women Preachers and Their Sermons, 1850–1979* (San Francisco: Jossey-Bass Publishers, 1998).

7. See Teresa L. Fry Brown in *Birthing a Sermon: Women Preachers on the Creative Process*, ed. Jana Childers (St. Louis: Chalice Press, 2001). The chapter details my sermon preparation.

1. Weary Throats

1. Julia Foote, *A Brand Plucked from the Fire: An Autobiographical Sketch* (Cleveland: Lauer & Yost, 1886) printed in *Spiritual Narratives*, ed. Henry Louis Gates Jr. (New York: Oxford University Press, 1988), 112-13.

2. Bettye Collier-Thomas, *Daughters of Thunder: Black Women Preachers and Their Sermons, 1850–1979* (San Francisco: Jossey-Bass Publishers, 1998), 226-27.

3. Catherine Wessinger, ed., *Religious Institutions and Women's Leadership: New Roles Inside the Mainstream* (Columbia: University South Carolina Press, 1996), 3-10.

4. Susan Hill Lindley, *"You Have Stept Out of Your Place": A History of Women and Religion in America* (Louisville: Westminster John Knox Press, 1996), 52-54.

5. Cheryl Townsend Gilkes, "The Role of Church and Community Women," in *If It Wasn't for the Women* (Maryknoll: Orbis Books, 2001), 63-75.

6. C. Eric Lincoln and Lawrence H. Mamiya, *The Black Church in the African American Experience* (Durham: Duke University Press, 1990), 274-75.

7. Richard J. Douglass-Chin, *Preacher Woman Sings the Blues: The Autobiographies of Nineteenth-Century African American Evangelists* (Columbia, Mo.: University of Missouri Press, 2001), 11, 206.

8. Darlene Clark-Hine, Elsa Barkley Brown, and Rosalyn Terborg-Penn, eds., *Black Women in America: An Historical Encyclopedia*, vol. 1 (Brooklyn: Carlson Publishing, 1993), 15.

9. Wessinger, *Religious Institutions*, 5-7.

10. Ibid.

11. Collier-Thomas, *Daughters of Thunder*, 12-43.

12. Bert James Loewenberg and Ruth Bogin, eds., *Black Women in Nineteenth-Century American Life: Their Words, Their Thoughts, Their Feelings* (University Park: Pennsylvania State University Press, 1976), 127-30. See also Jean McMahon Humez, ed., "Documents: Female Preaching and the A.M.E. Church, 1820–1852," in *Gifts of Power: The Writings of Rebecca Jackson, Black Visionary, Shaker Eldress* (Amherst: University of Massachusetts Press, 1981), 316-17.

13. Loewenberg and Bogin, *Black Women in Nineteenth Century*, 130.

14. Chanta M. Haywood, "Prophesying Daughters: Nineteenth-Century Black Religious Women, the Bible, and Black Literary History," in *African Americans and the Bible: Sacred Texts and Social Textures*, ed. Vincent Wimbush (New York: Continuum, 2000), 355-61.

15. Douglass-Chin, *Preacher Woman*, 35-76.

16. Foote, *Brand Plucked from the Fire*, 9-21, 65.

17. Ibid., 67.

18. Ibid., 66-67.

19. Ibid., 78.

20. Loewenberg and Bogin, Black Women in Nineteenth Century, 156-57.

21. Ibid., 133.

22. Ibid., 187, 189.

23. Brenda Stevenson, "Maria Stewart," in Hine, Brown, and Penn, Black Women in America, 3-6.

24. Mark Chaves, Ordaining Women: Culture and Conflict in Religious Organizations (Cambridge: Harvard University Press, 1997), 17.

25. Ibid., 16-17.

26. Cheryl Townsend Gilkes, "Together in the Harness: Women's Tradition in the Sanctified Church," in If It Wasn't for the Women, 48-54.

27. Chaves, Ordaining Women, 6-17, 24-27.

28. Collier-Thomas, Daughters of Thunder, 14-27.

29. Ibid., 26, 33.

30. Ibid., 33, 85.

31. Wessinger, Religious Institutions, 363, 373, 378, 381.

32. Collier-Thomas, Daughters of Thunder, 194.

33. See Jarena Lee, Religious Experiences and Journal of Mrs. Jarena Lee: "A Preachin' Woman," ed. A. Lee Henderson (Nashville: AMEC Sunday School Union/Legacy Publishing, 1991).

2. Singing in the Key of G-O-D

1. Samuel D. Proctor, The Certain Sound of the Trumpet: Crafting a Sermon of Authority (Valley Forge: Judson Press, 1994), 6-7.

2. James Earl Massey, The Burdensome Joy of Preaching (Nashville: Abingdon Press, 1998), 45.

3. William H. Meyers, "Disentangling the Call to Preach: Certainty, Ambiguity, Mystery," in Sharing Heaven's Music: The Heart of Christian Preaching, ed. Barry L. Callen (Nashville: Abingdon Press, 1995), 43.

3. Sight-Reading: Half Notes and Whole Notes

1. See Michael Dash, "The Bible in African American Spirituality," in The African-American Jubilee Edition, Contemporary English Version (New York: American Bible Society, 1995, 1999), 45-56. Dash provides a fuller discussion of spirituality and Bible reading in the Black church and culture.

2. James Earl Massey, "Reading the Bible from Particular Social Locations: An Introduction," in The New Interpreter's Bible, vol. 1 (Nashville: Abingdon Press, 1994), 150-53. See also Cain Hope Felder, ed., Stony the Road We Trod: An African-American Biblical Interpretation (Minneapolis: Fortress Press, 1991).

3. Hans A. Baer, "The Role of the Bible and Other Sacred Texts in African American Denominations and Sects: Historical and Social Scientific Observations," in African Americans and the Bible: Sacred Texts and Social Textures, ed. Vincent L. Wimbush (New York: Continuum, 2000), 92, 94-95, 98.

4. Carolyn Osiek, "Reading the Bible as Women," in Wimbush, *African Americans and the Bible*, 186-87. See Phyllis A. Bird, "The Authority of the Bible," in *The New Interpreter's Bible*, vol. 1 (Nashville: Abingdon Press, 1994), 35-36. Bird offers an extensive discussion on the history of the authority ascribed to the Bible and the potential for idolatry. See also Renita Weems, "Reading Her Way Through The Struggle: African American Women and the Bible," in Felder, *Stony the Road We Trod*, 57-77.

5. Cain Hope Felder, *Troubling Biblical Waters: Race, Class, and Family* (New York: Orbis Books, 1989), 88-91.

6. Elizabeth R. Achtemeier, "Canons of Sermon Construction," in *Sharing Heaven's Music: The Heart of Christian Preaching*, ed. Barry L. Callen (Nashville: Abingdon Press, 1995), 58-61.

7. Thomas G. Long, "Biblical Exegesis for Preaching," in *The Witness of Preaching* (Louisville: Westminster John Knox Press, 1989), 60-77. Long provides detailed steps for a method of exegesis.

8. Richard Hays, "Exegesis," in *Concise Encyclopedia of Preaching*, ed. William H. Willimon and Richard Lischer (Louisville: Westminster John Knox Press, 1995), 122-23.

4. Resting but Remaining in Tune

1. Olin P. Moyd, *The Sacred Art: Preaching and Theology in the African American Tradition* (Valley Forge, Pa.: Judson Press, 1995), 11.

2. James H. Harris, *Preaching Liberation* (Minneapolis: Fortress Press, 1995), 38.

3. Katie Geneva Cannon, *Katie's Canon: Womanism and the Soul of the Black Community* (New York: Continuum, 1995), 101-18.

4. H. Beecher Hicks Jr., *Preaching Through a Storm* (Grand Rapids, Mich.: Ministry Resources Library, 1987), 85-90, 100.

5. C. Kirk Hadaway, *Behold I Do a New Thing: Transforming Communities of Faith* (Cleveland: Pilgrim Press, 2001), 30-31, 83.

6. Christine M. Smith, *Preaching as Weeping, Confession, and Resistance: Radical Responses to Radical Evil* (Louisville: Westminster John Knox Press, 1992).

7. Teresa Fry Brown, "An African American Woman's Perspective," in *Preaching Justice: Ethnic and Cultural Perspective*, ed. Christine M. Smith (Cleveland: United Church Press, 1998), 49.

8. Fred Craddock in Ronald J. Allen, ed., *Patterns of Preaching: A Sermon Sampler* (St. Louis, Mo.: Chalice Press, 1998), 29-30.

9. James Harris, "Liberation Preaching," in ibid., 36-37. See also James Harris, *Preaching Liberation*.

10. James W. Cox, "Illustrations," in *Concise Encyclopedia of Preaching*, ed. William Willimon and Richard Lischer (Louisville: Westminster John Knox Press, 1995), 264-66.

5. Singing the Song in a Strange Land

1. Albert J. Raboteau, *A Fire in the Bones: Reflections on African American Religious History* (Boston: Beacon Press, 1995), 143-51.

2. Frank A. Thomas, *"They Like to Never Quit Praisin' God": The Role of Celebration in Preaching* (Cleveland: United Church Press, 1997), 30-37.

3. Part of the list is taken from my study notes. It is not verbatim but my understanding of what Dr. Adams imparted.

4. Jon Michael Spencer, "Folk Preaching (African American)," in *The Concise Encyclopedia of Preaching*, ed. William H. Willimon and Richard Lischer (Louisville: Westminster John Knox Press, 1995), 142-43.

5. Evans E. Crawford, *The Hum: Call and Response in African American Preaching* (Abingdon Press, 1995), 15-21.

6. Henry H. Mitchell, *Celebration and Experience in Preaching* (Nashville: Abingdon Press, 1990), 63-68, 87-88.

7. See Henry Mitchell, "African American Preaching," in *Concise Encyclopedia*, 2-8. Mitchell gives a brief history of "hooping" including the use of the "holy whine" used by Shubal Sterns and Daniel Marshall in South Carolina and influenced by the passionate preaching of George Whitefield during the Great Awakening revival movements.

8. Martha Simmons, "Avoiding Problems When Preaching on Controversial Issues," *African American Pulpit* (Summer 2001): 6-9.

9. Teresa Fry Brown, "Just Preach!" *The African American Pulpit* 3, no. 2 (2000): 59-64.

6. Choir Robes and Choreography

1. Joseph M. Webb, *Preaching and the Challenge of Pluralism* (St. Louis: Chalice Press, 1998), 17-30.

7. New Songs

1. Anna Julia Cooper, "The Higher Education of Women" in *A Voice from the South* (New York: Oxford University Press, 1988), 48-79.

2. Martin Luther King, Jr., "Remaining Awake Through a Great Revolution," sermon preached at National Cathedral, Washington, D.C. (31 March 1968).

Selected Bibliography

The African American Pulpit: Millennium Issue, Spring 2000, Volume 3, Number 2 (Valley Forge, Pa.: Judson Press, 2000).

The African-American Jubilee Edition, Contemporary English Version, (New York: American Bible Society, 1995, 1999).

Allen, Ronald J. Patterns of Preaching: A Sermon Sampler. St. Louis, Mo.: Chalice Press, 1998.

Callen, Barry L. Sharing Heaven's Music: The Heart of Christian Preaching. Nashville: Abingdon Press, 1995.

Cannon, Katie Geneva. Katie's Canon: Womanism and the Soul of the Black Community. New York: Continuum, 1995.

Carpenter, Delores C. A Time for Honor: A Portrait of African American Clergywomen. St. Louis, Mo.: Chalice Press, 2001.

Chaves, Mark. Ordaining Women: Culture and Conflict in Religious Organizations. Cambridge: Harvard University Press, 1997.

Childers, Jana. Birthing a Sermon. St. Louis, Mo.: Chalice Press, 2001.

Clark-Hine, Darlene, Elsa Barkley Brown, and Rosalyn Terborg-Penn. Black Women in America: An Historical Encyclopedia, vol. 1. Brooklyn: Carlson Publishing, 1993.

Collier-Thomas, Bettye. Daughters of Thunder: Black Women Preachers and Their Sermons, 1850–1979. San Francisco: Jossey Bass Publishers, 1998.

Crawford, Evans E. The Hum: Call and Response in African-American Preaching. Nashville: Abingdon Press, 1995.

Douglass-Chin, Richard J. Preacher Woman Sings the Blues: The Autobiographies of Nineteenth-Century African American Evangelists. Columbia, Mo.: University of Missouri Press, 2001.

Felder, Cain Hope. Stony the Road We Trod: An African-American Biblical Interpretation. Minneapolis: Fortress Press, 1991.

_____. Troubling the Biblical Waters: Race, Class, and Family. New York: Orbis Books, 1989.

Gates, Henry Louis, Jr. *Spiritual Narratives*. New York: Oxford University Press, 1988.

Harris, James H. *Preaching Liberation*. Minneapolis: Fortress Press, 1995.

Hadaway, C. Kirk. *Behold I Do a New Thing: Transforming Communities of Faith*. Cleveland: Pilgrim Press, 2001.

Hicks, H. Beecher, Jr. *Preaching Through a Storm*. Grand Rapids, Mich.: Zondervan, 1987.

Lee, Jarena. *Religious Experiences and Journal of Mrs. Jarena Lee: "A Preachin' Woman."* Nashville: AMEC Sunday School Union/Legacy Publishing, 1991.

Lincoln, C. Eric, and Lawrence H. Mamiya. *The Black Church in the African American Experience*. Durham, N.C.: Duke University Press, 1990.

Lindley, Susan Hill. *"You Have Stept Out of Your Place": A History of Women and Religion in America*. Louisville, Ky.: Westminster John Knox Press, 1996.

Loewenberg, Bert James, and Ruth Bogin. *Black Women in Nineteenth-Century American Life: Their Words, Their Thoughts, Their Feelings*. University Park: Pennsylvania State University Press, 1976.

Long, Thomas G. *The Witness of Preaching*. Louisville, Ky.: Westminster John Knox, 1989.

Massey, James Earl. *The Burdensome Joy of Preaching*. Nashville: Abingdon Press, 1998.

McGee, Lee. *Wrestling with the Patriarchs: Retrieving Women's Voices in Preaching*. Nashville: Abingdon Press, 1996.

McKenzie, Vashti M. *Not Without a Struggle: Leadership Development for African American Women in Ministry*. Cleveland: United Church Press, 1996.

Mitchell, Ella Pearson, ed. *Those Preaching Women: African American Preachers Tackle Tough Questions*, vol 3. Valley Forge, Pa.: Judson Press, 1996.

Mitchell, Henry H. *Celebration and Experience in Preaching*. Nashville: Abingdon Press, 1990.

Moyd, Olin P. *The Sacred Art: Preaching and Theology in the African American Tradition*. Valley Forge, Pa.: Judson Press, 1995.

The New Interpreter's Bible, volume 1. Nashville: Abingdon Press, 1994.

Norén, Carol M. *The Woman in the Pulpit*. Nashville: Abingdon Press, 1992.

Proctor, Samuel. *The Certain Sound of the Trumpet: Crafting a Sermon of Authority*. Valley Forge, Pa.: Judson Press, 1994.

Raboteau, Albert J. *A Fire in the Bones: Reflections on African American Religious History*. Boston: Beacon Press, 1995.

Schmidt, Frederick W., Jr. *A Still Small Voice: Women, Ordination and the Church*. Syracuse: Syracuse University Press, 1996.

Smith, Christine M. *Preaching as Weeping, Confession, and Resistance: Radical Responses to Radical Evil*. Louisville, Ky.: Westminster John Knox Press, 1992.

———. *Preaching Justice: Ethnic and Cultural Perspective*. Cleveland: United Church Press, 1998.

Thomas, Frank A. *They Like to Never Quit Praising God: The Role of Celebration and Preaching*. Cleveland: United Church Press, 1995.

Townsend, Gilkes, Cheryl. *If It Wasn't for the Women*. Maryknoll, N.Y.: Orbis Books, 2001.

Webb, Joseph. *Preaching and the Challenge of Pluralism*. St. Louis, Mo.: Chalice Press, 2001.

Weisenfeld, Judith, and Richard Newman. *This Far by Faith: Readings in African American Women's Biography*. New York: Routledge, 1996.

Wessinger, Catherine. *Religious Institutions and Women's Leadership: New Roles Inside the Mainstream*. Columbia: University South Carolina Press, 1996.

Willimon, William, and Richard Lischer. *The Concise Encyclopedia of Preaching.* Louisville, Ky.: Westminster John Knox Press, 1995.

Wilmore, Gayraud. *African American Religious Studies: An Interdisciplinary Anthology.* Durham, N.C.: Duke University Press, 1989.

Wimbush, Vincent L. *African Americans and the Bible: Sacred Texts and Social Textures.* New York: Continuum, 2000.

Zikmund, Barbara Brown, Adair T. Lumis, and Patricia Mui Yin Chang. *Clergy Women: An Uphill Calling.* Louisville, Ky.: Westminster John Knox Press, 1998.